ETHNIC AMERICANS

Preface

The original impetus for writing this book was Americans' heightened concern with, and glorification of, ethnicity and ethnic values at the end of the 1960s and the early 1970s. Both of us were brought up in the 1930s and 1940s when one learned that to become a "good American" one must shed one's foreign ties, culture, and religion, and adapt to what now might be called the values and beliefs of white, Anglo-Saxon Protestant (WASP) America. By the 1970s, however, ethnicity had become *chic*. People wore buttons announcing that they were proud to be Polish or Italian; reporters wrote favorably on the virtues and values of ethnic working class neighborhoods in cities like Baltimore and Pittsburgh; and people of a variety of backgrounds, instead of anglicizing their names, "ethnicized" them. In such a context we prepared the first edition, confident that Americans were showing renewed interest in the experiences of their immigrant forebears.

And we were right. The enthusiastic reception to the book encouraged us to do a second edition at just about the time that Americans ceased proclaiming their ethnicity and started seeking economic security in an economy with narrowed opportunities and greater emphasis on what an individual—male or female —could do and less awareness of one's "cultural baggage."

This third edition, however, is a result not only of renewed public interest and concern about immigration, but also of so much new scholarship that has been produced in the last decade. The celebration of the one hundredth birthday of the Statue of Liberty in 1986 gave rise to an extravaganza of events commemorating immigration. In the same year, Congress, after years of debate, passed legislation designed to stop the migration of undocumented individuals to the United States. While much public attention focused on undocumented aliens, the nation also was confronted with the task of formulating a fair refugee policy. The Reagan Administration only wanted to admit refugees from communism and was opposed to almost all others, while various ethnic and religious groups urged a more evenhanded position.

As in the earlier editions we have focused on those non-English people who came voluntarily to the New World after 1607. By limiting the topic in this fashion we have obviously excluded American Indians and blacks. Their history is in many respects unique and requires separate treatment. We have expanded Chapter 1, but the book still stresses the period after 1830 because 95 percent of America's immigrants entered during those years.

The new scholarship has greatly enhanced our understanding of several ethnic groups, and particularly of the women of those cultures. We now know so much more than we did only a few years ago of the Huguenots and Scots of colonial America, of the Irish and Norwegian emigration through the nineteenth century, of Italians in a wider variety of American cities, and of the unique experiences and responsibilities of the women of these, and other, backgrounds. As a result of this explosion of knowledge, we have attempted to revise this volume, incorporating as much of the recent scholarship as possible while revising and enhancing earlier interpretations based on a richer understanding.

Although all of the chapters have been revised to incorporate the newest findings of scholars, the greatest revision has taken place in the chapters dealing with the past 40 years. After the second edition appeared, David Reimers published an original study of third-world immigration to the United States, entitled *Still the Golden Door,* and Congress passed the most far-reaching immigration legislation since the Immigration Act of 1965. These features alone would warrant a new study, but combined with the most recent scholarship, there seemed to be no question but that a rewriting was necessary.

We would like to thank Fred Binder for reading the manuscript and Diana Hadley for her astute comments on Chapter 6. In addition, we would like to thank the reviewers of the manuscript: Christopher F. Armstrong, Bloomsburg University; William Griffin, Indiana State University; George E. Pozzetta, University of Florida; and R. Penn Reeve, Southeastern Massachusetts University. Finally, we also would like to thank the staff members of the University of Arizona History Department for their services: Bojana Aleman, Dorothy Donnelly, Mary Sue Passe, Micki Coburn and Patricia Marie.

We offer this third edition in the hope that it continues to be not only a brief summary of the immigrant experience but also a reflection of the most recent historical scholarship and public policies.

Leonard Dinnerstein
David M. Reimers

Contents

List of Text Tables

ETHNIC AMERICANS

A History of Immigration

THIRD EDITION

LEONARD DINNERSTEIN
University of Arizona

DAVID M. REIMERS
New York University

1817

HARPER & ROW, PUBLISHERS, New York
Cambridge, Philadelphia, San Francisco, Washington,
London, Mexico City, São Paulo, Singapore, Sydney

To Irene Rosenberg and to the Memory of Ben Rosenberg
    and
to Walt and Chris Wagner

Sponsoring Editor: Robert Miller
Project Editor: Donna DeBenedictis
Cover Design: Jean Wyckoff
Cover Photograph: Immigrants leaving Ellis Island, c. 1900. The Granger Collection.
Production Manager: Willie Lane
Compositor: ComCom Division of Haddon Craftsmen, Inc.
Printer and Binder: R. R. Donnelley & Sons Company
Cover Printer: Lynn Art

ETHNIC AMERICANS: A History of Immigration

Copyright © 1988 by Harper & Row, Publishers, Inc.

Library of Congress Cataloging in Publication Data

Dinnerstein, Leonard.
    Ethnic Americans: a history of immigration/Leonard Dinnerstein,
David M. Reimers.—3rd ed.
        p.   cm.
    Bibliography: p.
    Includes index.
    ISBN 0-06-041671-8
        1. United States—Ethnic relations.   2. Ethnology—United States.
3. United States—Emigration and immigration.   4. Americanization.
5. Immigrants—United States—History. I. Reimers, David M.
II. Title.
E184.A1D48 1988
305.8'00973—dc19   87–18810
                                                                         CIP

87 88 89 90 9 8 7 6 5 4 3 2 1

chapter 1

The Colonial Heritage

Never before—and in no other country—have as many varied ethnic groups congregated and amalgamated as they have in the United States. The original seventeenth-century settlers were overwhelmingly English, and it was they who set the tone for American culture. In spite of the English Protestant orientation of society, ethnic diversity also characterized the New World, even in the colonial period. After the 1680s millions of others, including Scotch-Irish, Germans, Scots, Irish, French, Dutch, Italians, Russians, Poles, Scandinavians, Greeks, Chinese, Japanese, Africans, and Latin Americans, eventually emigrated to America. Today most Americans are unable to trace any pure lineage. How many among us can say that we are 100 percent French or Dutch or English or German or any of the other strains that built America?

The English were the first Europeans to colonize successfully in the New World. The Dutch, French, and Spanish claimed large empires of land and established settlements earlier, but they were unable to induce significant numbers of their countrymen to leave their homes and live in America. On the other hand, the English, zealous in their pursuit of gold and silver, recognized that productive inhabitants increased the wealth of the nation. Even after the restoration of Charles II in 1660, when the English for a time were discouraged from leaving home, England established policies to encourage others to settle in her colonies. Whereas the French and Spanish ruled their overseas domains closely from Paris and Madrid and expected colonists to adhere to the Roman Catholic faith,

England rarely interfered with the American settlements, except for the regulation of trade. The English colonists, almost always short of labor and desirous
of populating the wilderness as a buffer zone against the Indians, French, and
Spaniards, shared the mother country's enthusiasm for immigrants. As a result
of English and colonial attitudes and policies, the greatest population movement
in history began. Eventually, over 40 million people left Europe in search of the
reported golden opportunities of America.

    During the colonial period, the vast majority of immigrants was European
Protestants who could eventually blend with the dominant English Protestant
culture. Between 1680 and 1760 a dramatic growth occurred in the British
mainland colonies as the population soared from approximately 250,000 to over
2 million. Little has been written about the English people who arrived during
that period, but scholars have devoted attention to several of the other groups that
helped the colonial people increase almost tenfold. Chief among these newcomers
were counted 250,000 Scotch-Irish (Presbyterian Scots who settled in Ulster
County, Ireland, early in the seventeenth century and whose descendants started
emigration to the American colonies in the eighteenth century), who constituted
the largest non-English group; 200,000 Germans were the second most significant
European minority. About 2,000 Huguenots (Protestants who were evicted from
France after the revocation of the Edict of Nantes in 1685 withdrew their privileges of worship there) made a much greater impact than one might surmise in
places like Boston, New York, and South Carolina. Untold numbers of Scots,
Dutch, and Swedes rounded out the European population of the colonies. Here
and there were small enclaves of Roman Catholics and—in the port cities of
Savannah, Charleston, Philadelphia, New York, and Newport—scatterings of
Jews.

    Despite the generally tolerant attitude of the English government toward
the newcomers, the English colonists, who were the dominant group in each area,
were not always as gracious as the officials in the mother country. Though they
too had come for economic opportunity and freedom to worship God as they
thought appropriate, they made no pretense of being tolerant to anyone who
deviated significantly from themselves. Hence the arrival of the Scotch-Irish
(whom colonists referred to as the "Irish"), the Germans, and others aroused
opposition. Americans of every generation have been frightened that newcomers
would subvert established customs and undermine the traditions of society, and
the dominant group in colonial America was no exception. In 1698 South Carolina passed a law giving bounties to newcomers but exempting the Scotch-Irish
and Roman Catholics. At about the same time, Maryland temporarily suspended
the importation of Scotch-Irish servants, and Virginia prohibited the sale of more
than 20 of them on any one river. In 1729 Pennsylvania placed a 20-shilling duty
on each imported servant. "The common fear," one Pennsylvania official said at

the time, "is that if they [the Scotch-Irish] thus continue to come they will make themselves proprietors of the Province."

Similar fears have been repeated generation after generation. Only instead of the Scotch-Irish being the "villains," different groups of Americans in different times and places have substituted Italians, Chinese, Jews, blacks, Poles, Puerto Ricans, Irish, Mexicans, and other ethnics. The paradox, which began in colonial America, is this: Whereas on the one hand we have welcomed strangers to work and live among us, on the other hand we have scorned and abused immigrants or minority groups who have deviated from the dominant culture.

Nevertheless, Americans through the twentieth century have actively recruited European, Asian, and Latin American people and emphasized the opportunities available to, rather than the hardships endured by, newcomers. Many colonies sought immigrants, and along with ship companies they sent agents (newlanders) to Europe to promote their attractions. The newlanders often dressed in fancy attire and wore pocket watches with heavy gold chains to attest to the wealth found in the New World. They carried tales of maids who became ladies, tenants who became landlords, and apprentices who became artisans only a few years after reaching the colonies. But "the best advertisement for the colonies," one historian has written, "was clearly the success of the pioneers. Messages they sent back home inevitably had the effect of removing the last psychological barrier from the minds of many already inclined to leave." "It is as Good Country as any Man needs to Dwell in," one Scotch-Irishman wrote back home in 1767, "and it is Much better than I expected it to be in every way." Going to America thus came to mean, as one scholar put it, not launching into the vast unknown, "but moving to a country where one's friends and relatives had a home."

But life in the colonies was rarely as wonderful as emigrants had anticipated. The wilderness had to be cleared and existence could be boring, barbaric, and demoralizing. Outside of the few towns there were no fairs, no markets, and no society to exchange pleasantries with; only a harsh workaday world that had to be faced from sunup through sunset. In 1734 an emigrant from Belfast noted in his journal, "We were oppressed with fears on divers accounts, especially of being massacred by the Indians, or bitten by snakes, or torn by wild beasts, or being lost and perishing in the woods." Many of his fellows also were taken ill and died quickly.

These experiences often came after the journey to the New World had presented travelers with untoward hardships. Part of their meager funds had to pay for passage to ports of embarkation, and once there, immigrants had to guarantee that the ships would sail to the final destinations on the agreed date. Extra days ashore meant added expenses for food and lodging. Finally, on board ship they faced weeks and sometimes months of dismal living conditions on overcrowded and disease-ridden vessels. Shipowners regarded their passengers as freight on which they hoped to maximize profits. The space between decks seldom exceeded five feet, and the immigrants, regardless of sex or marital relation, slept two or three in a berth; one rarely had an area of more than two feet by six feet to call one's own. Voyages lasted six weeks to six months. Stormy days forced passengers below deck, but portholes for light and ventilation were practically nonexistent. Overcrowding, disease, pestilence, brutal shipmasters, and shortages of food and water added to the tribulations of the ocean crossing. Many children under 7 sickened and died, and older folk too were lucky to reach the New World. In 1752 on a ship from the Netherlands to Pennsylvania, only 21 out of 340 passengers disembarked; the others had starved to death. On another voyage from Belfast in 1741, 6 of the 46 who died "were consumed by the sixty survivors." On yet another ship, many drank salt water and their own urine; and on another those who complained of hunger "were put in irons, lashed to the shrouds and flogged."

Despite these hardships, hundreds of thousands did reach their destinations. Many of those who came had lived in poverty in their old homes and were penniless. Shipping agents accepted indigents who signed an indenture agreeing to work in the New World for a period of three to seven years to pay for their passage money. The immigrants who came in this fashion were often "sold" on board ship, and not infrequently members of the same family wound up with different "masters." Some parents had to "sell their children as if they were cattle," and if parents or spouses died, the remaining members of the family had to serve extra time to pay for the deceased's passage. Unaccompanied children or those whose parents had died during the journey were usually indentured until the age of 21. At the end of their terms the freed servants received a small sum of money, tools, a new suit of clothes, and sometimes land. The sale of indentured servants continued until about 1820. One scholar estimated that about one-half to two-thirds of the white immigrants came to the English colonies in this manner.

Before the 1660s most colonists came directly from England. They laid the foundation and set the direction for the future development of American society. The settlement at Jamestown in 1607 resulted from the visions of some London-based fortune hunters who dreamed of large profits. By 1622 famines, pestilence, and Indian troubles practically destroyed the colony, and the English crown assumed possession.

In New England both Pilgrims and Puritans considered themselves good Christians. Like so many others who would follow, they were also influenced by economic factors in their decisions to settle there. They were plagued by a faltering European economy, and the move to the New World provided the opportunity to implant their own ways of life in a virgin territory and to improve their economic fortunes.

No other group, no matter how large, was ever as significant in the development of the United States as were the Pilgrims and Puritans. Their ideology emphasized the importance of the Protestant faith, diligent application to work, and individual accomplishment. They often paid homage to those who attained great wealth. They cherished the Anglo-Saxon legal heritage and revered the written compact. They brought the English language to the New World. All these aspects of their culture were firmly implanted in American soil, and they laid the foundations for American society. Every succeeding immigrant group that came to the English colonies, and later to the United States, had to absorb these aspects of the dominant culture before they in turn would be accepted as Americans.

After Charles I succeeded his father, James I, on the English throne in 1625, domestic concerns prevented him from giving much attention to the colonies. Nevertheless, he did grant an area of land north of Virginia to George Calvert, Lord Baltimore, which was christened Maryland. Calvert, a Roman Catholic, hoped the colony would be financially profitable and serve as a haven for his coreligionists. He died before actually receiving the grant from the king, and the deed went to his son Cecilius, who embarked on a voyage to the New World in 1634. From the beginning there were large numbers of Protestants in Maryland, and to protect Catholics in case of eventual discrimination, Lord Baltimore urged passage of the Toleration Act in 1649; it granted freedom of religion to all who believed in the divinity of Jesus Christ. Five years later, however, under the domination of a Protestant legislature the act was repealed and Catholics were denied the protection of the law. The repeal signified quite strikingly how the colonists, and in later centuries other Protestants, regarded the Roman Catholic faith.

Maryland was the last New World colony established by England before the domestic turbulence of the 1640s routed and then led to the beheading of King Charles I. Oliver Cromwell's protectorate lasted until 1660, when Charles II, son of the dethroned monarch, restored the crown to England.

After 1661 the new reign discouraged emigration. The mercantile theory, which held sway for the next century, dictated that the wealth of nations lay in their inhabitants and their production and that loss of population meant, in effect, loss of riches. The English colonists therefore had to seek other sources of population. In 1662 the Royal African Slave Company received a monopoly from the crown and began importing African slaves in increasing numbers. By 1680, however, William Penn received a grant of land from King Charles II and went to Europe to recruit settlers directly.

Penn printed hundreds of pamphlets in English, German, French, and Dutch, describing the wonders of Pennsylvania. Pennsylvania, the Europeans were told over and over again, was a land where crops never failed, where game roamed aplenty, where abundant supplies of wood stood ready for use in building houses, barns, and furniture, where religious freedom was guaranteed to all, and where no political restrictions harassed dissenters. Moreover, the colony promised universal male suffrage, a humane penal code, and no compulsory military service. As one historian later wrote, "Pennsylvania was in truth a land of milk and honey." No wonder that in the colonial era more immigrants sailed for Philadelphia than for all other ports combined.

Penn's promotional efforts appealed particularly to those affected by the intermittent wars in the German states during the seventeenth century. German Pietists and subsequently members of the Lutheran and Reformed churches left Europe for the beckoning opportunities in the New World. As a result of vigorous advertising, Pennsylvania became the mecca for German immigrants, though Germans settled in all other colonies as well.

Members of various German sects were found in English America, but the majority were members of the Lutheran or Reformed churches. They came to the New World for a combination of economic, religious, and political reasons: Some came to escape persecution in states where tyrannical princes had different faiths; others came because crop failures, famines, or never-ending wars made prospects for the future seem bleak. The relaxation of emigration restrictions in Switzerland and the German states in the eighteenth century also stimulated emigration, as did glowing letters from friends and relatives who had already gone to the English colonies.

Wherever the Germans went, they prospered. Their concern for their property was proverbial, and it was often said that a German took better care of his cows than of his children. After settling on good lands the Germans built sturdy houses and barns and tilled their farms with diligence and enthusiasm. One historian has written that they "produced in their children not only the *habits* of labor but a *love* of it." They fed their stock well, exercised frugality in diet and dress, and were known for their thrift, industry, punctuality, and sense of justice.

But the colonial Germans had little desire to blend with the rest of the population. They kept to themselves, continued speaking German, attended their own churches, and rarely took the opportunity to become British citizens. They maintained their own culture and feared that the use of English and contact with other groups would completely anglicize their children. Because of their aloofness they antagonized the dominant English group in the colonies, especially in Pennsylvania, who viewed them as dangerous elements in the community. Even Benjamin Franklin, an urbane and decent man, disliked the Germans who poured into Pennsylvania in the eighteenth century, and he demanded: "Why should the *Palatine Boors* be suffered to swarm into our Settlements, and by herding together, establish their Language and Manners, to the Exclusion of ours? Why should *Pennsylvania,* founded by the *English,* become a Colony of *Aliens,* who will shortly be so numerous as to Germanize us instead of our Anglifying them . . .?"

The Scotch-Irish, like the Germans, were Protestants who left their homes for religious and economic reasons. In the late seventeenth century English mercantile laws had prohibited the exportation of Irish woolens except to England and Wales, and this nearly crippled Ulster's profitable foreign trade. Then successive increases in rents, termination of farm leases, poor harvests, curtailed supplies of flax to linen manufacturers, increased food costs, and restrictions precluding Presbyterians from holding political offices piled woe upon woe. Furthermore, the English Parliament decreed that the children of all Protestants not married in the Church of England must be declared bastards. The absurdity of this ruling also resulted in " 'many persons of undoubted reputation' [being] prosecuted in the bishops courts as fornicators for cohabitating with their own wives." But not until 1717, when the fourth successive year of droughts ruined crops, were serious preparations begun for the migration to the New World.

The first group of Scotch-Irish to leave their homeland may have been motivated by religious as well as economic conditions, but, thereafter, glowing shipping advertisements, letters from friends and relatives in the colonies, and poor economic conditions in Ireland sparked further emigration. Intensive and protracted Scotch-Irish emigration to the American colonies correlated with the ebb and flow of prosperity in the linen industry in Ireland.

The original Scotch-Irish settlers went to Worcester, Massachusetts, and Londonderry, New Hampshire, where they met a chilly reception. New Englanders regarded them as "uncleanly, unwholesome and disgusting." Pennsylvania, on the other hand, because of its tolerance, received them readily. Perhaps even more important, the ships carrying flaxseed went to Philadelphia, and so the Scotch-Irish went there too.

Most of the Scotch-Irish arrived as indentured servants, but once their periods of service ended, they moved to the frontier, and their settlements predominated in central Pennsylvania and portions of Maryland, Virginia, and the Carolinas. Unlike the Germans, the Scotch-Irish were forever on the move.

The Scotch-Irish, although a colonial minority, left a mark on American society that remains to this day. Wherever they went, the church and the schoolhouse followed. Devoutly religious and with an intense desire for learning, they stressed the importance of an educated ministry and the dissemination of knowledge. Their stern morality pervaded the American scene. The Presbyterians frowned on dancing, card playing, the theater, breaking the Sabbath by any diversion, and engaging in frivolous pastimes. Later contact with other immigrant groups eventually mitigated the harshness of Scotch-Irish codes, but they still persist to some extent among some of the more devout Methodists and Southern Baptists, many of whom are descended from the colonial Scotch-Irish. It was common for Scotch-Irish to become Methodists and Baptists on the frontier because of their inability to find trained Presbyterian ministers and because the

New World loosened many Old World ties while facilitating new associations. On the other hand, not all of the Scotch-Irish were as dour as the aforementioned discussion might suggest. One scholar tells us that many among them "also danced, fiddled, sang, reveled, raced horses, gambled, got drunk and fought, celebrated St. Patrick's Day and shot off guns on New Year's Eve."

A number of other ethnic groups also populated the English colonies and in some areas their culture and values predominated. Because they constituted a smaller percentage of the total population than did the English, Scotch-Irish, and Germans, their influence, as well as their continued existence as separate groups, was not as lasting; but almost all made their mark in colonial America.

The Huguenots, who settled in virtually every region of the colonies but who concentrated in the port cities, stand out as the group that relinquished its heritage faster than any of the other peoples who came to British America. As a group they included a high proportion of professionals, merchants, and craftsmen and a very small number of indentured servants. Most of the Huguenots, who constituted the first major wave of newcomers from the European mainland, took non-Huguenot spouses, which ensured their disintegration as a separate people. As a result they quickly blended in with the most prominent colonists and not only occupied several important political offices but also became extraordinarily wealthy. Many of their contemporaries envied them and the phrase "rich as a Huguenot" was not always said without a tinge of bitterness.

The Dutch in New York and New Jersey, and the Scots, mostly in New Jersey and the South, are more representative of immigrants to America who held onto their cultures and values for several generations. They considered their heritage too important an aspect of their lives to relinquish it easily. Dutch influence lived on in New York's Hudson Valley and the eastern parts of Long Island, as well as in significant areas of New Jersey, long after the British had conquered New Netherland and renamed it New York. Worship in the Dutch language continued in some parts of New York and New Jersey until the 1820s and farmers continued usuing Dutch dialogue in some of their ethnic enclaves into the twentieth century. Education was quite important to the Dutch, and their children were taught not only the three Rs but also enough religion to make them God-fearing Christians. Instruction was in the Dutch language until approximately the middle of the eighteenth century. Girls were not given as sophisticated an education as boys, but they did learn to read and write and were taught needlework at home. They also were given particularly careful tutoring in the Bible and religious studies because inculcating religion in the children was considered the woman's responsibility.

Like most other ethnics, then and in subsequent centuries, the Dutch were exceedingly clannish and sought to isolate themselves from other colonists. In fact, many observers, regarded them as aloof but that did not seem to bother them nor did they alter their ways because of other people's perceptions. The Dutch relaxed by skiing, sleighing, and horse racing; they were known to enjoy drinking, and many of the women found pleasure in smoking tobacco. Economically they were quite successful.

The Scots were another group that not only kept to themselves but also welcomed newcomers from various regions of the old country and absorbed them into the ethnic community. They made their mark in the colonies in the organization of commerce, the development of mining, and advances in medical science. They were merchants and proprietors in a variety of businesses and, like the Dutch, valued education for their offspring. Most were overwhelmingly attached to the evangelical Presbyterian church, and family networks among Scottish settlers were an important source of religious unity.

One of their primary areas of settlement in British America occurred in the 1680s when approximately 600 Scots moved into east Jersey. By 1750 one-fifth of the population of New Jersey was made up of Scottish settlers and their descendants; by the middle of the eighteenth century, these people "turned central Jersey and the whole corridor from New York to Philadelphia into the center of Scottish Middle Colony life."

Although not as large in numbers as the Scotch-Irish from Ulster and the Germans, one scholar reminds us that

> In several particulars, the experience of Scottish settlers can serve as a model for that of many colonial ethnic groups. With a few striking exceptions—such as the Huguenots, who were notorious for submerging their national identity and attaching themselves to other Protestant communities—the confrontation with alien cultures in the New World helped to unify settlers from diverse and seemingly unconnected regional backgrounds under a common national banner. They often achieved that consolidation around a particular religious identity, such as Scottish Presbyterian, Dutch or German Reformed, or, in the next century, Irish Catholic. That process often created ethnic entities that seemed more Scottish, or more German, or even more English, than their European counterparts.

What this scholar really was saying, and what is less common today than it was even as late as the 1960s in some parts of the United States, was that in colonial America religious and ethnic identities were often intertwined. One was not merely French, Dutch, or Scottish, but French Huguenot, Dutch Reformed, or Scottish Presbyterian. Colonists thought of one another with these double identities and denounced each other more often in religious than in national terms. The governor of New York, for example, in 1686, complained that the colony contained too many Dutch Calvinists and French Calvinists, Dutch Lutherans, and "Singing Quakers, Ranting Quakers; Sabbatarians; Antisabbatarians;

some Anabaptists, some Independents; some Jews; in short all sorts of opinions there are some, and the most part, of none at all."

While the colonists noticed the arrival of large numbers of non-English newcomers, many persons from England continued to migrate to the New World in the eighteenth century. Emigration from Great Britian increased after 1760 and was heavy until the American Revolution. How many arrived in the eighteenth century is not known, but scholars have estimated that 30,000 English emigrated from 1760 to 1775 alone. Most of them settled in the 13 colonies that became the United States.

Historian Bernard Bailyn has studied in detail the records of those leaving in the early 1770s. The English immigrants of those years were usually young, single males who settled mainly in New York, Pennsylvania, North Carolina, Maryland, and Virginia. Like so many seventeenth-century English immigrants, they frequently came as indentured servants. While some were poor, the largest group was composed of skilled artisans. They had heard of the labor shortage in the colonies, and they came looking for a better life. Carpenters, farmers, bricklayers, shoemakers, tailors, and all skills were needed in America. As Bailyn tells us, "The forces of attraction were powerful, generated by the magnet of a labor-short American economy, which grew swiftly in certain regions and in certain kinds of activities."

Another source for colonial workers was convicts. Instead of imprisoning criminals, the British commuted their sentences to banishment to the colonies for periods of 7 to 14 years. It has been estimated that 50,000 such convicts found themselves in the colonies rather than in jail between 1718 and 1775. Some were no doubt hardened criminals, but many were tradesmen who had fallen on hard times and had run afoul of the law. Minor crimes at that time carried heavy sentences. The colonies were not always receptive to convicts, but the colonial governments could not halt this traffic. Besides, the convicts' labor was needed, and they were put to work in the New World.

While convicts were viewed with suspicion at times, no group was hated as much in the British colonies as were the Roman Catholics. Carrying with them to the New World their European traditions, some of which harked back to the Reformation, the Protestant settlers had tolerance for almost no deviants, but "the prospect of the arrival of Roman Catholics of any nationality," one scholar tells us, "curdled the blood of most provincials." The Roman Catholics constituted less than one percent of all of the colonists and half of them were in Maryland, but the numbers had nothing to do with the fears. Those who did not want them around exaggerated their influence and did not allow facts to alter their perceptions. Most Pennsylvanians, for example, imagined swarms of Irish and German Catholics in their midst even though statistics belied such apprehensions. One Pennsylvanian disinherited a daughter because she married a Roman Catholic.

Moravians in New York were "always viewed with suspicion," we are told, because of their missionary activities among the Indians and their allegedly pro-Catholic and anti-British sentiments. Catholics did live rather freely in the middle colonies, but in times of social crises, an inordinate amount of fear swept the towns in which they dwelled and their presence was deemed harmful to community harmony. This was especially true in the middle of the eighteenth century during the French and Indian War.

In December 1760, the Catholic church in Lancaster, Pennsylvania, was completely destroyed by enraged Protestants and Catholics were penalized in the colony in other ways as well. They were disarmed, prohibited from serving in the militia, and forced to pay double taxes. "And those residing in the colony," we are informed, "were registered so that their every movement could be scrutinized."

In the Revolutionary era this hostility toward Catholics knew no bounds and even as intelligent a man as John Adams, our second president, could write to his wife after visiting a Catholic church in Philadelphia

This Afternoon's Entertainment was to me most awful and affecting. The poor Wretches, fingering their Beads, chanting Latin, not a Word of which they understood; their Pater Nosters and Ave Maria's. Their holy Water—their Crossing themselves perpetually—their Bowing to the Name of Jesus, whenever they hear it—their Bowing and Kneelings, and Genuflections before the Altar. The Dress of the Priest was rich with Lace—his Pulpit was Velvet and Gold. The Altar Piece was very rich—little Images and Crucifixes about—Wax Candles lighten up. But how shall I describe the Picture of our Saviour in a Frame of Marble over the Altar at full Length upon the Cross, in the Agonies, and the Blood dropping and streaming from his Wounds. . . .

Here is every Thing which can lay hold of the Eye, Ear, and Imagination. Every Thing which can charm and bewitch the simple and ignorant. I wonder how Luther ever broke the spell.

Hostility toward Catholics may have been the most virulent prejudice but there was little affection between and among most groups. Jews and Catholics did not always enjoy the right to vote in colonial America; Jews in particular were proscribed from becoming physicians and attorneys in some places. Quakers and Jews did not have the legal right to testify in criminal court cases in New York City until after the American Revolution. Many colonies had an established church—Congregational in New England and elsewhere usually Anglican—and residents were taxed to support it.

To be sure, ethnic tensions and disputes in colonial America rarely took on the virulence that one would see in the late nineteenth and twentieth centuries, but they did exist. The English squabbled with the Germans, with the Palatines, and with the Swiss. Tensions between English and Scots, in fact, stood near the center of New Jersey's land riots of the 1740s. French Huguenots also saw their churches burned in South Carolina and one observer characterized the Dutch in this fashion: "Their notions were mean and contracted; their manners blunt and austere; and their habits sordid and parsimonious."

But community mores in most of the colonies generally were favorable to intercultural marriage as long as the non-English or non-Protestant member accepted the dominant religion of the spouse. As a result the commercially successful Huguenots and Jews, to name but two of the groups, often made alliances with the "best families" in the colonies and then raised their children as Anglicans or, later, Episcopalians. Consequently both the Huguenot and Jewish communities practically disappeared. In the United States today the only remnants of Huguenots are their historical and genealogical societies in places like South Carolina; New Rochelle, New York; and Rhode Island. As for the colonial Jewish population, it was absorbed into the dominant culture. Almost all contemporary American Jews trace their ancestries either to the great migrations from Eastern Europe in the late nineteenth and early twentieth centuries, or to the movement from the German states in the 1840s and 1850s.

In contrast, numerically larger colonial minorities like the Scotch-Irish and the Germans preserved and maintained their traditional ways well into the nineteenth century. Germans in places like Pennsylvania and the Carolinas continued speaking their own language, the Dutch maintained schools for their children in New York until after the Revolution, and a good deal of sectional controversy that has generally been attributed to geographical locale may in fact have its roots in ethnic differences. The Scotch-Irish on the frontier in Pennsylvania may have been angered by Quaker control in the Keystone State as much as by lack of military protection. The Regulator movement in the Carolinas, which pitted Scotch-Irish in the West against English descendants in the East, may also have had many more ethnic overtones than some historians have acknowledged.

As the colonial period ended, a rather distinctive ethnic picture could be seen. In New England an overwhelmingly English heritage predominated and aside from some Scottish, Huguenot, and Scotch-Irish elements, few other minority members could be found. The Middle Colonies, on the other hand, were ethnically diverse, and cities like New York and Philadelphia counted all sorts of people within their environs. The rural areas of these states, and New Jersey as well, seemed more Scottish, or Dutch, or Scotch-Irish, or German than one might originally have thought. As one proceeded south, a huge black population, almost all slaves, coexisted not only with the English but also with strains of all of the groups that might be found in the Middle Colonies as well.

By 1790 people of English stock still predominated in most of the states but Germans constituted fully a third of Pennsylvania's population and the Scots and Scotch-Irish totaled almost 37 percent of the remainder of the people in the

Keystone State. A recent analysis of ethnic groups in the new nation at the end of the eighteenth century still found English majorities in New York, New Jersey, and Maryland, but noted how strongly represented other groups were in those states' mixture of people. Nonetheless, the white minorities eventually blended their ways with those of the dominant English culture, and although there were varieties of Protestant churches, the children and grandchildren learned to tolerate differences within Protestantism.

The pattern of minority life developed in the English colonies in the seventeenth century set the standard for future European minorities in this country. The English colonists and later Americans of the majority group appreciated the labor that the newcomers could provide, but expected the immigrants to absorb the dominant customs while shedding their own as quickly as possible. Minority group members were sought for their labor yet were despised for their ignorance of English, their attachment to cultures and faiths prevalent in the Old World, and their lack of knowledge of the American way. Occasional groups of political refugees, like the 25,000 or so French-speaking immigrants who fled their Caribbean plantations in the 1790s in the wake of slave uprisings, might be given safe havens. But these newcomers, usually middle or upper class, brought a courtliness or sophistication that allowed them to mingle with the elite in American society. As a result they assimilated rather quickly and suffered much less from minority status than did those of lesser education, wealth, or position.

The passage of time, community pressures, and heroic endeavors have always worked against the maintenance of minority cultures in this country. The war for independence from England and the formation of a new American government had a nationalizing effect on the formerly separate colonies and their inhabitants. Many of the immigrants and their children were now quite proud to regard themselves as Americans, not as transplanted Europeans. Some ethnic groups—notably the Germans who lived between the Delaware and Susquehanna rivers in Pennsylvania, and the Broad and Saluda rivers in South Carolina—resisted Americanization for a longer time than others, but sooner or later most of them assimilated. The Napoleonic Wars, which began in the 1790s and lasted through 1815, slowed the pace of emigration from Europe, and this hiatus quickened the Americanizing process among the immigrant stock in the United States.

chapter *2*

The Old Immigrants

The century and a half following the Napoleonic Wars in Europe witnessed the greatest migration in the history of the world. Sparked by the Industrial Revolution, which forced peasants off the land and into the cities, the movement also gained momentum from many other factors in the social history of Europe. The European population doubled between 1750 and 1850. At the same time, intensified religious persecutions and a relaxation of emigration restrictions in various European nations combined with a transportation revolution to facilitate the movement of those who wanted to travel. Meanwhile, receptive countries in South Africa, Oceania, and North and South America sought people to exploit resources. Finally, two devastating world wars uprooted millions. More than 60 million people left their native countries during this period. Some went from one European or Asian country to another, but others sought riches in Africa, Asia, and South America. More than 15 million went to Canada, Argentina, and Brazil. About two-thirds of the migrants, who were primarily European but included considerable numbers of Asians and Latin Americans, chose the United States as their destination. Their arrival would be one of the most significant factors shaping the destiny of this country.

In the years between 1820 and 1930 America received more than 37 million immigrants, mostly from Europe. An analysis of time periods reveals that those coming from northern and western Europe predominated through the 1880s,

Table 2.1 IMMIGRATION TO AMERICA, 1820–1930

Decade	Germany	Ireland	England, Scotland, Wales	Scandinavia	Italy	Austro-Hungary	Russia and Baltic states	Totals
1820	968	3,614	2,410	23	30		14	8,385
1821–1830	6,761	50,724	25,079	260	409		75	143,439
1831–1840	152,454	207,654	75,810	2,264	2,253		277	599,125
1841–1850	434,626	780,719	267,044	13,122	1,970		551	1,713,251
1851–1860	951,657	914,119	423,929	24,680	9,231		457	2,598,214
1861–1870	827,468	435,697	607,076	126,392	11,725	7,800	2,515	2,314,824
1871–1880	718,182	436,871	548,043	242,934	55,795	72,969	39,287	2,812,191
1881–1890	1,452,970	655,540	807,357	655,494	307,309	362,719	213,282	5,246,613
1891–1900	505,152	388,416	271,538	371,512	651,783	574,069	505,281	3,687,564
1901–1910	341,498	339,065	525,950	505,324	2,045,877	2,145,266	1,597,308	8,795,386
1911–1920	143,945	146,199	341,408	203,452	1,209,524	901,656	921,957	5,735,811
1921–1930	412,202	220,564	330,168	198,210	455,315	214,806	89,423	4,107,209
Totals	5,947,883	4,579,182	4,225,812	2,343,667	4,751,311	4,279,285	3,370,427	

Source: Immigration and Naturalization Service, Annual Reports.

whereas the southern and eastern Europeans overshadowed the others after the 1880s. As Table 2.1 shows, the great surge came after 1880.

Not all these people can be treated in one chapter, of course. Hence a discussion of the different groups has been divided into three roughly chronological periods. The so-called old immigrants, those of northern and western Europe, are considered in this chapter along with the French Canadians and the Chinese, most of whom came in the nineteenth century. The next chapter deals both with the "new" immigrants from southern and eastern Europe and with the Japanese, whose major emigration occurred roughly between 1880 and 1920. Later chapters deal with the Hispanic migrants from Mexico and the Caribbean, whose presence is, for the most part, a twentieth-century phenomenon; the refugees coming as a result of Hitler's persecutions, World War II, and the cold war; and the new immigrants who have become eligible for admission to the United States because of congressional action since 1965.

Although foreigners arrived in the United States throughout the nineteenth century, statistics reveal that before 1880 the bulk was concentrated in two major periods: from 1845 to 1854, when more than 3 million persons landed at American ports, and from 1865 to 1875, when the numbers reached almost 3.5 million. Aside from these years, mass immigration is a phenomenon of the half century between 1880 and 1930, although the impact of more than 8 million newcomers from 1970 to 1987 suggests that a new surge may be in the offing. In the first period the Irish and Germans exceeded all others; in the second the English and Scandinavians figured heavily along with the first two; and after 1880 all these groups were joined, and then swamped, by southern and eastern European emigrants who pushed American immigration totals to new heights. Asians and Latin Americans, on the other hand, predominated after 1970.

Most immigrants came essentially because of poor economic conditions in Europe and prospects for a better life in the United States. Local concerns and variations, the pace of industrialization on the Continent, the disruptions of World War I, and the restrictive immigration quotas of the 1920s had much to do with the timing of the emigrants' departures. In Great Britain the industrial change began in the eighteenth century, and the British clearly dominated American immigration statistics until the 1840s; in the German states the transformation of the social order made its most profound impact in the second third of the nineteenth century; hence the Germans began to move after 1830; and in Scandinavia the decade of the 1880s, with its economic upheavals, proved most significant for migration. Nevertheless, the peaks and troughs in foreign arrivals after 1819 correspond roughly with the fluctuations in the business cycles in the United States. Good years such as 1854, 1873, 1892, 1907, and 1921 were high points for immigration, but they were followed by industrial depressions that resulted in correspondingly low totals for new entrants.

People do not cross continents and oceans without considerable thought, nor do they uproot themselves from family, friends, and familiar terrain without significant strain. The motivation to emigrate must be overwhelming before the fateful step is taken. In the nineteenth century, as in the seventeenth and eighteenth, poverty was the chief spur to movement. One eminent historian has written: "The most powerful factor impelling emigration was an extraordinary increase in population, preceding the ability of agriculture to feed it or of industry to give it jobs." The industrial and agricultural revolutions wrought such profound changes in Europe that large numbers of people were forced by circumstances beyond their control to relinquish ancestral dwellings and move to where they could find jobs. Yet one cannot ignore the variety of other impelling reasons. Religious intolerance, demeaning social gradations, political upheavals—all these pushed people across the Atlantic, and the ubiquitous "American letters" describing the Garden of Eden in the New World pulled countless thousands to America. Nevertheless, it must still be acknowledged that the economic factor was the most compelling for the majority of emigrants.

The Irish were the first of the impoverished Europeans to leave in the nineteenth century. The Irish Poor Law of 1838, the enclosure movement on the land, and finally the great famine at the end of the 1840s, when blight ravaged the potato crops and brought untold misery and starvation to millions, combined to increase emigration. A French observer who had visited both America and Ireland before the Great Hunger said the condition of the Irish was worse than that of black slaves. He concluded: "There is no doubt that the most miserable of English paupers is better fed and clothed than the most prosperous of Irish laborers." As hundreds of thousands starved to death during the famine, one of the few lucrative trades left in Tipperary was the sale of coffin mountings and hinges. One man lamented of the suffering, "Every day furnished victims, and the living hear, and endeavor to drive from their minds, as soon as they can, the horrifying particulars that are related. I have this day, returning to my house, witnessed more than one person lying in our district at this moment unburied. I have known of bodies here remaining in the mountainous parts, neglected for more than eight days." Many of the destitute Irish went to England, some to South America, but more than a million came to the United States. The majority of these people remained in the port cities of New York and Boston, where they landed, because they were too poor to move any farther; but others traveled west. As conditions improved in Ireland in the middle of the 1850s, emigration subsided, but another potato rot in 1863 and still another famine in the 1880s swelled the Irish emigration statistics. Almost 4 million Irish came to the United States in the nineteenth century. Their impact in this country has far exceeded both their numbers and their percentage of the population.

Along with the Irish came the Germans. But, unlike the Irish, they continued to be the largest ethnic group arriving in all but three of the years between 1854 and 1894. Before the end of the century more than 5 million Germans reached the United States; in the twentieth century another 2 million came. The exodus, at first primarily from the rural and agricultural southern and western regions of Germany, fits the general pattern of immigration. Crop failures, high rents, high prices, and the changeover to an industrial economy stimulated the move. Conditions were not as bad as in impoverished Ireland, but they were bad enough. One observer told of the "poor wretches" on the road to Strasbourg: "There they go slowly along; their miserable tumbrils—drawn by such starved dropping beasts, that your only wonder is, how can they possibly reach Havre alive." Relatives and friends who went first to America wrote glowing letters, for the most part, and this in turn stimulated further waves. Rich farmers who saw a bleak future in Germany, poor ones who had no future, peasants and paupers whom the state paid to leave, a handful of disappointed revolutionaries after 1848, and an assortment of artisans and professionals came in the 1840s and 1850s.

In late 1854 reports circulated in the German states of large numbers of shipwrecks and cholera epidemics at sea that resulted in death rates as high as 50 percent. At about the same time, nativist agitation in the United States reached a peak; and the American economy turned downward. These factors curtailed immigration in the late 1850s, and then came the Civil War, which deterred people already beset with troubles enough of their own.

Between 1866 and 1873, however, a combination of American prosperity and European depression once again increased German emigration totals. Congressional passage of the Homestead Act granting free land to settlers, the convulsions in the German states owing to Bismarck's wars in the 1860s, the high conscription rate, and low wages at home also prompted German emigration. When the United States suffered a severe depression between 1873 and 1879, immigration figures were correspondingly depressed. But when the American economy improved, anxious Europeans descended on our shores in the early 1880s. Germans who believed that prosperity would never be theirs at home left in record numbers; in 1882 more than 250,000 passed through the immigration stations here. The American depressions of the late 1880s and 1893–1894 cut emigration sharply, but by then an improved industrial economy in Germany provided greater opportunities than in the past, and fewer Germans felt compelled to seek their fortunes in the New World.

The Scandinavians—the largest northwestern European group, after the British and the Germans, to populate America in the nineteenth century— increased their numbers in the United States markedly after the Civil War. The first group of nineteenth-century Scandinavians arrived in the autumn of 1825, when about 50 Norwegians settled in Kendall, New York, about 30 miles southwest of Rochester. In 1841 a Swedish colony developed in Pine Lake, Wisconsin.

During the next decades, Scandinavians continued to come but never in the numbers that either the Irish or the Germans did. For example, Scandinavian immigration totaled only 2,830 in 1846 and not much more in 1865. After 1868, however, annual immigration from Norway, Sweden, Denmark, and Finland passed the 10,000 mark. Jacob Riis, the famous social reformer and friend of Theodore Roosevelt, for example, left Denmark for America in 1870. Like so many other immigrants, he arrived with little but "a pair of strong hands, and stubbornness enough to do for two; [and] also a strong belief that in a free country, free from the dominion of custom, of caste, as well as of men, things would somehow come right in the end." Other Danes and Scandinavians obviously agreed, for annual immigration from Scandinavia did not fall below the 10,000 mark until the disruptions caused by World War I. In the 1920s, when other Europeans resumed their exodus, the Scandinavians joined them.

As in the case of the Irish and the Germans, Scandinavian immigration can be correlated to a large extent with economic conditions at home and in the United States. Sweden enjoyed a period of good crop production between 1850 and 1864; the years between 1865 and 1868, however, culminated in a great famine that coincided with particularly bountiful times in the United States. During those years, the numbers of emigrants increased sharply, doubling from 1865 to 1866 and tripling from 9,000 in 1867 to 27,000 in 1868. The exodus from Norway, a large percentage of the nation's entire population at that time, can be explained almost wholly by the industrial transformation and the consequent disruptions at home. Norwegian migration can be grouped into three significant periods: from 1866 to 1873, when 111,000 people came; from 1879 to 1893, when the figures went over 250,000; and from 1900 to 1910, when the numbers totaled about 200,000.

Industrialism came earlier in Denmark than in either Norway or Sweden, and the rural upheaval sent people into the cities and towns. But there were simply not enough jobs for those willing to work, and many artisans and skilled laborers sought opportunities in America. Wisconsin was the first state to attract Danes in any substantial number, but subsequently large contingents could be found in Iowa and Illinois as well. Before 1868 families generally emigrated from Denmark as a unit, but thereafter unmarried, young adult male immigrants exceeded married ones by an almost 3:1 margin. A plurality of these Danes was farmhands but there was also a sprinkling of small landholders, craftsmen, and unskilled factory laborers as well. By 1920 United States census figures recorded 190,000 Danish-born in this country.

Although economic factors overshadow all others for the Scandinavians, it would be misleading to overlook social difficulties as motivating forces for the emigrants, except in the case of the Danes, who had no serious political or religious problems. In Sweden and Norway church and state were aligned, and both dissenters and nonconformists were penalized. There was no universal suffrage, and tightened conscription laws bothered many young men and their families; one scholar noted a particularly high proportion of emigrants among those eligible for military service in Sweden in the 1880s. Swedes in particular also abhorred the hierarchy of titles and the rigidly defined class system. After living in the United States, one Swede wrote home that his "cap [is not] worn out from lifting it in the presence of gentlemen. There is no class distinction between high and low, rich and poor, no make-believe, no 'title-sickness,' or artificial ceremonies. . . . Everybody lives in peace and prosperity."

Another compelling, perhaps decisive, reason was something called "American fever." After Europeans left their homelands, they wrote to their compatriots and described the wonders of America, or the "land of Canaan." Nowhere did these letters have a greater impact than in the Scandinavian countries. They were passed carefully from family to family, published intact in the local newspapers, and discussed avidly from the pulpits on Sundays. The influx of favorable mail inspired whole villages with the fervent desire to emigrate to America. Not all the letters from the United States glowed with praise, however, and many in fact did complain of the adjustment to the New World. But as one emigrant succinctly put it, "Norway cannot be compared to America any more than a desert can be compared to a garden in full bloom."

The Irish, the Germans, and the Scandinavians constituted the main non-English European immigrants during this period, but others chose to emigrate to the New World for similar reasons. Between 1815 and 1850 the predominantly rural Welsh endured severe agricultural discontent as the nation began industrializing. A depression hit Wales after 1815. The winter of 1814 had been the coldest in memory; and in 1816, "the year without summer," Wales began to feel the effect of a population explosion. By mid-century the nation's inhabitants, like those in the rest of Europe, had doubled. The high birth rate, the increase in illegitimate births, and the pauperization of the peasants compounded the discontent. When one looked at the United States, however, where an individual could go for £2 or £3 from Liverpool in 1836, there seemed to be a pot of gold at the end of the rainbow. The availability of land, the growth of American industry—especially in iron making and mining, where many Welshmen could use their skills—and the increasing number of "American letters" tempted those most inclined to seek a better life.

Dutch religious dissenters also considered American economic opportunities inviting, and beginning in the 1840s they founded colonies in Michigan, Wisconsin, Iowa, and what would later be South Dakota. Their departures corresponded with the potato blights and economic depression in Holland. By 1902 more than 135,000 Dutch, most of whom had arrived in the 1880s and 1890s, lived in the United States.

Several other groups, including the French from France, French Canadians, Chinese, and German Russians, also made significant impressions on the United States. Overpopulation at home and the diminishing size of agricultural plots that had been divided and subdivided for generations finally induced French Canadians to start emigrating in the 1830s, although most left Canada between 1860 and 1900. The approximately 300,000 emigrants settled for the most part in the mill villages and factory towns of New England, although scattered communities developed in New York and the upper Midwest.

The discovery of gold in California in 1849 had a great impact on the Chinese. News of the strike reached China by way of American merchant ships, but only the people of Toishan, a depressed agricultural province about 150 miles northwest of Hong Kong, responded. Toishan's agricultural output could feed its population for only about one-third of the year, and floods and typhoons frequently devastated the community. As a result, many Toishanese moved into commercial activities and came in contact with Westerners in Hong Kong and Canton, the two major cities closest to this agricultural province. They were therefore receptive to the opportunity for enrichment in the United States, and a number of the more adventurous males made the long journey. Only a few women accompanied the men. During subsequent years, more than half the Chinese in the United States came from Toishan, and a large percentage of the others came from areas surrounding that province. Lack of contact with Americans probably deterred other Chinese from going to the United States.

German Russians, Germans who had settled in western Russia several generations earlier and who had been allowed not only to maintain their cultural heritage but also to be free from military service as well, began arriving in the United States in the 1870s after the Russian government abrogated earlier agreements and tried to incorporate these people into the nation's broader society. Most of these Germans traveled to what later became North and South Dakota, but others could be found in Montana, Kansas, and Nebraska. Almost all were Lutherans, Mennonites, and Hutterites and some of their colonies today are more in tune with the values of yesteryear than they are with contemporary American culture.

The tremendous physical and economic growth of the United States in the nineteenth century made it mandatory for Americans to turn to the new settlers and laborers for cheap labor to plow fields, build canals and railroads, dig mines, and run machinery in fledgling factories. Without the newcomers the vast riches of the nation could not have been exploited quickly.

Fantastic efforts and inducements were made to lure Europeans, French Canadians, Chinese, and, later, Latin Americans to the United States. Their strong backs and steadfast enterprise were necessary to turn American dreams into American accomplishments. At the forefront of these efforts were the state and territorial governments, the railroads, and the various emigrant-aid societies, which were buttressed by federal legislation.

Just as the Atlantic seaboard states had made efforts in the colonial period to attract settlers, so in the nineteenth century practically every state and territory of the American West, plus several others, sought to entice select groups of Europeans to their area. More people meant more schools and post offices, larger federal appropriations for internal improvements, larger markets for goods, faster economic development, "and the speedy arrival of the eagerly desired railroad."

In 1845 Michigan became the first state to provide for the appointment of an immigration agent to recruit settlers at the New York docks, and Wisconsin followed suit seven years later. After the Civil War, though, the competition among states for Europeans intensified, and efforts to attract them expanded on a vast scale. At least 33 states and territorial governments eventually set up immigration bureaus, advertised in European and American foreign-language newspapers, sent agents to northern and western Europe, and published their brochures, guidebooks, and maps in English, Welsh, German, Dutch, French, Norwegian, and Swedish. Each state elaborated upon its virtues, "the likes of which," one historian has written, "had never been known—except to other states seeking immigration." Minnesota, proud of its "beautiful lakes, forests, prairies and salubrious climate"—and quiet about its subzero winters—offered two prizes for the best essays on the state as a place for European immigrants and then published them in seven languages. Kansas specifically exempted the Mennonites from militia service, and thousands of them moved there from central and eastern Europe in the 1870s. In 1870 the movement came to a head when several mid-western governors organized a national immigration convention at Indianapolis. Delegates from 22 states and the District of Columbia discussed how the federal government could be more helpful in recruitment, and they petitioned Congress to establish a national immigration bureau. The heyday for the state bureaus ended with the depression of 1873, but several continued into the 1880s and 1890s. On the eve of World War I, Louisiana officials still distributed enticing brochures in several foreign languages to those disembarking at New Orleans, and the legislatures of Michigan, Wisconsin, and South Dakota continued to make appropriations to induce foreigners to settle in their states.

The railroads worked as hard as the states to attract immigrants and in fact, in the words of historian Carl Wittke, were "probably the most important promotional agencies at work for some years around the turn of the century." After 1854, but especially in the 1870s and 1880s, most of the transcontinental railroads actively promoted immigration to the areas where they owned lands. The more people who settled in any given location, the more business and profits for the trains. Crops and merchandise would have to be moved and with additional markets and sources of labor, industrialists and governmental aid would surely follow. Like the states, the railroads subsidized agents in Europe, advertised and printed brochures in many languages, and played up the virtues of their respective territories. In addition, some gave free or reduced passage to prospective settlers, established immigrant receiving houses near their terminals, and built churches and schools for fledgling communities.

The first railroad to seek foreigners aggressively, the Illinois Central, inaugurated its program in 1854. The line sent special agents to the German states and the Scandinavian countries, and these men attended fairs and church services, arranged meetings, advertised in the local press, and promised fabulous inducements to prospective settlers. Not only did they help secure ocean passage, but they also provided free railroad transportation to Illinois for prospective land purchasers and their families. If the immigrants then bought land from the company, the Illinois Central allowed for long-term payments at 6 percent interest, gave discounts to the farmers for shipping their future crops on the line, and agreed to pay all land taxes until payments were completed. Immigrants preferred buying railroad lands to homesteading free governmental acreage because of these inducements, as well as the fact that the railroads often offered choicer properties.

The Illinois Central had almost completed its efforts in 1870, when most railroads were inaugurating their land and development bureaus. Some functioned as agents for states; the Burlington line, for example, represented Iowa, and the Northern Pacific line acted as Oregon's East Coast representative. They also published monthly newsletters in various northern and western European languages, and the Northern Pacific even set up its own newspapers in Germany, Switzerland, and England. From 1882 to 1883 alone, the company printed 635,590 copies of its publications in English, Swedish, Norwegian, Danish, Dutch, and German and also distributed a monthly newsletter for immigrants, *Northwest.* The Burlington's efforts resulted in the sale of nearly 3 million acres in Iowa and Nebraska, and the Northern Pacific is credited with having more than doubled the population of Minnesota, the Dakotas, Montana, and the Pacific Northwest between 1880 and 1900.

Working together with the railroads and state agencies to encourage immigration were the various emigrant-aid societies. But unlike the state agencies and railroads, these semiphilanthropic organizations were more interested in assisting departing Europeans and easing their travails in a foreign land by providing interpreters, clean boardinghouses, and employment bureaus in the United States than in encouraging them to come to America. This aid was clearly necessary, for as one Swedish emigration agent explained, "most of the emigrants are entirely ignorant about how to come to America."

Numerous steamship lines also vigorously promoted their own interests by seeking out immigrants. By 1882, 48 steamship companies traversed the Atlantic, each competing furiously with the others for the immigrant traffic. Fares were relatively cheap. One could go from England to the United States, for instance, for about $12 to $15, from Copenhagen to New York for about $30, and from Odessa to Dakota territory for $75. In many cases minor children accompanied their parents at no extra cost. Publicity and services attracted customers. The Red Star, Anchor, and Hamburg-American lines, among others, received patronage by establishing more than 6,500 agencies in the United States to sell prepaid tickets. As early as the 1850s the Irish were sending more than a million dollars a year—about half in prepaid tickets—to their relatives and friends at home, and other immigrant groups were no less diligent. In the 1880s estimates are that most of the Scandinavians emigrating to the United States came on prepaid tickets or purchased them with money specifically sent for that purpose. Although there are no exact statistics available, historians assume that 25 to 70 percent of all immigrants in the late nineteenth and early twentieth centuries received either prepaid tickets from the United States or money specifically designated to facilitate the journey.

Although the companies vied for the immigrant traffic, few felt compelled to make the voyage comfortable for steerage passengers. Before the 1850s immigrants came in sailing vessels quite similar to those the colonists had arrived in a century or two earlier and under similar filthy conditions. The average journey across the Atlantic took about 44 days, although voyages of four to six months were not uncommon. Like their forebears, many of those arriving in the nineteenth century, especially on English packets, which had been built for carrying cargo and not people, suffered inhumane treatment. Overcrowding, filth, stench, and poor ventilation were standard on almost all vessels, and tales of starvation and brutal assaults stand out in the accounts of many of the crossings. Over and over again one reads of the lack of sufficient food and water, of crew members beating and kicking helpless passengers, and of rampant disease. In 1846 a Danish man who sailed to New York on a German ship wrote home, "Steerage became a regular brothel. We had four prostitutes and five thieves." Dysentery, cholera, typhoid fever, lice, and "the itch" also presented problems. Those housed in the ship's bowels slept and ate on wooden bunks, which looked like dog kennels, and had straw-stuffed mattresses. One mid-century ship from Ireland possessed only 36 berths for 260 people; another had only 32 for 276. After one Irish ship had docked in New Orleans, customs officials found passengers and pigs lying together in "filth and feculent matter." One observer wrote that "it was a daily occurrence to see starving women and children fight for the food which was brought to the dogs and the pigs that were kept on the deck of the ship." An emigrants' guide in 1851 likened the fate of steerage travelers to those on the African slavers; and as a surgeon who had served on six emigrant ships wrote,

"The torments of hell might in some degree resemble the suffering of emigrants, but crime was punished in hell, whereas in an emigrant ship it flourished without check or retribution."

With the advent of steamships, however, conditions and amenities improved. The average crossing lasted 14 days in 1867 and only 5½ days in 1897. On the steamers all passengers had their own berths, women slept separately from men, and the galley provided three meals a day. Overcrowding and foul odors still existed, and the turbulence of the North Atlantic still forced many passengers to their knees to pray for divine assistance; but temporary inconvenience for two weeks or less could be endured with greater ease than the much longer and more difficult passage on the sailing ships. Moreover, between 1855 and 1875 both European and American governments established more stringent rules to improve conditions for emigrants and restrict abuses by shipmasters.

Immigrant traffic followed commercial routes. Because of the Canadian timber trade a number of vessels went to Boston, mostly British ships carrying Irish. British officials also concluded that the fastest way to send mail to Canada was via Boston, which also explains in large part how the Irish wound up in Massachusetts. The Mississippi trade made New Orleans the major Southern port and also resulted in its receiving more immigrants than any other Southern city. But the journey to Louisiana took an extra two or three weeks; moreover, the climate in the lower South was muggy, and the possibility of disease was great, so most Europeans shunned that route. New York, the nation's major commercial center, also served as its chief immigration depot. From 1816 on it accommodated more than 70 percent of the newcomers, and its reception centers at Castle Garden and later at Ellis Island became world famous.

Regulation of foreigners entering British America had been a function of the individual colonies and later, by tradition, of the states. The federal government did require the collecting of vital statistics in 1819 but otherwise allowed immigrants to enter unfettered until 1882, when it imposed additional regulations.

New York State, where most of the newcomers landed, passed a series of laws, beginning in 1824, requiring ship captains to post bonds indemnifying the state for any expenses incurred in connection with paupers disembarking there. Later the state required a $1 head tax on steerage passengers to finance an immigrant hospital. In 1847 New York established the State Board of Commissioners of Immigration. The law creating the board granted the commissioners the power to collect vital statistics, board and inspect incoming ships, establish and manage an immigrant hospital, and quarantine those who had communicable diseases. The commissioners, who served without pay, made every effort to assist the newly arrived foreigners. In 1855 they set up Castle Garden, a model reception center, through which everyone disembarking in New York had to pass. In this way the foreigners were counted, and their ages, occupations, religions, and the value of property they brought with them were recorded. The immigrants at the centers had to bathe with soap and water, and afterward they could purchase items like bread, milk, and coffee and use the extensive kitchen facilities to prepare their own food. Officials encouraged everyone to leave the depot within hours of arrival, but those who wished could sleep overnight in the galleries. Beds were not provided, but a few thousand could be lodged. Immigration officials had already inspected and licensed numerous New York City boardinghouses, and they posted lists of suitable accommodations. Before this time many "green-horns," as the immigrants were called, had been fleeced by boardinghouse agents and cheated by phony ticket sellers and other swindlers. To counteract this, Castle Garden also provided money exchanges and railroad and canal ticket booths for those going inland and disseminated information about the United States and employment opportunities throughout the country.

Castle Garden remained the nation's chief immigrant depot for more than 35 years. In 1876 the United States Supreme Court forbade New York State to collect bonds from ship captains on the ground that they were equivalent to head taxes, and for the next six years New York State financed the reception center out of its general funds. In 1882 Congress levied a 50-cent head tax on newcomers and defrayed New York's expenses out of the monies collected. In 1890 the federal government finally took charge of immigration and relieved the state of its role in this area. Ellis Island replaced the abandoned Castle Garden as the gateway to America for millions of Europeans.

Once through Castle Garden or Ellis Island, foreigners dispersed quickly. (See Table 2.2.) Those too poor to go anywhere else remained in New York. Others, determined to reach the wooded regions and fertile prairies of the Midwest, obtained the necessary railroad or canal tickets and proceeded on their journeys. A favorite route began with a boat ride up the Hudson River to Albany and then across the Erie Canal to Buffalo, then by water, rail, or wagon to the ultimate destination. Most of the nineteenth-century newcomers from Germany and Scandinavia wanted their own farms; the Homestead Act, the invitations from the states and the railroads, and the letters from relatives drew them to the north central plains, where land was either free or cheap. (As late as 1879 some Wisconsin land sold for 50 cents an acre.)

Those who were too poor to finance any trip once they had arrived in America—like many Irish—accepted the offers of canal and railroad builders to be taken along to construction projects. Eventually, as a result, pockets of Irish existed in every region of the country. Most Irish, however, remained in the port cities where they landed or in their environs. By the end of the nineteenth century,

Table 2.2 THE URBAN IMMIGRANT, 1870

Irish, German, and English Populations in American Cities

Name of city	Total population	Irish	Germans	English
1. New York, N.Y.	942,292	202,000	151,203	24,408
2. Philadelphia, Pa.	674,022	96,698	50,746	22,034
3. Brooklyn, N.Y.	376,099	73,985	36,769	18,832
4. St. Louis, Mo.	310,864	32,239	59,040	5,366
5. Chicago, Ill.	298,977	40,000	52,316	10,026
6. Baltimore, Md.	267,354	15,223	35,276	2,138
7. Boston, Mass.	250,526	56,900	5,606	6,000
8. Cincinnati, Ohio	216,239	18,624	49,446	3,524
9. New Orleans, La.	191,418	14,693	15,224	2,005
10. San Francisco, Calif.	149,473	25,864	13,602	5,166
11. Buffalo, N.Y.	117,714	11,264	22,249	3,558
12. Washington, D.C.	109,200	6,948	4,131	1,231
13. Newark, N.J.	105,059	12,481	15,873	4,040
14. Louisville, Ky.	100,753	7,626	14,380	930
15. Cleveland, Ohio	92,829	9,964	15,855	4,530
16. Pittsburgh, Pa.	86,076	13,119	8,703	2,838
17. Jersey City, N.J.	82,546	17,665	7,151	4,005
18. Detroit, Mich.	79,577	6,970	12,647	3,282
19. Milwaukee, Wis.	71,440	3,784	22,600	1,395
20. Albany, N.Y.	69,422	13,276	5,168	1,572
21. Providence, R.I.	68,904	12,085	596	2,426
22. Rochester, N.Y.	62,386	6,078	7,730	2,530
23. Alleghany, Pa.	53,180	4,034	7,665	1,112
24. Richmond, Va.	51,038	1,239	1,621	289
25. New Haven, Conn.	50,840	9,601	2,423	1,087
26. Charleston, S.C.	48,956	2,180	1,826	234
27. Indianapolis, Ind.	48,244	3,321	5,286	697
28. Troy, N.Y.	46,465	10,877	1,174	1,575
29. Syracuse, N.Y.	43,051	5,172	5,062	1,345
30. Worcester, Mass.	41,105	8,389	325	893
31. Lowell, Mass.	40,928	9,103	34	1,697
32. Memphis, Tenn.	40,226	2,987	1,768	589
33. Cambridge, Mass.	39,634	7,180	482	1,043
34. Hartford, Conn.	37,180	7,438	1,458	787
35. Scranton, Pa.	35,092	6,491	3,056	1,444
36. Reading, Pa.	33,930	547	2,648	305
37. Paterson, N.J.	33,600	5,124	1,429	3,347
38. Kansas City, Mo.	32,260	2,869	1,884	709
39. Mobile, Ala.	32,034	2,000	843	386
40. Toledo, Ohio	31,584	3,032	5,341	694
41. Portland, Me.	31,413	3,900	82	557
42. Columbus, Ohio	31,274	1,845	3,982	504
43. Wilmington, Del.	30,841	3,503	684	613
44. Dayton, Ohio	30,473	1,326	4,962	394
45. Lawrence, Mass.	28,921	7,457	467	2,456
46. Utica, N.Y.	28,804	3,496	2,822	1,352

Table 2.2 (*Continued*)

Name of city	Total population	Irish	Germans	English
47. Charlestown, Mass.	28,323	4,803	216	488
48. Savannah, Ga.	28,235	2,197	787	251
49. Lynn, Mass.	28,233	3,232	17	330
50. Fall River, Mass.	26,766	5,572	37	4,042

Source: U.S. Census, 1870.

Irish colonies existed in San Francisco and New Orleans, but the majority were in Massachusetts, New York, Pennsylvania, and Illinois.

The Germans, who, as was noted previously, were the most numerous of the nineteenth-century immigrants, had originally hoped to plant a new Germany in America: Missouri in the 1830s, Texas in the 1840s, and Wisconsin in the 1850s were the states that they had hoped to make their own. But American expansion and ideology quickly frustrated such visions. Americans were unwilling to allow any group to carve out its own exclusive territory in the United States, and subsequent waves of immigrants showed no respect or tolerance for the wishes of those Germans who wanted to insulate their settlements. Germans toiled as farmers in rural areas and as both skilled and unskilled laborers in the urban communities. Nearly half of them settled in Illinois, Michigan, Missouri, Iowa, and Wisconsin, but Texas published its laws in the German language in 1843, and Germans constituted one-fifth of the white population there four years later. Many of the counties of west Texas owe their beginnings to German immigrants, and by 1900 about one-third of the state's white population had German origins. Germans also dominated the foreign-born statistics and lent a particular flavor to cities like St. Louis, Cincinnati, and Milwaukee. Even in New York City they outnumbered all other foreign elements in the nineteenth century. One observer described New York's German section in the 1850s: "Life in *Kleindeutschland* is almost the same as in the Old Country. . . . There is not a single business which is not run by Germans. Not only the shoemakers, tailors, barbers, physicians, grocers, and innkeepers are German, but the pastors and priests as well. . . . The resident of *Kleindeutschland* need not even know English in order to make a living." A recent chronicler, in fact, made the same observation about people in and around Fort Wayne, Indiana. Until World War I, it was possible

> to go throughout one's life, and to expect one's children to do the same, living a German-American life—attending German-language parochial or public schools, dozing through long German sermons from the pulpit, reading Fort Wayne German newspapers, purchasing one's grocery, hardware, and agricultural supplies from German stores which prudently employed German-speaking clerks, attending German band and choral performances, sharing a "grawler" of locally-brewed German beer and locally-packed German sausages with

one's fellow workers at one of the one hundred and seventy friendly ethnic saloons, and ultimately to take one's final rest in an exclusive German Lutheran, Catholic, or Jewish cemetery.

Before 1890 the Scandinavians went mostly to the wheat-growing regions of Illinois, Wisconsin, Iowa, Minnesota, the Dakotas, Kansas, and Nebraska. The rich and fertile soil, the open spaces, and the harsh winter climate reminded them of their European homes, and with each successive wave of settlement there was the added attraction of living near friends and relatives from the old country. The solicitations from the actively recruiting states and railroads steered them into the Midwest, and the boom times of the early 1880s kept them there. Minnesota's population, buttressed by a heavy migration from Germany and Scandinavia, soared from 8,425 in 1860 to 101,109 in 1870 and 1,301,826 in 1890. Wisconsin, Iowa, Illinois, and the Dakotas showed similar rises. But the bitter winter of 1886–1887 and the successive years of failing wheat crops slowed the incoming pace. Beginning with the early 1890s Scandinavians responded to the industrial opportunities in the Northeast and the Middle Atlantic States as well as in the lumber camps and sawmills of the Pacific Northwest. The influx of Scandinavians and others into the state of Washington, for example, reached such proportions that the state population jumped from 75,000 in 1880 to over 1 million in 1910. Every census after 1910 shows more than 60 percent of the Swedish-born and their children living in urban areas. In 1917 Chicago had the largest number of Swedes and Norwegians in the world next to Stockholm and Oslo, respectively, and 13 years later the federal census found a sizable Norwegian population comfortably established in a middle-class neighborhood of Brooklyn.

Other nineteenth-century newcomers went to both urban and rural areas. The French Canadians had established small communities in Winooski, Vermont, and Woonsocket, Rhode Island, as early as 1814 and 1815, respectively, and later settlements in Madawaska and Burlington, Vermont, before 1850. By the end of the nineteenth century they constituted one of the major minorities in New England and much smaller ones in the cities of northern New York, Michigan, Illinois, and Wisconsin. The Welsh who came to America headed for the mining camps in Pennsylvania and Ohio. The Dutch, who went to the wooded and lake regions of southwestern Michigan, northern Illinois, and southern Wisconsin, also had settlements in Iowa, New York, Wyoming, and Arizona. The Czechs, on the other hand, went mostly to the prairie lands in Wisconsin, Nebraska, and Texas. Some of the mountain states in the West attracted English, Scottish, and Welsh settlers, and the Mormons in Utah were particularly successful in converting some Dutch and Scandinavian peoples who then went on to places like Ogden and Salt Lake City. Immigrants from the British Isles, Germany, and the Russian Empire found the coal mines of the foothills of the Kiamichi Mountains in southeastern Oklahoma compelling because of the relatively high wages they could earn there.

Even in the South—whose officials and some businessmen desired northern and western Europeans to fill the labor ranks (white Southerners commonly considered blacks unsuitable for any work other than farm and domestic service) but whose population in general did not want intruders—received contingents of foreigners. Swedes went to Thornsby, Arkansas; Danes farmed in Mississippi; Italians worked in Louisiana, Mississippi, and Tennessee; the Irish bolstered the populations of several Southern cities; a Slavic community developed near Petersburg, Virginia; and some Chinese planted themselves in Mississippi. In the 1900 census of Alabama, Italians were the most numerous foreigners in Mobile County, the Irish stood out from all the rest in Bibb County, and Germans ranked at the top of Europeans living in Colbert, Montgomery, and Culliman counties.

Wherever they went and whoever they were, the immigrants lived and worked under conditions that were far from idyllic. In rural areas, loneliness and desolation were common problems for all groups, as were prairie fires, blizzards, the pestilence of grasshoppers, and the ravages of storms or long spells of dry weather. Food was not always plentiful and sacrifices had to be made in other areas also. Many Danes in Nebraska wore wooden shoes; among too many of the pioneers, who depended upon the homespun garments that their women made for them, underwear was also considered a luxury that the hardier settlers did without. A German in Indiana wrote back home in 1842, "We have reduced our requirements for luxuries very sharply: We drink coffee on Sundays only, go barefoot all summer and make our own clothes because we keep sheep and can also make flax."

Mass immigration resulted in new social problems for newcomers to urban communities also, especially in congested cities like New York City and Chicago. Many immigrants were either unemployed or underemployed, and disease and poverty were common. Inexperienced with such problems, these immigrants proved unable to cope with them except superficially.

Immigrants generally found work easily in the United States but often in unskilled jobs. In cities like New York, Boston, and Chicago immigrants composed the bulk of the unskilled laborers, porters, street cleaners, bartenders, waiters, draymen, cabmen, carmen, livery workers, and domestics. The Irish could be found as stevedores on docks at every major port in the country. In New England they replaced young American women in the mills and later stepped aside for the French Canadians. Two-thirds of the domestics in Boston by 1860 were Irish, usually young women, and the census of that year also noted that Irish men and women held most of the city's common laboring jobs. Germans in New York held menial positions but also qualified as tailors and skilled craftsmen in the furniture, cabinetmaking, and bookbinding firms; in Cincinnati they were dominant in the stove and musical-instrument industries. Those Norwegians who did not farm worked in the iron mines and lumber camps in Michigan, in the sawmills and fisheries in the Pacific Northwest, and at other industrial tasks in places as diverse as Tacoma, Cleveland, and Brooklyn.

Workers were always needed until the completion of the canals and railroads, and strapping Irishmen won a reputation for talent and skill in these construction industries. Irish laborers built the Illinois Central Railroad before the company employed German hands. The Union Pacific used Mexicans, Germans, Chinese, and Irish to get its lines going. Scandinavian, Irish, and German women had no qualms about serving as domestics, but French Canadians shunned personal service for factory work. The mainstay of the late nineteenth-century New England textile mills, the French-Canadian family, insisted that all its members be employed at the same establishment. They put little premium on education and thought that children as well as adults should contribute to the family coffers. One overseer in a textile mill recalled telling a French-Canadian family that the law prohibited the hiring of children under the age of 10, "and the next day they were all ten." In the West the Chinese were forced to accept the menial jobs that whites shunned in mines, in domestic service, and on farms. Chinese also opened restaurants and laundries, and they made up half of California's agricultural workers by 1884.

Some immigrants were excluded from unions; others, unfamiliar with American laboring practices and the advantages of unions, worked as scabs and strikebreakers. Chinese laborers showed little regard for the white man's union, and when white miners struck in 1875, the Union Pacific brought 125 Chinese to mine in Rock Springs, Wyoming. Ten years later a similar problem resulted in the further importation of Chinese workers, who refused to join the Knights of Labor. This no doubt precipitated the September 1885 massacre in Rock Springs, where whites killed 28 Chinese laborers, wounded 15 others, and chased several hundred out of town.

The conditions under which Americans and immigrants labored were often appalling. Since American wages were much higher than those in Europe and Asia, emigrants did not realize that there could be economic hardships in the United States. In Sweden farmhands earned $33.50 *a year,* plus room and board. It is no wonder, therefore, that a salary of $40 *a month* in the Pennsylvania coal mines, $1.25 to $2.00 a day on a railroad construction gang, or $200 a year as an American farmhand would be appealing. Not until they reached the United States and had to cope with the realities of urban squalor or rural depression did the emigrants realize that the American laborer did not lead a princely existence.

In the Midwest during the boom times after the Civil War, farm income was relatively high. Wheat sold for $1.50 a bushel, and hard work seemed to ensure prosperity. But in the 1890s wheat prices fell on the world market to 50 cents a bushel. Countless thousands were ruined. There is no doubt that the failure of wheat crops in places like Kansas, Nebraska, Minnesota, and the Dakotas contributed to the decline in migration to those areas in the late 1880s and early 1890s.

Employees in industrial enterprises fared just as badly as those on the farm. In the nineteenth century there was a chronic labor shortage even though at times a city like Boston had more people than jobs. But the pay in most occupations failed to sustain even a modest standard of living. In 1851 *The New York Times* and the New York *Tribune* published estimated budgets for a family of five. The first came to about $600 a year, the second to $539. Yet the wage scales reveal that most employees' yearly incomes fell far short of these figures. A skilled tailor might earn $6 to $9 a week but did not work a 52-week year. Cabinetmakers earned $5 a week, and common laborers took home $20 to $30 a month. A journeyman dressmaker earned $1.25 to $1.50 for a 14- to 16-hour day. In Boston, in 1830, when the annual cost of living was $440, the average workingman's salary was $230; in 1864, when the cost of living rose to $810, the average unskilled laborer earned only $465. Real wages increased in the decades after the Civil War, but many immigrant families earned only a few hundred dollars a year and had to struggle to maintain even a modest standard of living.

With such low wages and yearly incomes one can understand why so many immigrants, as well as many native-born Americans, lived in quite humble and often downright squalid dwellings. The typical Norwegian in the upper Midwest built a log cabin 12 feet by 12 or 14 feet, with a height of 7 to 14 feet, for himself and his family. The early Dutch pioneers of Michigan lived under bedsheets framed on hemlock branches, with a cooking pot outside. When they earned enough to build a more commodious abode, several families shared a one-room log cabin. The German Russians in North Dakota put together homes representative of many others on the Great Plains. Inexpensively built, they had interior walls plastered with a straw- or prairie-grass clay mud and limewashed. Few of the homes had wooden floors since lumber was too expensive and the original occupants did not expect to remain long in these modest abodes.

Urban enclaves also left much to be desired. In small cities like Fall River and Holyoke, Massachusetts, French Canadians crowded into dark, dank, rat-infested tenements, which one chronicler pronounced "worse than the old slave quarters." Housing in most of the major urban centers was also appalling. In Boston the Irish resided in "crammed hovels . . . without furniture and with patches of dirty straw" or in damp cellars that flowed with raw sewage after heavy rains or in reconverted factory lofts with leaking roofs, broken windows, and no running water. Historian Oscar Handlin, who vividly chronicled their experiences, tells us that in winter the Boston Irish often remained in bed all day to protect themselves from the cold or "huddled together like brutes, without regard to sex, or age, or sense of decency. . . ."

Similar hovels existed in New York as well. In the middle of the century

18,000 people lived in cellars without light, air, or drainage, and even those who lived above them had to use outdoor, and often malfunctioning, privies—winter and summer. Overcrowding was proverbial; half a million people lived in 16,000 dilapidated tenements. The Irish often grouped five or six families in a single flat. Three-quarters of the city had no sewers; garbage and horse droppings littered ghetto streets.

The appalling overcrowding of immigrants and lack of proper sanitation led to continual bouts with disease. The newcomers suffered from consumption, cancer, pneumonia, diarrhea, and bronchitis. They were also victims of periodic epidemics of typhoid, typhus, and cholera, which spread through the slums like fires in a parched forest. Cities having the largest immigrant populations—New York, St. Louis, Cincinnati, and New Orleans—suffered the most from these outbreaks. In 1851 a cholera epidemic hit Chicago, and in one three-block section where 332 Scandinavians (mostly Norwegians) lived, *everyone* died from the disease. Hospitals and lunatic asylums housed disproportionately high numbers of newcomers. In New York in the 1850s, 85 percent of the foreign-born admitted to Bellevue Hospital were Irish; so were most of the admissions to Blackwell's Island, the city's asylum.

In rural areas, too, settlers, poorly versed in the need for proper sanitation, preventive measures, and the benefits of quarantines during bouts with contagious diseases, often fell prey to the ravages of rampaging epidemics. In 1898 a wave of diphtheria spread through McIntosh County, North Dakota, yet all of the German Russians insisted that every member of the family attend all of the funerals of neighbors who perished. As a result all of the adults and children in the community either had the disease or had been exposed to it. One cabinet-maker there, who worked day and night building coffins, had to construct three for his own children, ages 12, 10, and 3, who died within a week of one another.

Poverty was another common affliction for the immigrants. Rural folk would sometimes benefit from the generosity of their neighbors but in the larger cities many of the poor turned to almshouses. Those forced to accept charity also had to tolerate the sanctimonious declaration that they were merely "the indo-lent, the aged, and infirm who can earn their subsistence nowhere, [but must] become a burden, and often because of their vices, a nuisance to the community." The foreign-born outnumbered the native-born in the poorhouses of the nation in 1850; in some states, like New York, the ratio was greater than 2:1. And the problem became worse as more and more immigrants arrived.

Among the most serious difficulties encountered by the immigrants was American intolerance for ethnic differences. Each immigrant group experienced hostility in countless ways. The best jobs were closed to them, and employers posted signs saying "No Irish Need Apply" or some variation on that theme. Institutions dealing with the foreign-born—almshouses, hospital dispensaries, employment bureaus—treated their clients with "a ridiculous, often brutal disdain." Hardly any minority escaped the barbs of the prejudiced. The Germans received abuse from several sides. Temperance advocates did not like their making merry, drinking beer, and ignoring the Puritan Sabbath. Conservative Americans distrusted radical and reform-minded German exiles from the abortive revolutions of 1848 who supported the abolition of slavery, women's rights, and other liberal causes in America.

Economics in part explains ethnic intolerance. The increase in immigration, especially of many poverty-stricken refugees from Ireland, aroused American fears of having too many poor people. And large numbers of unskilled laborers, it was argued, would also depress wages and the American standard of living. Americans also deplored what they considered the immigrants' striking personal deficiencies. A Massachusetts Bureau of Labor Statistics report in the 1880s censured the French Canadians for their lack of "moral character, their lack of respect for American institutions, their failure to become naturalized, and their opposition to education."

Before the Civil War the most important source of conflict between native-born and immigrant was religion. More precisely, the key battles were fought over American objections to Irish Catholics. The underlying issue revolved around the American belief that Roman Catholicism and American institutions, which were based on Protestant concepts, were incompatible. In this view, if Catholics "took over" America, the pope in Rome would rule and religious and political liberty would be destroyed. Samuel F. B. Morse, the inventor of the telegraph, believed that there was a Catholic plot to destroy the United States. He held that the Church was sending Jesuit-controlled immigrants to America. Writing in 1835 he asked his countrymen not to be any longer "deceived by the pensioned Jesuits, who have surrounded your press, are now using it all over the country to stifle the cries of danger, and lull your fears by attributing your alarm to a false cause. . . . To your posts! . . . Fly to protect the vulnerable places of your Constitution and Laws. Place your guards; you will need them, and quickly too.—And first, shut your gates."

Morse was not the only impassioned enemy of Catholicism. Militant Protestants published sensational exposés of the Church. The most famous of the anti-Catholic accounts was Maria Monk's *Awful Disclosures of the Hotel Dieu Nunnery of Montreal,* published in 1836. This gothic horror tale was frequently reprinted and sold several hundred thousand copies. According to her inflammatory story, the author was compelled to live in sin with priests in the nunnery and witnessed the execution of nuns for refusing to submit to the carnal lusts of priests. She even insisted that babies were strangled and buried in the basement of the Hotel Dieu Nunnery. Such yarns created inevitable controversy. On the one hand, her work was cited by anti-Catholics as proof of their worst fears, and on the other hand, indignant Catholics and skeptical Protestants denounced the book as a fraud. Investigations turned up no evidence to support her charges, and Maria Monk was personally discredited as a prostitute. Nevertheless, many believed her story, and the book continued to inflame the passions of the anti-Catholic crusade. Her success encouraged others to publish similar hair-raising studies, and she herself added to the literature by writing *Further Disclosures,* also about the Hotel Dieu.

These accounts fanned the passions of the day and contributed to violence. In August of 1834 an angry mob burned the Ursuline Convent outside of Boston. Nativist violence occurred in other places in antebellum America, including a riot in Philadelphia in the summer of 1844. Most conflicts did not lead to violence but involved controversies over control of church property, religious teaching in the schools, and the general issues of separation of church and state.

Not satisfied with exposés and agitation, the nativists turned to state and national politics for weapons against the detested Catholics. A few nativist political organizations and parties existed prior to 1850, but the major nativist party was the American party of the 1850s. Called the Know-Nothings, this large secret organization suffered from a number of sectional disagreements and eventually fell apart as a national movement, but at its peak it was held together by a suspicion of the Roman Catholic church. In 1854 the party scored victories at the polls, won control of several state governments, and sent dozens of congressmen to Washington. The major strength of the Know-Nothings lay in the Northeast and the border states. Once in office the nativists proposed a number of bills to restrict the franchise and to make naturalization a longer process. They also established legislative committees to investigate alleged misconduct in Catholic institutions. Many Know-Nothings who took Maria Monk seriously were convinced that nuns were virtual prisoners in convents, and they petitioned state governments to free these women.

The proposals and investigations produced few results, nor did the agitation lead to immigration restriction. The movement failed in part because the party was fragmented, in part because discussions concerning the morality and extension of slavery consumed American political attention in the late 1850s. But most important, despite fear of Catholics and other alleged evils of immigration, was the fact that Americans welcomed immigrants because they were needed to help the nation expand and develop economically.

Yet even without native hostility, foreigners and their children preferred living in ethnic enclaves and often resisted moving into the mainstream. In some Norwegian communities a "yankee was almost an alien" and a visitor to Scandinavia, Wisconsin, in 1879–1880, noted: "On the streets, in stores, one heard only Norwegian. The church was a replica of those at home; the minister wore the vestments of the State Church; the hymnbooks were the same as those used in Norway." A more recent commentator wrote that although his grandparents lived in the United States for more than 60 years, "There's no evidence that they had more than glancing contact with anyone who was not Norwegian."

Several groups, including the Irish, Germans, and Scandinavians, established parochial schools to preserve traditions and thwart assimilation. The French Canadians feared that the loss of their particular language would mean loss of faith, which to them meant absolute loss of identity. For the Irish, language presented hardly any problem, but their church claimed their staunchest allegiance. To them nothing seemed as important as keeping the faith. Many sermons and religious tracts of the Irish Catholics, historian Hasia Diner tells us, "linked common schooling with Protestantism, atheism, sexual depravity, and social unrest." In the Upper Midwest, among other places, Germans and Scandinavians maintained Lutheran parochial institutions of learning, and in Minnesota alone in 1917 over 350 elementary and secondary schools were counted, where 270 different German-language texts were in use. Fewer than one-third of all the parochial schools in Minnesota on the eve of World War I taught their children in the English language. Most of these places utilized German but there were also schools conducted in Polish, French, Norwegian, Danish, Dutch, and Czech.

Schooling and language were closely tied to religion, and many religious groups split over the appropriate course of behavior and action. Most usually opted for the maintenance of established values. Among Catholics, liberal cardinals like James Gibbons of Baltimore and John Ireland of St. Paul argued for a gospel of success and accommodation with the members of the dominant society. They favored assimilation, opposed parochial schools, and frowned on Catholic insularity. But the more conservative theologians of the Northeast, like Bishop Bernard McQuaid of Rochester, Archbishop Michael Corrigan of New York, and William Cardinal O'Connor of Boston, did not agree with their more open counterparts. "Clinging to medieval visions of church and society," prize-winning historian Kerby Miller tells us, "The conservatives revered tradition, order, and authority both religious and secular." They feared socialism and progressive change and aligned themselves "with the most reactionary elements of native society. Likewise their refusal to attribute social and spiritual ills to any source other than 'Anglo-Saxonism' (their synonym for Protestantism and materialism) impelled conservatives to segregate their flocks behind rigid ideological and institutional barriers."

Protestants suffered from similar battles. One chronicler of newcomers to South Dakota noted, "The central role of the church as a conservative force that defended cultural continuity with the past cannot be overstated. It was the key to cultural maintenance and local identity in all immigrant communities." Constant admonitions from Scandinavian clergymen that "Language saves faith" and knowledge of English promotes loss of one's heritage permeated the region.

Germans especially clung to their religious traditions and fought bitterly any attempt to interfere with their cultural heritage. In 1889 when Wisconsin and Illinois passed laws requiring some of the education of school-age children to be conducted in English, both Lutheran and Catholic Germans denounced the new measures. Their united opposition led to Republican electoral defeats in both states and the subsequent repeal of the offensive acts. The strong German stand against compulsory education in English reinforced prevailing views about their clannishness. What is more, they did little to alter this impression. Great efforts were made to maintain the Old World culture. In Nashville, Tennessee, observers noted that the newcomers "used the German language as a weapon to ward off Americanization and assimilation and used every social milieu—the home, the press, and the church—in the fight to preserve the German language and German customs among their children and grandchildren." Historian Andrew Yox, who studied the newcomers in the North, reiterated almost the same point.

> The German immigrants who came to America in the mid-nineteenth century established a counterculture they called *Deutschtum*. In medium-sized cities like Buffalo, Cincinnati, and Milwaukee, the German quarter consisted of Gothic steeples, rows of small frame cottages, open-air markets, and the ubiquitous saloon. Unlike the sedate neighborhoods of the Anglo-Americans, the German district rustled with sounds. Beer gardens, brass bands, shops, dance halls, and "slumber-breaking" bells, installed in the steeples to rouse the artisans for work, teamed up to deprive the Yankees of their once-quiet weekends. The German community was younger, more tolerant with regard to beer and dancing, and more populated than the native American sectors. With respect to other immigrant enclaves, the German colony was larger and more developed. In major cities, *Deutschtum* consisted not only of stores and saloons, but banks, hospitals, orchestra halls, and elite social clubs.

Efforts were made to keep everything German and women in particular were admonished "that they must seek to preserve the German spirit in their children." A Texas grandmother, who had come to this country as a 10-year-old girl in 1846, published her memoirs, *Was Grossmutter Erzählt* (1915), in her native tongue and reminded readers that "German family life stands for the preservation of an ideal culture, which can only continue to exert its influence if respected from generation to generation." Most German Americans obviously felt the same way, for at the beginning of the twentieth century it was still rare for Midwestern Germans to choose mates from other ethnic groups, and on the eve of World War I, 70 percent of the Lutheran churches in St. Louis still conducted their services in German. In some German-Russian areas of North Dakota, moreover, church services and Sunday schools in the German language continued into the early 1950s.

The intense concern for preserving the culture of the *Vaterland* also led to vigorous organizational activities. German Americans maintained the most news-papers, fraternal organizations, gymnastic and cultural societies, choral and athletic groups, and benevolent organizations.

Newspapers not only preserved cultural identity but also explained the American scene, helped promote settlement, urged readers to become citizens, and related quantities of information about the homeland to homesick emigrants. By 1900, over 750 German-language newspapers existed in the United States, 64 of them in North and South Dakota alone. In fact, in 1905 the *Dakota Freie Press* had more subscribers than any English-language newspaper in South Dakota. Needless to add, numerous German daily and weekly papers dotted the landscape in all of the major American cities.

The Germans also enjoyed their ethnic theater, their beer, their convivial picnics, their pleasure-filled Sundays, and their melodious music. While parks all over America had bandstands filled by German oompah bands, their *Liederkranz* (singing societies) and *Sangerbünde* (regional and national associations of song groups) made an even more significant national impact. The *Liederkranz* groups were among the most popular cultural societies in the nation between the end of the Civil War and the advent of World War I. Composed of all-male choruses (some cities had female auxiliaries), they promoted not only choral song but also classical music, opera, and philharmonic concepts as well. These singing societies were a major force on the cultural scene in cities like Chicago, Buffalo, Philadelphia, Pittsburgh, Cincinnati, and many other cities as well. In Louisville, Kentucky, "the Liederkranz was the most prestigious of all the musical organizations," while in Wheeling, West Virginia, there were 11 different German singing societies from 1855 until their demise in 1961 and, we are told, "for many of Wheeling's German citizens the singing societies were a way of life."

Yet the coming of World War I marked the decline of the hyphenated German-American culture. The country then demanded 100 percent loyalty and denounced everything and everyone that smacked of "the Hun." Though many resented the pressures upon them, German Americans made a strong effort to conform to the dominant customs and thereby weakened their own heritage.

Scandinavians, who were mostly Lutheran, were more devout and more straitlaced than the Germans. No one caricatured them as jolly or frolicsome. Their faith, a stern one that frowned on drinking, dancing, and levity, also provided a complete philosophy of life stressing piety along with the work ethic. This influence was so pervasive and persistent that in 1934 fully two-thirds of all the Protestant church members in Minnesota, Wisconsin, and the Dakotas still belonged to the Lutheran church.

The security derived from the family, ethnic neighborhood, school, church, society, and newspaper hastened the day when immigrant children or grandchildren could stand securely on their own and move into the mainstream of American life. Having been nurtured in relative security, they had the strength to meet head-on new challenges of becoming Americanized. They knew, however, that the customs that provided a secure ground for their parents or grandparents would not suffice for them in the United States. The girls and women, more sheltered from the outside world than the boys and men, took their cues from fathers and husbands, changing their ways to the extent that the head of the household dictated.

But no sooner is such a statement declared than disclaimers must be made. To be sure, in the German and Scandinavian households traditional values and life-styles prevailed. In most of these homes women were respected and appreciated for what they were—"good, laborious, submissive, and silent housewives." But among some of the German Russians in the Dakotas, women were somehow thought to be of considerably less value to a family unit, and one popular saying among them went

> When women die, it is not a tragedy
> But when horses die, it is a disaster.

Among the Irish, however, women stood out as the dominant factors in family life. Perhaps because "the tone of male-female relations within Irish families was indeed characterized by intense animosity," as historian Hasia Diner tells us, as well as "a high rate of domestic violence and discord, [and] the frequent desertion of the male breadwinner," wives and mothers emerged as the strong and stable forces in the family. And because so much violence and disorder occurred in Irish families, a larger percentage of Irish females than those of any other immigrant group, sought work outside of the home and delayed or refrained from marriage. Political activist Elizabeth Gurley Flynn recalled: "A domestic life and possibly a large family had no attraction for me. My mother's aversion to both had undoubtedly affected me profoundly. She was strong for her girls 'being somebody' and 'having a life of their own.'"

And of those who did marry, Irish women more than any other ethnic females except blacks appeared in census rolls as heads of family. For example, in 1870 in Philadelphia 16.9 percent of Irish women headed families compared to only 5.9 percent headed by German females. (Only black families had a higher percentage of female heads in Philadelphia that year.) The tradition of strong, assertive Irish women provided excellent role models for their daughters, many of whom later became successful as nurses and teachers.

Thus, as we summarize the lives, experiences, and adventures of the old immigrants, we reiterate the points that the complexities, the inequities, and the incongruities of so many immigrants' lives combined with the dynamics of American society to foster a new type of individual in the United States. Almost always rooted in, and committed to, their ethnic heritage, and often desperate to preserve their native cultures intact, these newcomers frequently discovered that the realities of life in both urban and rural America eventually intruded on the values they wished to continue. To a certain extent, of course, modicums of the culture were preserved. But each successive generation viewed itself as more American and less ethnic than previous ones. And the advent of World War I in 1917 proved a mighty blow to ethnic life in the United States. This was true for both the old immigrants, whom we have just discussed, and the new immigrants, who comprise the text of the next chapter.

chapter 3

The New Immigrants

As the nineteenth century progressed, industrialization moved southward and eastward in Europe. Uprooted peoples left their farms and villages, moved into towns and cities, crossed national boundaries, and traversed the oceans. The movement was worldwide, and millions of Europeans dispersed themselves throughout Europe and the Western Hemisphere. Warsaw, Berlin, Vienna, Naples, and London were as much inundated by the newcomers as were New York, Chicago, and Philadelphia. Germany, France, Brazil, Argentina, and Great Britain received hundreds of thousands of immigrants. However, the United States with its higher standard of living and reputation for being a land of golden opportunity attracted the largest number of the immigrants. Between 1880, when southern and eastern Europeans began making their significance felt on American immigration statistics, and 1930, when the combination of immigration restriction laws and a major depression put barriers in their way, the United States received a total of 27 million immigrants.

After 1890 newcomers from northern and western Europe continued coming to American shores; but they did not have the same impact in either numbers or percentages that the immigrants from southern and eastern Europe had. In the nineteenth century, for example, 1882 was the peak year of immigration. Of the 788,992 immigrants of that year, 250,630 were from Germany, whereas only 32,159 were from Italy, 27,935 from the Austro-Hungarian Empire, and 16,918 from Russia and the Baltic countries. In 1907, the peak year for twentieth-century migration, of the 1,285,349 recorded entrants only 37,807 came from Germany, whereas 298,124 came from Italy, 338,452, from the Austro-Hungarian Empire, and 258,943 from Russia and the Baltic States.

These southern and eastern Europeans, the so-called new immigrants, were trying to escape from economic strangulation and despair just as the Germans, Irish, and Scandinavians had before them. The southern Italians, especially, fled horrendous conditions. Unemployment, high birth rates, overpopulation, cholera and malaria epidemics were among the problems besetting these people. Many Italian peasants lived in houses of straw or even in rock caves and abandoned Greek tombs. Often, one-room shacks housed people and livestock together. An agricultural laborer earned 8 to 32 cents a day in Sicily but rarely worked an entire year. Furthermore, while the population in Italy increased by 25 percent from 1871 to 1905, the economy slackened. Wheat, citrus fruits, and wine, commodities that were the mainsprings of the Italian rural economy, declined drastically in price on the world market. The resulting poverty made some Italian arrivals in the United States declare afterward, "We would have eaten each other had we stayed."

Some northern Italians had left the country earlier in the nineteenth century. After national unification in 1859, though, relaxed emigration restrictions and expanded steamship advertising combined with a depressed economy to induce southern as well as northern Italian men and boys and a few women to seek their fortunes in the New World. Many went to Brazil and Argentina, but depressions in those countries in the 1890s directed the traffic to the United States. The comparative prosperity and opportunities here, which were communicated in letters and reported by returning immigrants, finally resulted in a deluge of emigrants, many of whom left Italy through Naples. Between 1876 and 1930 more than 5 million Italians sailed for the United States. Table 3.1 indicates the peak years and the numbers of Italian immigrants at those times.

Table 3.1	ITALIAN IMMIGRATION IN PEAK YEARS, 1905–1920
Year	Number
1905	316,797
1906	358,569
1907	298,124
1909	280,351
1912	267,637
1913	376,776
1920	349,042

Source: Immigration and Naturalization Service, *Annual Reports.*

Jews ranked second to the Italians among the new arrivals. In the late nineteenth and early twentieth centuries over 2 million of them left eastern Europe, more than 70 percent of these coming from Russia. Over 90 percent of the Jews headed for the United States, the remainder going to cities in central and western Europe, Canada, and Latin America. If others were victimized by a changing agricultural economy, the Jews were aliens in the land of their birth. Russian laws, with few exceptions, restricted them to life in enclosed settlements (mostly in eastern Poland and western Russia), curtailed their educational and occupational opportunities, and conscripted Jewish youths at the age of 12 for 31 years of military service. Things were made still worse by violence. The assassination of Czar Alexander II in 1881 set off a wave of government-condoned pogroms—brutal beatings, killings, and lootings—which lasted for about 30 years. Jews never knew where or when the terror would strike next. A particularly devastating pogrom in the city of Kishinieff in 1903 involved 2,750 families; 47 people were killed and 424 were wounded; many Jewish homes were burned, and Jewish shops were pillaged. The massacre received worldwide attention and vastly increased the number of Jews emigrating from Russia. As a consequence of these East European migrations, the Jewish population in the United States soared from about 250,000 (mostly of German descent) in 1877 to more than 4 million in 1927.

The Slavic groups—which included Russians, Ruthenians (Ukrainians), Slovaks, Slovenes, Poles, Croatians, Serbs, and Bulgarians—together accounted for about 4 million of the new arrivals in the United States. Each of these ethnic groups had a distinctive language, set of customs, and historical experience, but most dispersed themselves throughout the country and either set up separate enclaves or blended in with other Slavic groups. Many were mistakenly identified in the census tracts or lumped together as Slavs and otherwise ignored.

The Poles, the largest of the Slavic groups, were counted separately after 1899, and as a result we know that after the Italians and the Jews, they were the third largest element among early twentieth-century immigrants. Well over 1 million Poles arrived before World War I; their coming can be attributed to the acute poverty in territory controlled by Russia and the suppression of Polish culture and nationalism in the sections of Poland under Austrian domination. The Poles, like practically all other Europeans, were influenced by what they heard from compatriots who had already settled in the United States. "It would be difficult to overestimate the importance of the letters exchanged across the Atlantic," two scholars have written. "Many were published in newspapers, others circulated hand-to-hand in the villages thus expanding an informal contact network."

Several other groups came to the United States for reasons similar to those that spurred the Jews and Slavs. Among them were found about 1 million Magyars from Hungary, perhaps 400,000 Greeks, 233,000 Portuguese, 105,000

Czechs, 70,000 or 80,000 Armenians, and thousands of Syrians escaping from Turkish tyranny; about 90,000 Japanese came from the Orient and Hawaii. World War I temporarily interrupted the major flow, but in the 1920s another 800,000 Italians, 160,000 Scots (more than the entire colonial migration from Scotland), almost 500,000 legally accounted-for Mexicans (as many more crossed the border illegally), and over 400,000 Germans streamed into this country.

One of the most overlooked groups was the Basques who settled in the Great Basin (the area roughly between Salt Lake City and the Sierra Nevada Mountains in eastern California, which includes most of Nevada, southeastern Oregon, and southwestern Idaho) at the end of the nineteenth and the beginning of the twentieth centuries. Their homeland, Basque country on the Iberian peninsula in Europe, was taken over partially by France in 1789 but mainly by Spain in 1839. Since generation after generation of Basques produced larger families than the local economy could absorb, grown children frequently emigrated. There are Basques in many Latin American countries, and the Basques also populated California during the Spanish and Mexican periods. Today Boise, Idaho, houses the largest Basque contingent outside the Iberian peninsula. Other Basque colonies are in eastern Oregon, California, Nevada, Wyoming, and Colorado. Since the Basques are Caucasians, they have not been enumerated separately in either immigration figures or census returns. One scholar estimated in 1970 that there were about 12,000 to 15,000 Basques, including members of the second and third generations, in the Idaho-Oregon area. It is unlikely that the entire Basque population in this country exceeds this figure; with intermarriage occurring it may even be less.

The majority of the immigrants, old and new, consisted of males who came without families; among the Irish, though, females exceeded 50 percent of the group's total. Of the European immigrants 78 percent of the Italians and 95 percent of the Greeks were males, while many Jews came as families. From Asia the Japanese immigrants, like the Chinese before them, were overwhelmingly male. Although many men sent for their wives and children afterward, others hoped to make their fame and fortune and return. Few made fortunes, but many did return.

Intelligent estimates of how many foreigners returned to their native countries range from a high of nearly 90 percent for the Balkan peoples to a low of 5 percent for the Jews. We do know that in the period between 1908 and 1914, immigration officials recorded 6,703,357 arrivals and 2,063,767 departures. During these years, more than half the Hungarians, Italians, Croatians, and Slovenes returned to Europe. For the most part returnees included a high percentage of single men. A number of Italian men annually migrated to Italy in the fall, returning to the United States the next spring. The availability of jobs determined their movement. During the winter months, many Italians in railroad, construction, and mining work saw no point in remaining unemployed in the United States. From 1908 through 1916, 1,215,998 Italians left the United States. This back-and-forth migration virtually ceased by the mid-1920s after the quota system went into effect.

Eighty percent of the new immigrants settled in the northeastern section of the United States, roughly delineated by Washington in the southeast, St. Louis in the southwest, the Mississippi River, Canada, and the Atlantic Ocean. Two-thirds of the immigrants could be found in New York, New England, Pennsylvania, and New Jersey; sizable numbers also gravitated toward states like Illinois and Ohio. Relatively few went to the South.

The major cities, especially New York City and Chicago, proved particularly attractive because of the jobs available, because of their location as major transportation depots, and because they were inhabited by compatriots who could help the immigrants adjust to the New World. A majority of the Jews and many Italians remained in New York. Other groups also found city life desirable. According to the census records of 1910, about three-quarters of the population of New York City, Chicago, Detroit, Cleveland, and Boston consisted of immigrants and their children. Foreign enclaves also dominated cities like Philadelphia, Milwaukee, Buffalo, Baltimore, Pittsburgh, and Providence. In 1916, 72 percent of San Francisco's population spoke a foreign language.

Although some habitats naturally had more to offer than others, no *area* of the United States escaped the immigrants' attention or proved totally unsuitable to all groups. Thus one could find—then as now—Italians in Louisiana, Michigan, and Colorado, Hungarians and Greeks in Florida, Slavs in Virginia, Mexicans in Illinois, Irish in Montana, Armenians in Massachusetts and California, Basques in Idaho and Oregon, Serbs and Croatians in Nevada, German Russians in North Dakota, and Jews in Arizona and New Mexico. Foreigners, including the English, Russians, Lithuanians, Poles, Magyars, and Italians, outnumbered the native-born throughout the Oklahoma coalfields by a margin of 2:1 in 1890. One Oklahoman noted, "You name it and they were all workin' together here. And they got along just fine too." Certainly, these immigrants constituted minorities in the states where they lived, but it is significant that so many places in the United States afforded opportunities to the venturesome.

The immigrants came with high hopes, and although in some places they got on well, in general they were unprepared for the coolness with which so many Americans received them. Like others who had come earlier, the new immigrants were often stereotyped as representatives of some kind of lower species. None of the newer groups escaped contempt. Greeks were physically attacked in Omaha, Nebraska, and they were forced out of Mountain View, Idaho. A New Englander, observing some Poles weeding rows of onions, commented: "Animals, they work under the sun and in the dirt; with stolid, stupid faces." On the West Coast the people of San Francisco created an international incident by segregating fewer than 100 Japanese students in the city's schools.

Italians, who outnumbered all other twentieth-century European immigrants, were one of the most despised groups. Old-stock Americans called them wops, dagos, and guineas and referred to them as the "Chinese of Europe" and "just as bad as the Negroes." In the South some Italians were forced to attend all-black schools, and in both the North and the South they were victimized by brutality. In 1875 *The New York Times* thought it "perhaps hopeless to think of civilizing them, or keeping them in order, except by the arm of the law." Other newspapers proclaimed that Italians were criminal by nature, and a supposedly intelligent and sympathetic observer wrote that Italians "are as a race simple-minded and often grossly ignorant." University of Wisconsin sociologist E. A. Ross, one of the Progressive era's most outspoken bigots, explained that crime in Italy had declined significantly since the migrations began "because all the criminals are here." Americans were fortified in their beliefs about southern Italians because many northern Italians, who had arrived here decades earlier, also regarded their compatriots from the south as "an army of barbarians encamped among us."

Jews experienced similar problems. In colonial America, Jews had not been allowed to vote, and the restriction lasted, in some states, well into the nineteenth century. Not until New Hampshire removed its barriers in 1877 did American Jews have the franchise in every state. Even where there were no Jews, prejudice and misconceptions were widespread. On the stage the Jew almost always appeared as a scoundrel. To have portrayed him in a sympathetic or admirable vein, one scholar tells us, "would have been in defiance of the centuries-old tradition that in the drama the Jew must be the villain or the object of derision."

When the East European Jews arrived, they were often scorned, even by German Jews. The German Jews who had arrived in the mid-nineteenth century did not want Russian, Galician, and Rumanian Jews in their midst. German Jews had achieved considerable success in the United States and had absorbed the nation's values, and many had even refurbished their religious practices, bringing them more into line with Protestantism. The stampede of East European Jews with their long beards, peculiar clothing, and staunch devotion to an orthodox faith that seemed strange to many Americans threatened members of the established Jewish community. They envisioned, correctly, an increase in anti-Semitic feeling, which would affect their hard-won respectability. Their views were most specifically stated in an 1894 issue of the *Hebrew Standard:* "The thoroughly acclimated American Jew . . . has no religious, social or intellectual sympathies with the East European Jew. He is closer to the Christian sentiment around him than to the Judaism of these miserable darkened Hebrews." But the American Jews could do nothing to stem the East European tide, nor could they stop other

Americans from lumping all Jews together. Once they recognized these facts, they reversed their position and did what they could to help the newcomers adjust to life in America.

Although the German Jews eventually reconciled themselves to having their brethren from eastern Europe in the United States, other Americans did not. Beginning in the 1870s the latent, or often privately uttered, anti-Semitism emerged into the open and struck first at those Jews who were the most Americanized. The New York Bar Association blackballed a Jew who applied for membership in 1877; a City College of New York fraternity did the same thing a year later; and a major resort hotel in Saratoga Springs, New York, barred a longtime guest, Joseph Seligman, one of New York City's leading bankers. Thereafter, clubs, resorts, and private schools increasingly turned away Jewish patrons. Hostility toward Jews knew no geographical bounds. In the 1890s, Jewish merchants in the South had their stores wrecked and were harassed by threats to leave town. In a New Jersey mill town several days of rioting resulted after a local firm hired 14 Jews. By the Progressive era, open discrimination prevailed in housing and employment. Hotels displayed signs proclaiming "No Jews Allowed," and job advertisements specified "Christians Only."

No amount of prejudice or hostility toward the newcomers, however, prevented employers from putting the greenhorns to work. The industrial sections of the country needed cheap labor continually, and the numerous foreigners provided the necessary hands. Older immigrants and native-born workers would not tolerate conditions the immigrants had to accept, and so toward the end of the nineteenth century Slavs and Italians replaced British, Irish, and Germans in Pennsylvania coal mines; Portuguese, Greeks, Syrians, Armenians, and Italians worked alongside French Canadians in the New England textile mills; East European Jews and southern Italians took over the jobs formerly held by the Irish and Germans in New York City's garment factories; and the Japanese on the West Coast did the agricultural and menial tasks that had formerly been the province of the Chinese. The United States was certainly not paradise for the foreigners. However, one immigrant residing in Chicago probably summarized the majority feeling when he wrote to his mother in Europe: "Nowhere there is heaven, everywhere misery, in America no good, but still better than in the [old] country."

Because immigrants felt more comfortable working and living among friends and relatives, ethnic groups concentrated in particular industries and occupations. The Slavic groups located in the mining and industrial regions of western Pennsylvania, Ohio, Illinois, Michigan, and New York. They also provided the bulk of the labor in Chicago's slaughterhouses and Pennsylvania's steel mills, where they were considered desirable because of "their habit of silent submission, their amenability to discipline and their willingness to work long hours and overtime without a murmur." Or, as the Pittsburgh *Leader* bluntly put it, the East European immigrant made "a better slave than the American." About one-third of the Poles also went into farming in the Northeast and the Midwest. They did truck gardening on Long Island, cultivated tobacco, onions, and asparagus in the Connecticut Valley, and planted corn and wheat in the north central Midwest.

The Greeks avoided farming but went into industry or operated small businesses of their own. One survey at the beginning of the twentieth century found that about 30,000 to 40,000 of the 150,000 Greeks in the United States were laborers in factories or in railroad construction gangs. But others peddled fruit and vegetables or maintained shoeshine and ice-cream parlors, flower shops, restaurants, or confectioneries. The association of Greeks with candy and food was proverbial. Chicago became the center of their sweets trade, and in 1904 a Greek newspaperman observed that "practically every busy corner in Chicago is occupied by a Greek candy store." After World War II the Greeks still maintained 350 to 450 confectionery shops and 8 to 10 candy manufacturers in the Windy City. Most Americans still connect the Greeks with restaurants, and for good reason. Almost every major American city boasts fine Greek eating establishments, a tradition that goes back more than half a century. After World War I, for example, estimates were that the Greeks owned 564 restaurants in San Francisco alone.

The Italians settled everywhere and entered almost every occupation, or so it seems at first glance. They built subways in New York, manufactured cigars in Florida, and made wine in California. In Chicago they manned the stockyards, and in San Francisco they caught fish. They constituted a large segment of New England's textile workers and were second only to the Jews in New York's garment trades. They provided gang labor on railroads and construction projects and worked underground in the bituminous coalfields of Illinois, Kansas, and Oklahoma, the iron mines of Michigan and Minnesota, and the copper and silver mines of Colorado, Arizona, and Montana. In 1894 they constituted all but one of New York City's 474 foreign-born bootblacks; in 1897, 75 percent of the city's construction workers. They moved into major sanitation departments in New York, Chicago, and Philadelphia. In 1911 a federal commission found that they accounted for the largest number of common laborers of any ethnic group in America.

But the Italians also yearned for the security of their own businesses, and as soon as they were able, they bought pushcarts or opened small stores. In New York City they dominated the fruit business in all its phases from produce market to retail outlet. They opened shoe-repair shops, restaurants, groceries, and bakeries. Some made spaghetti, others made candy. Many cut hair, and by 1910 more than half the barbers in New York City were Italian.

Unlike the Italians, who left Europe for the most part illiterate and unskilled, 67 percent of the Jewish males who arrived in the early part of the twentieth century were classified as skilled workers. This figure compared with an average of 20 percent for all other male immigrants. Most of the Jews utilized their craftsmanship in New York's garment trades, which contained half the city's Jewish workers. On the eve of World War I, in fact, 70 percent of all workers in New York's clothing industry were Jews. Other Jewish workers found jobs in cigar factories and distilleries, as printers and bookbinders, and as skilled carpenters. For the unskilled a peddler's pushcart often opened the path to settled retail trade throughout the country, while the enormous numbers of Jews, with their special dietary needs, gave rise to the establishment of kosher butchers, grocers, and neighborhood candy stores, which also sold soda water, newspapers, stationery, tobacco, and sundries. The Jews also found opportunities for themselves in music and the theater, and in the early decades of the twentieth century they made up half the actors, popular songwriters, and song publishers in New York City.

Outside the big cities, in the Rocky Mountain area for example, the Basques have been associated with sheep raising in the West's Great Basin. They have been herders, foremen, buyers, transporters, and ranch owners. When they arrived in the 1870s and 1880s, they were valued for their shepherding skills but despised as a minority. Some people referred to them derogatively as "Bascos," likened them to "Chinamen," and described them as filthy, treacherous, and meddlesome. Nevertheless, they maintained their calm and went about their work. Shepherding is a lonely, monotonous task, but the Basques excelled at it. Their culture values people who succeed in physically arduous tasks that also require grit and determination. One analyst opined that the Basque "sees physical labor and adverse working conditions as a personal challenge which affords an opportunity to merit the approbation of his peers." The Basques dominated the western sheep industry from the end of the nineteenth century, but they also entered a wide variety of industrial and professional activities. Paul Laxalt, for example, former governor of, and United States Senator from, Nevada, is descended from one of the French Basques.

Wherever the newcomers labored, employers sapped them of their energies before replacing them with fresh recruits. Industrial accidents were common. The infamous Triangle shirtwaist factory fire of New York City in 1911 took the lives of 146, mainly young women. One fireman who watched the women leap to their deaths told of the horror. "They hit the pavement just like hail. We could hear the thuds faster than we could see the bodies fall." Construction and railroad workers also frequently met with fatal injuries, as did newcomers in the Pittsburgh steel mills. Even where workers were fortunate to escape fatal injuries, working conditions often ensured irreparable damage to health. In Riverside,

California, Armenian cement makers inhaled dust and poisonous gases emitted in the large, overheated grinding rooms. In Chicago, Greek teenagers slaved in shoeshine parlors from six A.M. through nine P.M. Afterward the boys had to clean the stores before being allowed to return to barracks-like dwellings for a supper of stale bread and watery soup. The yearly earnings of a shoeshine boy were $160 to $180. A Hungarian immigrant complained about his experiences in a Pittsburgh steel mill: "Wherever the heat is most insupportable, the flames most scorching, the smoke and soot most choking, there we are certain to find compatriots bent and wasted with toil." In New York home sweatshops, whole families bent over coats and suits with their sewing needles.

In the labor camps, where many immigrant men came to work, conditions were as bad as in the cities, if not worse. Armed guards patrolled isolated labor camps in Georgia and West Virginia, and beatings with iron bars and gun butts kept the men at their jobs. When a Hungarian immigrant tried to escape from a Georgia lumber camp, his bosses went after him with trained dogs. When they caught him, he was horsewhipped and then tied to the buggy for the return trip. Peonage, though illegal, was widely practiced. Eventually, charges were brought against this particular lumber camp and the owners had to stand trial. As the Hungarian peon recalled, a peculiar kind of justice was enacted. "Of all things that mixed my thinking in America," the Hungarian later wrote, "nothing was so strange as to find that the bosses who were indicted for holding us in peonage could go out free on bail, while we, the laborers, who had been flogged and beaten and robbed, should be kept in jail because we had neither money nor friends." In a West Virginia labor camp Italian workers slept in wooden boxcars where "the dirt of two years covered the mattresses. Roaches and bedbugs livened the walls and held undisputed sway of the beds and their immediate surroundings. . . . All doors were closed at night. No windows, no air. Nothing seemed to have been left undone to reduce human beings to animals." The workday for these men lasted from five A.M. to four P.M. with an hour off for lunch. They were never given morning breaks because the padrone who controlled them resisted: "The beasts must not be given a rest. Otherwise they will step over me."

Not all oppressors were native-born Americans. Greek and Italian padrones, or labor agents, exercised great control over the immigrants. The padrones, who had come to the United States earlier, spoke English and arranged jobs and found living accommodations for their later-arriving compatriots. Men and boys were sent off to railroad and construction gangs, lumber camps, and factories. A padrone collected the salaries of everyone under him, or else a prior fee for placement, and kept a portion for himself as his commission. He also performed sundry tasks like writing letters and sending money back home for those unable to do so themselves. Often, and accurately, accused of taking advantage of those who placed their trust in him—the record of abuses committed by the padrones is replete with reports of decrepit rooming houses and vanishing payrolls—the padrone nonetheless performed the valuable services of easing the adjustment to the New World and of obtaining a man's initial position for him. In 1897 two-thirds of the Italian workers in New York were controlled by padrones, but as the immigrant numbers increased and the states began to regulate labor agents, the need for these intermediaries lessened. By the beginning of the twentieth century in Chicago and on the eve of World War I in New York, the number of padrones had declined considerably.

Although the new immigrants had little trouble finding jobs—either with or without the assistance of the padrones—the wages paid rarely provided for a family's subsistence. One scholar discovered that in a Pittsburgh steel district where a family needed $15 a week to survive, two-thirds of the recent immigrants earned $12.50 a week, while another third took home less than $10. Tales abound of garment workers earning 8 cents an hour; others made $1.25 for a full week's work. Prior to World War I, residents of New York City required a yearly wage of $876 to maintain a minimum standard of living; yet most families earned less. Although the immigrants earned low wages, some did better than others. In 1901 a government commission reported that Armenians, Jews, and Greeks fared better than Poles, Slovaks, southern Italians, and Serbs.

Wages were especially low for immigrant women who found jobs in the garment industries, in laundries, or as domestics. Yet these jobs were more desirable than others. Some immigrant girls who arrived alone and without money ended up as prostitutes in the nation's red-light districts. Indignant and moralistic reformers sometimes exaggerated the extent of the "white slave" traffic, but prostitution certainly grew in the late nineteenth and early twentieth centuries. One muckraking journalist described the plight of the poor immigrant young women in New York City.

> Just north of Houston Street are the long streets of signs where the Polish and Slovak servant-girls sit in stiff rows in the dingy employment agencies, waiting to be picked up as domestic servants. The odds against these unfortunate, bland-faced farm girls are greater than those against the Galician Jews. They arrive here more like tagged baggage than human beings, are crowded in barracks of boarding-houses, eight and ten in a room at night, and in the morning the runner for the employment agency takes them with all their belongings in a cheap valise, to sit and wait again for mistresses. . . . Just below this section of Poles and Slavs lies the great body of the Jews. . . . These girls are easily secured that in many cases the men who obtain control of them do not even speak their language.

With life so desolate, union organization made firm headway. Garment workers in New York and Chicago went out on strike in 1910 and after long struggles finally won the right to collective bargaining. In an industry run by tyrannical foremen and profit-hungry owners, unions like the Amalgamated Clothing Workers and the International Ladies' Garment Workers' Union (ILGWU) pioneered the efforts to establish safety and sanitary codes and to obtain shorter hours and higher wages. The people in the garment trades— owners, workers, and union organizers—were predominantly Jewish (and second-arily Italian), and this was the case well into the twentieth century. In 1924 Jews constituted 64 percent of the ILGWU members, and as late as the 1940s they made up 75 percent of the members of Dressmakers Local 22 in New York City. As the decades passed, however, Jews became concentrated in the upper echelons of management in both factories and unions and were replaced in the rank and file by blacks and Puerto Ricans.

The beginnings of union organization and the continuous replenishment by newer immigrants at the lowest job levels provided the minorities with the oppor-tunities to upgrade their positions and to move away from the slums. It is remarkable, in retrospect, to contemplate how people survived and continued to work and hope for better lives when they were mired in such depressed condi-tions. Whole neighborhoods were filthy, foul smelling, and overcrowded. In cities like Boston, New York, and Chicago houses adjoined stables, and offal, debris, and horse manure littered the streets. Piles of garbage in front of buildings or in narrow passageways between houses gave rise to stomach-turning odors and a large rat population. The population density was astronomical, some sections of Chicago, for example, having three times as many inhabitants as the most crowded portions of Tokyo and Calcutta. In 1901 a Polish neighborhood in the Windy City averaged 340 people per acre, and a three-block area housed 7,306 children! In the late nineteenth and early twentieth centuries the Italian sections of New York, Philadelphia, and Chicago seemed little better. One survey taker found that 1,231 Italians were living in 120 rooms in New York; another reporter could not find a single bathtub in a three-block area of tenements. In Chicago a two- or three-room apartment might house an Italian family of parents, grandpar-ents, several children, boarders, and cousins. A 1910 survey revealed that many of Philadelphia's Italian families had to cook, eat, and sleep in the same room, while most shared outhouses and a water hydrant—the only plumbing facility available—with four or five other families. In addition, many Italians kept chick-ens in their bedrooms and goats in their cellars. A Jewish girl in a New York tenement described her dwelling as "a place so dark it seemed as if there weren't no sky." In 1901 New York passed a tenement-house law requiring that all new buildings have windows 12 feet away from the opposite building, toilets and running water in each apartment, and solid staircases within each structure. But it took many years before a majority of the newcomers occupied such houses.

Although the members of various minority groups shared similar laboring and housing conditions, it would be a mistake to suggest that they also had common aspirations. All, of course, desired decent homes, well-paying jobs, and the opportunity to maintain their own life-styles free of strife. But the ethnic groups differed in cultural ethos and the ways in which each chose to attain its goals. Their attitudes toward family, education, religion, success, philanthropy, and community affairs differed considerably. Moreover, the values that the varying groups possessed frequently collided with the dominant strain in this country, a factor that sometimes created new problems for them in the United States.

The non-British minority groups spoke a foreign language when they arrived in America, and this placed an immediate stigma upon them. For their own emotional security they chose to live, like the old immigrants, in neighborhoods inhabited by their compatriots; and as a result they had even less reason to learn English quickly. Immigrant women felt particularly isolated because they rarely left the insulated community. Even the men were cut off from interaction with other groups. This was especially true when they worked with their compatriots in similar occupations, a situation that further retarded the assimilation process. As one Italian put it, "When I arrived in New York I went to live with my *paesani* [countrymen]. I did not see any reason for learning English. I did not need it for everywhere I lived, or worked or fooled around, there were only Italians." Habits of dress, food preparation, and religious practices were also retained by the immigrants. But the young children, educated in the United States, could not accept or feel completely at home with all of their parents' values. Children of immigrants did not usually sever all of the Old World ties, nor did most have any desire to do so, but they did try to harmonize as much of their parents' culture as they could with the demands of American society. Inevitably, such harmonization created intergenerational conflicts and strains. Moreover, the demands of one generation were sometimes in almost total variance with the values of the other.

Italians, for example, placed little importance on *individual* success or accomplishment. A person was supposed to enhance the family's fortune or honor, not his own. Only members of the family and their close blood relations were considered important and could be trusted. All others outside the family were strangers to whom one had no responsibilities. Family honor had to be defended to the death, if necessary, but society's laws were of little moment. "Individual initiative was virtually unknown," one scholar tells us, and "all actions had to receive the sanctions of tradition and custom." Most of the Italian immigrants seemed to follow the advice contained in a southern Italian proverb: "Do not make your child better than you are."

The Italian *contadini* (peasants), who had a history of oppression, linked education with class, status, and nobility. It was regarded as something that peasants—and women—could not aspire to. Education might be financed with surplus wealth, but most immigrant families could barely sustain themselves on what they earned. The *contadini* also had other reasons for being wary of the schoolhouse. In Italy, historian Rudolph Vecoli tells us, "educated persons were regarded with mistrust; in the old country, the priest and professor had been among the exploiters. Immigrant parents prized education solely for its utilitarian value; reading in itself was thought to be an idle, and perhaps injurious, pastime." Southern Italian immigrants therefore did not encourage their children to excel in reading. As soon as the law allowed, their offspring were pulled out of school and sent to work. Material, not cultural, advancement was what counted—the family as a whole mattered, not the individual child.

Some Italians, of course, did not subscribe to these views. The first American of Italian descent to become a governor and a United States senator, Rhode Island's John O. Pastore, had a mother who was impassioned with achieving American middle-class respectability. She made her sons wear fresh shirts every day and admonished them, "Make yourself liked; make people respect you." New York City's first Italian-American school principal recalled his father's urging, "Go to school. Even if it kills you." But these were the exceptions. Before World War II, few immigrant Italians graduated from high school or attended college. One survey of Italian children in St. Louis found that they went beyond the sixth grade for the first time in the 1930s. In 1940 only 1 percent of the residents on the Hill—the Italian area in St. Louis—had graduated from high school and only 18 percent of the inhabitants there had done so by 1970.

The southern Italian attitude toward religion and the church also differed considerably from that of most Americans and other immigrants. Nominally Roman Catholic, the Italians as a whole did not share the Irish dedication to the faith. Unlike American Protestants, who are not always dutiful in their attendance at church services but who maintain a respect for the institution and its members, the Italians—partly out of resentment of its Irish domination—regarded the Church as "a cold and almost puritanical organization." Moreover, they looked upon the priests as they had in Italy, "as lazy, ignorant hangers-on who merely earned their living off the community." It was not that Italians lacked religious beliefs but rather that their customs were quite different from those of the dominant Irish Catholics. They were flexible about doctrine, ignorant of many traditional aspects of Roman Catholicism, and devoted to the festivals and *festas,* which were more significant to most of them than any part of formal church services. The southern Italian immigrant feared "the evil eye" and its effects, and, as one historian tells us, "through the use of rituals, symbols, and charms, they sought to ward off evil spirits and to gain the favor of powerful deities." Inevitably, they were not avid churchgoers, though the women were more faithful than the men. An 1884 census of 50,000 Italians in New York City showed that 48,800 of them "neglected church services." Only as later generations of Italians became Americanized did they adhere more closely to the dominant standards of the Roman Catholic church in the United States.

Another point about the Italians that is less true for other immigrants and minorities was their inability to unite for community action. Southern Italians were devoted to their families and had some loyalty to members of their villages or communities in Italy, but they lacked an overall ethnic commitment. Italian mutual-benefit societies did exist in the United States, but for the most part each one helped comparatively small numbers of Italians. Regional dialects and lack of widespread written communication, as well as a diversity of thought, actions, and life-styles, divided Italians of different provinces and regions and made any kind of group organization almost impossible in the United States. Not until 1967, in fact, did the Italian-American Civil Rights League band together to protect and defend those of Italian descent in this country from abusive treatment by other Americans.

On the other hand, the success of the Jews in this very area won the admiration of numerous groups, particularly the Italians. In 1908 when the New York City police commissioner asserted that many criminals were Jewish, the Jewish community of the city protested immediately. A New York Italian newspaper remarked approvingly: "The Jews are all connected to each other, and, when they believe a patent offense has occurred to their colony, they act as one man."

The pogroms in Russia from 1903 to 1906 provided a focus for organized Jewish efforts to help their brethren in distress, and out of this came the American Jewish Committee, an organization composed of and representing the Americanized German Jewish community. The committee pledged itself to protect the civil rights of all Jews throughout the world. In 1913 Jews organized another defense organization, B'nai B'rith's Anti-Defamation League (ADL), four weeks after an Atlanta jury convicted a Jew of murder primarily, as B'nai B'rith and other Jews saw it, because he was a Jew. The ADL, dedicated to combating prejudice in the United States wherever it existed, was the first such general defense organization founded in this country and over the years has been quite successful in curbing the effects of prejudicial behavior.

Jews also differed from Italians in a number of other ways. They were more religiously observant, and, unlike the Italians, becoming more American for Jews meant a weakening rather than a strengthening of religious ties. The Jewish faith, however, embodies ethical prescriptions that make charity a social obligation, and no matter how loose the formal religious bonds, most Jews still regard philanthropic activities as an absolute necessity. Moreover, those who seek honor and prestige within the Jewish community know that they will receive both in direct proportion to their generosity and involvement in humanitarian endeavors. It is not surprising, therefore, that by 1909 there were well over 2,000 Jewish charities in the United States in addition to the fraternal organizations, mutual-benefit associations, cemetery groups, Jewish unions, and Zionist-oriented organizations. Jewish philanthropists in that year spent well over $10 million for charity among their coreligionists; the annual budget for Jewish philanthropy now tops a billion dollars.

Even the German or Americanized Jews, who at first had no desire to see their East European brethren in the United States, engaged in vast philanthropic endeavors to aid the newcomers. Motivation for such activities resulted partly from a sense of noblesse oblige and partly from a fear that their East European coreligionists might become a burden to society and thereby intensify existing anti-Semitism. They established orphanages, educational institutions, homes for delinquents and unwed mothers, hospitals, and recreational facilities. They were instrumental also in developing the Jewish Theological Seminary to train Americanized rabbis and a Yiddish language newspaper in the New York City ghetto to help Jewish immigrants adjust to the folkways and mores of this country.

East European Jews accepted whatever assistance they got, but in addition they endeavored to provide their own facilities. They too established charitable organizations to help the needy. They also devoted themselves to the quest for culture. Between 1885 and 1915 they started over 150 Yiddish-language newspapers, journals, and yearbooks. The best known of those was Abraham Cahan's *Forward.* At its height before World War I, it was the ghetto's leading journal and over the years the most widely read Yiddish newspaper in this country. In addition Jews established successful theater groups, and participants like Paul Muni, Jacob Adler, and Molly Picon went on to Broadway and Hollywood. East European Jews attended concerts and lectures and afterward moved on to the most popular cultural institution on the Lower East Side, the café or coffeehouse, where they would debate endlessly about plays, poets, pianists, politics, and the direction society was taking.

More than anything else, however, the Jews sought knowledge. New York City's Educational Alliance had a regular daily attendance of 500 and a waiting list of 1,000 for English classes, which were given at all hours of the day and 6 evenings a week. The poorest families saw to it that their children attended the public school, and teachers generally praised the youngsters for their industry and deportment. By 1915 Jews made up 85 percent of the student body at New York's free but renowned City College, one-fifth of those attending New York University, and one-sixth of the students at Columbia.

Jews who lived outside New York City did not have the million-plus coreligionists to support a full and rounded community life separate from the dominant groups in society. Accordingly, they generally relinquished Old World customs at a faster pace. It is for this very reason, in fact, that first- and second-generation New York City Jews remained where they landed. Rural areas, small towns, and even some of the bigger cities simply could not provide the cultural and educational opportunities as well as the Jewish sense of community so essential to these East European newcomers.

Other immigrants also sought to maintain their own cultures in the United States. For the Magyars in America both social and religious life revolved around the church. The Poles were also devoted to the Roman Catholic church and supported the institution generously. On the other hand, they thought less highly of education or advancing their children's positions in society. For most of the East Central European Catholic peasants home ownership was clearly the desired goal. Children may have been expected to learn to read and write, may have been tutored in the group's rich history and traditions, and may have been inculcated in the precepts of their faith, but as one Polish-American second-generation male complained, "Immigrant parents often thoughtlessly sacrificed their children's future to the exigencies of their own survival, sending them off to jobs when they should still have been in school or college."

Some parents, however, made the decisions about education deliberately and without qualms, and in this regard their views were reinforced by the local priest who "urged 'hard-working creatures of God' to exercise humility and patience suitable for their condition planned by 'Almighty Providence.' " And many ethnics agreed with such pronouncements. Too much education, they believed, was inappropriate for their youth.

Two scholars, Ewa Morawska and Helene Lopata, have written extensively on this phenomenon. Morawska explained that among East Central European Slavs:

> Popular consensus in the village still considered education acquired by formal schooling to be a pursuit for the nobility, a fancy of the higher orders; "It is all right for the rich man, but not for a poor, stupid peasant." In the virtually unanimous testimony of eyewitnesses—peasant-born memoirists, writers, publicists, and politicians—prolonged schooling and too visible concern with formal education alienated those peasants who possessed it from the rest of the village. For most, the only accepted and comprehensible purpose of schooling for a peasant son at the turn of the century was still the priesthood.

And Helene Lopata, writing about the Poles, described the almost identical thought patterns.

> The traditional peasant attitudes toward formal education were very negative, intellectual matters being defined as the province of the nobility and the intelligentsia, schooling was seen as an economic waste and a source of intergenerational problems. . . . The only school system the immigrants trusted to rear their children was the parochial school, which was expected to teach them Polish Catholicism and moral values.

Among most of the Slavs and southern Italians, education past the age of 14 was deemed wasteful and resulted in the family's loss of their children's income. Morawska found in her research, in fact, that many priests in Johnstown, Pennsylvania, as a matter of course signed papers indicating that underage children were in fact a year or two older so they could legally obtain work. Such views about education seem not to have been exclusively those of southern and eastern Europeans. Many religious Catholics, like Mexicans and French Canadians, shared these views. One scholar has written, in fact, that among French Canadians "formal schooling was devalued. Education beyond a basic level—reading, writing, and simple arithmetic—was required only for children who would join a religious order." It would take several generations before these views began to change and not until after World War II, and especially since the 1960s, do we find significant reevaluations of such attitudes among the descendants of the Slavs, Italians, and French Canadians. (The Mexicans will be discussed in a subsequent chapter.)

On the other hand, for those groups that recognized the importance of education both as a value in itself and as a tool for socioeconomic advancement, children and grandchildren of immigrants moved into the middle and upper classes much more quickly than did individuals whose parents frowned on too much learning. Among those who prized education were the Czechs, Japanese, Armenians, and Greeks. Japanese immigrants, who by law could never become citizens themselves, often made incredible sacrifices so that their children might go to high school and college. Armenians surpassed all other incoming groups between 1899 and 1910 with a literacy rate of 76 percent. Once in this country they, along with the Japanese and Greeks, "devoured" education. A common admonition of the Armenian parent to his child went "My son, don't be ignorant like me—get an education and be a man." "The Czechs," on the other hand, "came from a country where universal compulsory education was strictly enforced. A sense of literacy was thus ingrained in the Czech immigrant, and it was not unusual for parents to aspire toward a college education for their children in the United States." Greek children, no matter how poor their parents or how lowly their status, were "socialized to postpone immediate gratifications for a future goal. For a majority of Greek parents, that goal was to see their children . . . move up the social scale through the avenue of education, business, and commerce outside the Greek ethnic community."

The Greeks also tried to instill in their children the language and heritage of the old country while at the same time making sure they became accomplished in the United States. They encouraged their offspring to prepare for the professions, especially law and medicine, because in Greece these were considered the most prestigious fields. One scholar tells us that among Greek Americans "education of the young became a byword in community after community," while a Chicago schoolteacher claimed, "I think I have found the Greeks the brightest and quickest to learn." Greek-American children performed their required chores, but when someone asked one man why his 14-year-old son was not out working, the father responded, "My boy will stay in school. He must study at home after school. He must be a good student; he must become a good man."

In the Greek-American community the *kinotitos,* or community council, was the governing body of the people. It provided for the establishment of churches and schools, hired and fired priests and teachers, and exerted a continuing influence on Greek affairs. One could almost always gauge the feelings of the group by the actions and statements of the *kinotitos.* For recreation the Greeks flocked to their *kuffenein,* or coffeehouses. These served as community social centers where men smoked, drank, conversed, and played games in what became literally a place of refuge after a hard day of work or an escape from dank and dreary living quarters. No Greek-American community was without its *kuffenein,* and one chronicler reported that in Chicago before World War I "every other door on Bolivar Street was a Greek coffee house."

Many of the ethnic groups that came to the United States felt an attachment or loyalty to their native countries, but none surpassed the Greeks in their devotion to, or involvement with, the homeland. In the United States Greek Americans divided into factions and argued vigorously the ramifications of politics in Greece. Many Greeks did not expect to remain long in the United States, and their fervent attachment to the mother country continued unabated. Although large numbers of Greeks did stay in the United States, they were slow to take out American citizenship, which to many of them meant a renunciation of their heritage.

Like the Greeks, the East Central European Slavs remained attached to their compatriots and were reluctant to become American citizens. The ocean crossing did not lead to changed values or outlooks and unlike the fiercely independent Greeks, the Slavs, in general, did not perceive the United States to be a place where additional efforts would increase their opportunities to move up the socioeconomic ladder. Nor did they seem to consider social mobility as a realistic possibility for their children. They accepted the so-called natural superiority of the upper classes as part of God's order on earth and these views, which were sanctioned by both religion and custom, were deeply ingrained in them. They resisted pressures to Americanize and lived the life encapsulated by an old Galician village proverb: "There is not equality among angels in heaven; there will never be any on earth. A peasant is always a peasant, a gentleman a gentleman: Amen."

The numerous fraternal and social organizations immigrants established further attested not only to their reluctance to relinquish their heritage and beliefs but also to their desire to enrich their lives in America among compatriots who shared their philosophies and values. The South Slav Socialistic Federation played a key role in trying to further the aspirations of Yugoslav workers in the United States; the Ukrainian Women's Alliance (which became the Ukrainian Women's League of America in 1925) taught illiterates how to read while also promoting the goal of a national Ukrainian state in Europe; and the Croatian Catholic Society, formed in Gary, Indiana, in 1922, were among those groups actively promoting the maintenance of traditional cultures. The Greeks had two major ethnic associations: GAPA (Greek American Progressive Association) and AHEPA (American Hellenic Educational Progressive Association), organized in Atlanta in 1922. The former strove to perpetuate the Greek culture, the latter wanted to help smooth the path to acculturation. The variety of ethnic associations across the country also included the Garibaldina Society (Italian, formed in Los Angeles in 1885), the Young Men's Serbian Society of Tonopah, Nevada, and the Hungarian Verhovay.

Along with the ethnic societies were found numerous newspapers that recorded the groups' events. In the larger cities, like Chicago and New York, the different immigrants often had a choice of several daily and weekly newspapers in their own languages. In some of the smaller communities, however, foreign-language newspapers existed but the choices were understandably smaller or nonexistent. Among some of the numerous periodicals that recounted events in the old country and offered suggestions for coping with life in America were the *Ukrainian Chronicle,* the *Slovenian Proletarac,* and the *Bolletino del Nevada.* In the 1920s, among the foreign-language press in Utah, an observer listed *Beobachter* (German), *Bikuben* (Danish), *Utah Nippo* (Japanese), and *To Fos* (Greek).

In another area of the West, the Basques also took pride in their culture. Their language is Europe's oldest, although the Spanish takeover of Basque lands in 1839 caused it to become diluted with Spanish words. The language is so complex that in this country most of the children speak English. Although the Basques married one another during the first generation, the passage of time and their involvement with other people made this arrangement difficult to continue. Nonetheless, the Basques do get together periodically as a group. Since 1928 they have held an annual Sheepherder Ball in Boise, and there is also a midsummer St. Ignatius Day picnic to honor their patron saint. Many western universities have made an effort to preserve Basque culture. The University of Oregon has a collection of Basque songs and stories; the University of Nevada offers a course in the Basque language; and the University of Idaho collects Basque historical items.

Affection for Old World languages and customs, however, generally did not thwart the process of Americanization among the second and third generations. Once begun, assimilation could not be stopped. For most groups each succeeding generation possessed fewer ties to the old country and was more directly involved with American society. They forgot the language of their grandparents, moved away from the urban ghettos, and gained a strong foothold in the mainstream of American life.

chapter 4

Ethnic Conflict and Immigration Restriction

Although immigrants contributed to the accelerated pace of American growth and development, native-born Americans did not always consider their presence an unalloyed blessing. Periodically, different groups of Americans wanted to curtail the immigrant traffic, but the overriding national need for more people and the commitment to the idea of America as a haven for the distressed prevented serious legislative curbs. During the colonial period, the Scotch-Irish and the Germans aroused the ire of some, which led to hostile barbs and selective taxation. While John Adams was president, in 1798, the period of naturalization for foreigners was increased from 5 to 14 years, but the law was repealed a few years later. In the middle of the nineteenth century, as we noted, the Know-Nothings again raised the issue of too many foreigners, but their party evaporated before it could mount a lengthy campaign.

Between 1875 and 1924, pressure groups succeeded in getting Congress to reduce the number of immigrants allowed to enter the United States. Congress enacted its first restrictive law in 1875 when it banned prostitutes and alien convicts from American shores. Seven years later a more comprehensive law excluded lunatics, idiots, and persons likely to become public charges. In 1884 further legislation eliminated contract laborers. These measures, though reflecting a growing fear of certain types of people, kept out relatively few of those who sought entry into the United States.

More important, the Chinese Exclusion Act of 1882 was the first proscription of an ethnic group. The enactment of this law was the culmination of a vigorous West Coast campaign against the Chinese, and it reversed the welcome they had received during the gold rush in the late 1840s. When, in 1852, the governor of California was seeking new sources of labor for his growing state, he characterized the Chinese as among "the most worthy of our newly adopted citizens."

The negative picture of the Chinese originated with American missionaries, merchants, and diplomats who had sent back derogatory pictures of China and the Chinese before they came to America. These images were not widely known at first. They did, however, help prepare public opinion for the growing hostility toward Oriental immigrants that developed as their numbers increased from approximately 40,000 in 1860 to over 100,000 in 1880. Although a few opponents of the Chinese acknowledged that Chinese laborers were virtual slaves in this country, most West Coast workers, whether native or foreign-born, insisted that Chinese laborers depressed their wages and consequently provided unfair competition. In the 1860s, when the race to complete the transcontinental railroad was in full swing and jobs were abundant, this charge was ignored. When the job was finished, and especially during the depression of the 1870s, anti-Chinese feelings became virulent in California. One legislative committee in the state, appointed in 1876 to investigate the Chinese in their midst, concluded that "the Chinese are inferior to any race God ever made. . . . [They] have no souls to save, and if they have, they are not worth saving."

Behind much of the anti-Chinese sentiment was racism, the belief that there were vast cultural and racial differences between whites and Orientals. The Chinese were accused of having low morals, specifically of practicing prostitution and smoking opium, of low health standards, and of corrupt influences and practices. One advocate of restriction told a congressional committee in 1877:

> The burden of our accusation against them is that they come in conflict with our labor interests; they can never assimilate with us; that they are a perpetual, unchanging, and unchangeable alien element that can never become homogeneous; that their civilization is demoralizing and degrading to our people; that they degrade and dishonor labor; that they can never become citizens.

The movement to ban the Chinese from America centered in California. Mobs assaulted the Chinese; legislatures burdened them with special head taxes; and city ordinances harassed their hotels and laundries. The most vigorous opposition came from Dennis Kearney and the Workingmen's party in the 1870s. One manifesto of this group declared, "The Chinaman must leave our shores. We declare that white men and women, and boys, and girls, cannot live as the people of the great republic should and compete with the single Chinese coolie in the labor market. . . . To an American, death is preferable to life on a par with the Chinaman."

In response to the intense pressure from people on the West Coast, Congress passed the Chinese Exclusion Act of 1882. Loopholes in the law allowed for some immigration, however, and this sparked further agitation and violence in the West. In 1885 a Tacoma, Washington, mob drove out its Chinese residents and burned their homes, and incidents of violence occurred elsewhere in the West. More Chinese were harassed in Arizona in 1886 than in any other year. While awaiting further congressional action California passed its most far-reaching anti-Chinese law. This measure barred all Chinese except governmental officials from entering the state and required those already there to register with state officials. In 1892 additional congressional legislation virtually ended Chinese immigration and restricted the civil rights of those still in this country.

Following these restrictions, overt violence against the Chinese ceased, and agitation for tighter laws and controls gradually subsided. Yet the prejudice against the Chinese remained. Discrimination in jobs and housing was common after 1890, and derogatory images of Chinese Americans appeared in the media. Newspapers played up stories of prostitution, gambling, and opium dens in Chinatowns. "Chinks" and "John Chinaman" were sobriquets frequently used to describe Chinese Americans. The prejudices and discrimination lasted well into the twentieth century. State laws against interracial marriages, for example, were part of the legacy of racial prejudice, and Chinese aliens were not eligible for citizenship until after 1943.

In part, Americans transferred their prejudice after the Japanese began arriving in California and Hawaii in the 1890s. Again the focus of hostility and agitation was California, where most of the continental Japanese lived. Arguments similar to those used against the Chinese were employed to assail Japanese immigrants. "The Japs must go," shouted one demagogue; and the United States Industrial Commission reported in 1901 that the Japanese were "far less desirable" than the Chinese. "They have most of the vices of the Chinese, with none of the virtues. They underbid the Chinese in everything, and are as a class tricky, unreliable and dishonest."

And yet the racism directed against the Japanese was not the same as the anti-Chinese feeling. Whereas the Chinese were considered coolies who depressed American wages, at times the Japanese were considered too successful, especially in California agriculture, in which they became efficient workers and growers. Unlike China, Japan was becoming a world power at the beginning of the twentieth century. Instead of showing contempt for Japan, many racists became alarmed by her growing power. The fear was expressed in the "yellow peril" scare just after 1900. The yellow peril was a visionary invasion of the United States by hordes of Asians. Congressman Richmond Pearson Hobson of Alabama insisted that the yellow peril was already here, and he further warned of war: "The Japanese are the most secretive people in the world" and are "rushing forward with feverish haste stupendous preparations for war. . . . The war is to be with America." The Hearst press in California insisted that "every one of these immigrants . . . is a Japanese spy."

Growing fear of and antagonism toward Japanese immigrants reached a crisis after the turn of the century. Led by labor groups, delegates gathered in San Francisco in 1905 to organize the Asiatic Exclusion League. A year later, the San Francisco Board of Education ordered the segregation of all Oriental pupils. Of the city's 25,000 schoolchildren only 93 were Japanese, but the public was outraged at reports that older Japanese boys were sitting next to little white girls in classes. The Japanese government protested the order, and Theodore Roosevelt's administration found itself faced with a full-fledged diplomatic crisis. Federal pressure on the San Francisco school board led to the rescinding of the new policy. In return the Japanese, in the Gentlemen's Agreement of 1907, promised to restrict exit visas for laborers who wanted to go to the United States. The agreement, though it short-circuited a confrontation, did not prevent those Japanese already here from pursuing the American dream. Reputedly hard workers and shrewd businessmen, they amassed a great deal of property before the California legislature, in 1913, prohibited aliens ineligible for citizenship from acquiring land. The act, based on a provision of the naturalization laws limiting citizenship to incoming whites and descendants of Africans, failed in its purpose because the Japanese continued acquiring property in the names of their American-born children or under legal corporate guises.

Californians may have been especially concerned with Asian minorities but the most widespread American hostility was directed at Roman Catholics. The growing Catholic immigrant population after 1880 once more stirred up Protestant bigotry. Even more than before the Civil War, the Roman Catholic church appeared aggressive and powerful as Irish Catholics succeeded in politics and Catholic leaders spoke without restraint in public.

School issues in particular kindled ethnic tensions. Catholics found the Protestant orientation of American public schools offensive and developed their own parochial schools. Although the Church encouraged all Catholics to send their children to these schools, only a minority of Catholics—mostly of Irish background—chose, or could afford, to do so. This led in turn to Catholic demands for state aid for parochial schools, a proposal that further enraged Protestants. Local elections often centered on the school issue, as did the 1880 elections in New York City, for example. The Democrats had nominated William R. Grace, a Roman Catholic, for the mayoralty, and this incensed a number of the city's Protestants. *The New York Times* stated the prevalent anxieties clearly:

If the Irish Catholics should happen, for instance, to control the Mayoralty, the Controllership, and the Board of Aldermen, they would very soon be able to

> reconstitute the Board of Education, to place Catholic Trustees over certain schools, to put in Catholic teachers, to introduce Catholic textbooks, to convey public funds to Church schools under some guise which would elude the law, and, in fact, to Romanize our whole system of public education.

In the end Grace won the election, and the fears expressed by *The New York Times* proved groundless. But the anxieties remained.

Boston, with its large Irish population, was also a hotbed of dispute. In 1889 a teacher in a public high school defined indulgences in a manner that was considered offensive by a Catholic pupil. The Church protested and the Boston School Committee reprimanded the teacher, transferred him from history to English (a "safer" subject), and dropped a disputed text. Aroused Protestants organized and in the next election won control of the school committee.

At the national level the issue over religion and the schools intruded and divided political parties. In 1875 James G. Blaine, the House Republican leader, proposed a constitutional amendment to ban governmental property or financial aid for the use of any school or other institution under the control of any religious sect. Although the amendment never passed, the issue prompted considerable debate.

At bottom much of the conflict centered on the belief held by many Protestants that Catholicism was a menace to American values and institutions. This view was not as strong as it had been before the Civil War. Nevertheless, many Protestants believed that a large proportion of American Catholics were under the thumb of Rome and were unwilling to accept American values. Some champions of militant Protestantism insisted that Catholics had divided loyalties and should be denied the ballot until they took an oath of allegiance renouncing the supremacy of the pope. A prominent Protestant clergyman, Josiah Strong, expressed much of this anxiety in his popular *Our Country: Its Possible Future and Its Present Crisis* (1885), in which he argued that Catholics gave their foremost allegiance to the Church, not to the United States of America. Protestants like Strong were also agitated because of the Roman Catholic church's opposition or indifference to the temperance crusade.

The largest anti-Catholic organization to appear in the late nineteenth century was the American Protective Association (APA). Founded in 1887 in Clinton, Iowa, by Henry Bowers, the APA had a large following until the mid-1890s; at its peak it claimed 2.5 million members. Appealing mainly to working-class Protestants in the Rocky Mountain States and the Far West, the APA pledged its members' support of public schools, immigration restriction, and tougher naturalization laws.

To fight the so-called Roman menace, APA members organized boycotts of Catholic merchants, refused to go on strike with Catholic trade unionists, and vowed never to vote for a Roman Catholic for public office. The growing political power of Catholics was especially alarming to the organization, which claimed that "although only one-eighth of the population of the United States was Catholic . . . one-half of all the public officeholders were Catholics . . . , Catholics were favored in the Civil Service examinations, and . . . all civil servants were forced to contribute to Catholic charities."

Hysteria peaked in 1893 when many believed a rumor that the pope had written a letter ordering Catholics to exterminate all heretics in the United States. Some Protestants armed themselves, and the mayor of Toledo called out the National Guard to halt the coming slaughter. The rumor soon proved groundless and fraudulent, of course, but members of the APA quickly found other examples of Catholicism to fight.

The association never formed a political party, but it did enter politics. It supported candidates, usually Republicans, who were against the Catholic church and lobbied for particular pieces of legislation. The association backed state compulsory school-attendance laws and, at the national level, became embroiled in a dispute over Indian schools. Under federal policy established during the Grant administration, contracts were granted to church groups to operate Indian schools. Thus federal funds were going to parochial schools, a policy that horrified the APA. The association threw its support behind efforts to eliminate the contract system and substitute public schools for the church-supported ones.

In spite of the widespread hostility to Catholicism among non-Catholics, the appeal of the association was limited. The movement crested in the 1890s and then fell apart. Other issues were more important to American voters in the 1890s, and the APA found itself plagued by internal disputes. The Republicans used the APA, but they discovered that it was not important politically. Anti-Catholicism took other forms after 1895.

In addition to the religious prejudice directed at Catholics, as we have noted, hostility toward Jews also grew in the late nineteenth century. Anti-Semitism was aggravated by the economic depressions that plagued Americans, on and off, from 1873 through 1896. The German Jews, who arrived in the United States in the middle of the nineteenth century, prospered despite the existing prejudices because there were few, if any, economic barriers to those who were enterprising. Their prosperity in the face of widespread unemployment and despair reinforced the old Shylock image of a cunning and avaricious Jew demanding his pound of flesh. One southern patrician noted, for example, "It is quite the fashion to caricature the Jew as exacting his interest down to the last drachma." He then pointed out, perhaps half in envy and half in respect, that in the hardest of times the Jew "has money to lend if not to burn and before he is ready to execute his will he owns the grocery store, the meat-market, the grog-shop, the planing-mill, the newspaper, the hotel and the bank." The extremist fringe in the free-silver movement saw the Jew as the arch enemy foisting an international gold standard on beleaguered American farmers who were fighting for silver, "the people's money."

The presence of East European Jews, who started coming to the United States in the 1870s, aggravated existing anti-Semitic feelings; and as already noted, all Jews faced growing social and economic discrimination. As Jewish immigration from eastern Europe increased, this anti-Semitism helped to kindle the movement for immigration restriction. In 1906 a member of President Theodore Roosevelt's immigration commission told an investigator that the "movement toward restriction in all of its phases is directed against Jewish immigration. . . ."

Alongside religious antagonisms, economic conflicts also confronted the immigrants. Many workers opposed immigrants on the grounds that the newcomers depressed wages and were potential strikebreakers. The Knights of Labor called for a ban on contract labor, as did a number of labor leaders. Organized labor, with a high proportion of foreign-born workers, was reluctant to support general immigration restriction, but labor leaders were becoming more critical of immigration in the 1880s and in the economically depressed 1890s. In 1897 the American Federation of Labor (AFL), America's largest labor union, finally supported a literacy test as a means of limiting immigration.

Although employers needed workers for the nation's growing industries, at times they were uneasy about immigration. Labor disturbances, fairly common occurrences in the late nineteenth century, were frequently blamed unfairly on foreign agitators. In 1886 policemen broke up a peaceful protest meeting in Chicago. Before the crowd could be dispersed, however, a bomb exploded, killing seven policemen. Although no one knew who threw the explosive, the press placed the blame upon foreigners. One newspaper declared, "The enemy forces are not American [but] rag-tag and bob-tail cutthroats of Beelzebub from the Rhine, the Danube, the Vistula, and the Elbe." Another said the German anarchists accused of the crime were "long-haired, wild-eyed, bad-smelling, atheistic, reckless foreign wretches, who never did an honest hour's work in their lives."

Especially important in the growth of nativism was the fact that Americans became aware of the increased immigration from southern and eastern Europe. As previously noted, Americans considered these new immigrants to be undesirable, unassimilable, and hostile or indifferent to American values. Stereotyped images of Slavs, Italians, and Jews predominated. A retired superintendent who had worked in the Pennsylvania steel mills from the 1880s through the 1930s recalled, "Racism was very distinct then. . . . We all called them Huns, Dagos and Polacks." To the nativist, Italians suggested an image of crime and violence. As a Baltimore newspaper put it, "The disposition to assassinate in revenge for a fancied wrong is a marked trait in the character of this impulsive and inexorable race." Anti-Italian sentiment led to the lynching of 11 Italians in New Orleans in 1891. After the murder of a police superintendent, suspicion focused on the local Sicilian community and several Italians were indicted. City officials called for stern action, but the jury refused to convict. An angry mob then took matters into its own hands and lynched the accused men.

Late nineteenth-century Americans were increasingly receptive to pseudoracial thinking that classified Europeans into different races. In other words, Slavs, Jews, and Italians constituted races rather than nationalities or ethnic groups. This kind of thinking emphasized differences and deemed one "race" to be superior to another. This point of view became more important in the early twentieth century. Not surprisingly, racists found the old immigrants more desirable than the new. As one alarmed nativist said, "It is only in recent years that new, more ignorant and therefore more dangerous elements have entered into the problem of immigration. . . . The Irish and German tides were ebbing, while those of Southern and Eastern Europe were both increasing and threatening. None but an optimist . . . can view it without concern."

Just as religious prejudice, economic rivalry, and intellectual racism generated opposition to immigration, so did politics. Urban reformers noted with apprehension the rise of the Irish and then other ethnic minorities in urban politics. Reformers, usually those of old stock, believed that political machines built on immigrant votes were corrupt and inefficient, the protectors of prostitution, graft, and saloons. Prostitution was considered a virtual immigrant monopoly. A reform group in the 1890s declared, "Unless we make energetic and successful war upon the red light districts . . . we shall have Oriental brothel slavery thrust upon us. . . . Jew traders, too, will people our 'levees' with Polish Jewesses and any others who will make money for them. Shall we defend our American civilization, or lower our flag to the most despicable foreigners— French, Irish, Italians, Jews, and Mongolians?" When the power of the immigrant-supported machine was broken, they argued, American cities would be reformed.

Not all reformers regarded the immigrant as the cause of corruption; many attributed political corruption to business influence, and they noted that immigrants supported machines because the machines helped them. Clean up the immigrants' environment, they said, and the machine would lose its following. Yet graft and the social ills of American cities, combined with the concentration of immigrants in the urban ghettos, too often led native-born Americans to blame political chicanery on immigrants.

Conflicts also arose among the immigrants themselves. Many of the newcomers distrusted and disliked one another. Irishman Dennis Kearney, leader of the California Workingmen's party, led the assault on the Chinese, and English-born Samuel Gompers of the AFL favored immigration restriction. Within the ranks of labor some foreign-born unionists did not want members of ethnic groups other than their own in their unions. Foreign-born Protestants, as within the APA, did not trust Catholic immigrants. Within the Catholic church itself, Germans, French Canadians, Italians, and Poles resented Irish domination. As one Polish journal remarked in 1900, "Is it that the Irish want to dominate the Catholic world? Can't Polish Catholics have as much freedom as the other nationalities? Isn't the United States a land of Freedom? It is, but that is no reason that the Irish should have more preference than any other nationality."

Europeans came to America bringing their fears and prejudices with them, and these did not simply disappear. When German votes killed a proposal to teach Bohemian in a Chicago school, Bohemians retorted, "Finally, since impudence, selfishness, obstinacy and insolence is excessively rooted in the minds of all Germans, almost without exception, how then could we expect, even in this land of freedom to receive any support from them." An American writer of Norwegian ancestry recalls his grandmother admonishing members of the family never to trust a Swede. "The essence of her counsel," the grandson wrote, "was that Swedes were a strange, cold, selfish, sneaky lot and that any contact with them could only have unhappy consequences."

The intense xenophobia in the United States, both among older Americans and more recent arrivals, pointed inevitably in one direction: immigration restriction. Although the Chinese were banned in 1882 and the first general federal immigration law of that year had excluded certain classes of immigrants, these laws did not greatly affect the flow of immigration traffic. Bigots called for drastic limitations. The time had come, they insisted, to decide whether the nation was "to be peopled by British, German and Scandinavian stock, historically free, energetic, progressive, or by Slav, Latin and Asiatic races, historically downtrodden, atavistic, and stagnant." The most popular scheme for stemming the tide was the literacy test. Led by the Immigration Restriction League, founded in Boston in 1894 by Boston blue bloods, agitation for federal action grew. The literacy test, which required immigrants over 16 to be literate in some language, made no distinctions among nationalities or races, but the intent of the proposal was clear. Since proportionately more northern and western Europeans than southern and eastern Europeans were literate, the literacy requirement would have barred the latter groups of immigrants from the United States.

The literacy test, supported by the Republican party, finally did pass in 1896, only to be vetoed by President Grover Cleveland, who insisted that America should remain an asylum for the oppressed of Europe. The president also rejected the inference that the new immigrants were less desirable than the old: "It is said," he declared, "that the quality of recent immigration is undesirable. The time is quite within recent memory when the same thing was said of immigrants who, with their descendants, are now numbered among our best citizens." The literacy test's proponents attempted to muster the votes to override the veto, but they failed. And then the tide of nativism ebbed somewhat after 1896 as prosperity returned.

But it quickly reappeared, and by 1901 President Theodore Roosevelt was speaking in a vein quite different from that used by Cleveland only a few years earlier. Stirred by the recent assassination of President William McKinley by an anarchist, Roosevelt called for a comprehensive immigration act to keep out "not only all persons who are known to be believers in anarchistic principles or members of anarchistic societies, but also all persons who are of a low moral tendency or of unsavory reputation" and "all persons . . . who are below a certain standard of economic fitness to enter our industrial field as competitors with American labor." The president also wanted a careful educational test to ascertain the capacity to "appreciate American institutions and act sanely as American citizens." Roosevelt insisted that his proposals would decrease the "sum of ignorance" in America and "stop the influx of cheap labor, and the resulting competition which gives rise to so much of the bitterness in American industrial life, and it would dry up the springs of the pestilential social conditions in our great cities, where anarchist organizations have their greatest possibility of growth." Congress responded in part to the president's request by excluding anarchists in 1903 and "imbeciles, feeble-minded [persons] and persons with physical or mental defects which might affect their ability to earn a living" four years later.

In 1907 Congress also appointed a joint Senate-House commission to investigate the entire immigration problem. The new commission, known by the name of its chairman Senator William Paul Dillingham of Vermont, issued a 42-volume report in 1911. Its main assumption was that the newer immigrants from southern and eastern Europe were more ignorant, more unskilled, more prone to crime, and more willing to accept a lower standard of living than the older immigrants from northern and western Europe. The newcomers, the commission announced, were "content to accept wages and conditions which the native American and immigrants of the older class had come to regard as unsatisfactory." Although the Dillingham Commission did not favor a direct ban on the new immigration (it preferred a literacy test instead), it did suggest that restrictive legislation could be based on a percentage of each nationality group already in the United States. This alternative was ignored at the time but would be revived a decade later.

Congress responded to the Dillingham report with the passage of another literacy bill in 1913, but once again a president would not sanction it. William Howard Taft, heeding protests from friends favoring liberal immigration policies, acknowledged an "abiding faith" in American institutions to exert a positive influence upon newcomers "no matter how lacking in education they may be. . . . The second generation of a sturdy but uneducated peasantry," he continued, "brought to this country and raised in an atmosphere of thrift and hard work, and forced by their parents into school and to obtain an instrument for self-elevation, has always contributed to the strength of our people, and will continue to do so."

The outbreak of World War I and American entry into the war in 1917 broke the dam holding back the tide of nativism. On the eve of America's declaration of war Congress again passed a literacy bill, and when President Woodrow Wilson for a second time refused to approve it, Congress overrode his veto. The act also created an Asian "barred zone," which excluded most Asians and added to the list of banned immigrants.

In the heated atmosphere of wartime, patriots insisted upon 100 percent Americanism. Radical opponents of the war and German Americans who were suspected of having pro-German sentiments or of being secret agents of the kaiser became targets of unrestrained hysteria. Theodore Roosevelt led the attack on German Americans and insisted that "the men of German blood who have tried to be both German and American are not Americans at all, but traitors to America and tools and servants of Germany against America." Superpatriots attacked German Americans, their organizations, and their press. Libraries removed German books from their shelves, and several states, among them Delaware, Iowa, and Montana, prohibited public schools from teaching German. Sauerkraut became "liberty cabbage," orchestras refused to perform German music, and towns, business firms, and people hastily anglicized their German-sounding names. The governor of Iowa issued a proclamation urging citizens not to use foreign languages in public and the governing body of Nye County, Nevada, passed a resolution to the effect that use of another language in a publicly designated area would be deemed evidence of disloyalty. Angry mobs sometimes smashed German stores or burned German books. That most German Americans were loyal to the nation and supported the war did not seem to matter.

Although they were not as suspect as German Americans, some Irish Americans also came under attack. Many people of Irish ancestry were unenthusiastic about fighting a war in alliance with Great Britain, regarded as the enemy and oppressor of Ireland. A few Irish Americans who were critical of the Wilson administration found themselves in difficulty with the law.

The xenophobia unleashed by the war reached new heights in the 1920s. Although German and Irish Americans now found more acceptance, immigrants and their children were generally suspect. The nation assumed an isolationist mood; old-stock Americans rejected Europe and her peoples and insisted on conformity and loyalty to the United States. Terms like "wop" and "Jap" appeared regularly in newspapers like the *Pocatello* [Idaho] *Tribune* and about the only time minorities found stories about themselves in the daily newspapers was when they were involved in crimes, industrial accidents, or sports events. Ewa Morawska observed, "The same young men from Slavic and Magyar homes who, as American soldiers fighting in Europe during World War I, had been praised by the *Johnstown* [Pennsylvania] *Tribune* as 'our Johnstown boys' and lauded for heroism in the struggle 'in defense of their country' (the United States) were again labeled 'foreigners' after they returned to the city" at the end of the war. The Russian Revolution, a by-product of the war, added to the fears of things foreign. Americans believed that radical ideology, which was considered a foreign import, had to be stamped out or suppressed. Radical groups were hounded and physically assaulted, and Attorney General A. Mitchell Palmer's Justice Department rounded up aliens in spectacular raids and deported them during the Red Scare of 1919. Patriotic groups bombarded Congress with petitions proclaiming that the time had arrived "when Americans should assert themselves and drive from these shores all disloyal aliens."

While conservative and patriotic groups feared radical agitators flooding America with their Bolshevik ideas, labor leaders feared cheap labor. The 1920s were lean years for organized labor, as the unions lost more than a million members. In 1918 the AFL, anxious about the problems of industrial reconversion after the war, called for a two-year halt in immigration. Some labor union leaders not only used the old cheap-foreign-labor argument, but they also warned about the social dangers of immigration. The English-born Gompers, president of the AFL, defended restriction: "America has not yet become a nation." He noted that it was "honeycombed with 'foreign groups' living a foreign life," and this would continue if the nation's door remained open to all comers.

The 1920s have been described as a tribal era during which ethnocentrism and xenophobia ran wild. No development better illustrates this situation than the activities of the Ku Klux Klan, the largest nativist organization of the 1920s, which claimed over 4 million members at its height. Founded in Georgia in 1915, the Klan had a spectacular growth rate in the early 1920s and for a brief period exerted considerable political clout in several states, including Indiana, Alabama, Texas, and Florida. Klansmen thundered at liberal Protestantism and modern ideas and demanded prohibition enforcement and compulsory Bible reading in the public schools. But the focus of their credo was anti-black, anti-Semitic, anti-Catholic, and anti-immigrant. Hiram W. Evans, the Klan's imperial wizard, believed that the "old-stock Americans," the "Nordic race" of peoples, had "given the world almost the whole of modern civilization." And he insisted that the aliens from eastern and southern Europe should be kept out of the United States.

The Klan's response to immigration and minorities was merely an extreme version of what many old-stock white Protestants believed. Prohibitionists, for example, insisted there was a sinister connection among liquor, the city, and the immigrant. One liberal clergyman proclaimed, "National Prohibition is the highest mark of distinctively American morality and citizenship" and warned, "There is already too much congestion of immigrants in the great cities. . . . If we are to have an American civilization we must assimilate the stream of newcomers. If we do not assimilate them they will adulterate us with an admixture of old-world morals. A straw in the wind is afforded by the recent referendum in Massachusetts on the liquor issue. The entire state went overwhelmingly dry except the large immigrant filled cities, and they went so overwhelmingly wet as to give the state as a whole a wet majority."

From Michigan, Henry Ford's *Dearborn Independent* published anti-Semitic diatribes similar to those of the Klan. Included in the *Dearborn Independent*'s vitriolic writings was the *Protocols of the Elders of Zion.* This fake document, concocted by the Russian secret police at the turn of the century, charged there was a Jewish plot to establish a world dictatorship. During the decade, anti-Semitism even reached the hallowed gates of Harvard University when the university's administration established a Jewish quota, thereby prompting one Jew to dub the school an "intellectual Ku Klux Klan."

Discriminatory practices and thoughtlessness characterized Americans throughout the country in the 1920s and 1930s, and people of a variety of foreign ancestries suffered through many humiliating experiences. A number of individuals changed their foreign-sounding names to anglicized versions, either for better economic opportunities or merely to avoid unnecessary comments from others. Sam Divanovich of Tonopah, Nevada, for example, became Sam Devine because he thought it would "sound better and not cause as much comment." In Morrelville, Pennsylvania, in the 1930s, teachers often incorrectly characterized students of East Central European descent as "Slavish." "At school I went as Thomas," one man later recalled, "because my teacher would not pronounce or spell my own [name]." His wife had a similar experience. Her surname was "Tomasovich, but the teacher spelled it Tumoski; she did not bother to get it right." A child of Polish-American parents remembered that she never raised her hand in elementary school to speak. "I was afraid I'd make a mistake. . . . American children called us 'Hunky.' . . . We felt inferior." One man voluntarily misidentified himself and explained why: "I usually say I'm Russian. If you say you're Ukrainian, the guy tells you, 'Jesus Christ, what's that?' and you have to go into the whole history of Ukraine and explain to the guy what you mean. It is easier to just say that you are Russian."

Ideological racism, another facet of American nativism, peaked in the early 1920s. The eugenics movement in America after 1900 had warned of the dangerous effects of bad heredity. Eugenicists said that it was poor hereditary factors rather than environmental factors that produced unalterable human inequalities. Some anthropologists and other social scientists supported racist thinking. Racist popularizers, such as Madison Grant, enjoyed a vogue in the 1920s. Grant's *The Passing of the Great Race,* first published in 1916, and Lothrop Stoddard's *The Rising Tide of Color* preached a racism that could easily be applied to immigration restriction. Grant declared

> These new immigrants were no longer exclusively members of the Nordic race as were the earlier ones who came of their own impulse to improve their social conditions. The transportation lines advertised America as a land flowing with milk and honey, and the European governments took the opportunity to unload upon careless, wealthy, and hospitable America the sweepings of their jails and asylums. The result was that the new immigration . . . contained a large and increasing number of the weak, the broken, and the mentally crippled of all races drawn from the lowest stratum of the Mediterranean basin and the Balkans, together with hordes of the wretched, submerged populations of the Polish Ghettos.

A follower of Grant argued that continued immigration would inevitably produce "a hybrid race of people as worthless and futile as the good-for-nothing mongrels of Central America and Southeastern Europe," while a psychologist, flushed with uncritical use of intelligence test results, proclaimed that the "intellectual superiority of our Nordic group over the Alpine, Mediterranean and Negro groups has been demonstrated."

Given the intense nativism of the 1920s, the issue was not *whether* there would be immigration restriction but *what form* it would take. Aside from the recent immigrants, few Americans, regardless of background, resisted restriction. Congressmen representing urban areas with heavy concentrations of the foreign-born, however, attacked the proposed laws and their racist assumptions, but they lacked the votes to sustain their views. Over 800,000 newcomers arrived in 1921, and foes of immigration had visions of another immigrant invasion after the wartime lull. Stories circulated of between 5 and 20 million Europeans ready to descend upon the United States.

In 1921 Congress finally established the principle of restriction based on nationality and placed a ceiling on immigration from Europe. The 1921 law, for a one-year period, limited the number of entrants of each nationality to 3 percent of the foreign-born of that group in America based on the 1910 census. Under this stopgap measure approximately 358,000 were eligible to come from Europe. Congress extended the law twice before passing the Johnson-Reed Immigration Act of 1924.

The Johnson-Reed law continued the qualifications enacted in the past, such as the exclusion of anarchists, prostitutes, illiterates, and those likely to become public charges, and it also tightened the quotas established three years earlier. It cut the number of immigrants to 2 percent of the foreign-born of that group based on the 1890 census, and this further discriminated against southern and eastern nations, which was exactly what Congress wanted to do.

One need look only at the Greeks to see how moving the base year back from 1910 to 1890 and lowering the percentage helped Congress accomplish its purpose. In 1910 there were 101,282 Greeks in the United States. Under the 1921 act, they were therefore entitled to a yearly quota of 3,038 people (3 percent of 101,282). But the 1924 act, by lowering the percentage and setting the base year back to 1890 when the census takers counted only 1,887 Greeks in this country, cut the quota to 38 (2 percent of 1,887), or about 1 percent of what the 1921 law had allowed. Similar cuts affected Italians, East European Jews, and Slavs alike. Thus an ostensibly objective change of base years, and a one-point deviation in the percentage, drastically curtailed immigration opportunities for those that the Congress had no desire to welcome. The quota based on the 1890 census was meant to be temporary. In 1929 when the final yearly immigration quota of 153,714 people for all European groups went into effect (Asians were already barred in 1924, Western Hemisphere natives were not restricted, and Africans came in under the quotas for the European nations that controlled them) the northern and western Europeans received the bulk of the allotments.

A presidential commission, created by the 1924 act, asked a panel of experts to assist in determining each national allocation. The experts concluded that of the 94.8 million whites in the 1920 population, 41.3 million were of colonial stock and 53.5 million of postcolonial stock. Over three-quarters of the colonial group were of British origin, and of the postcolonial group 65 percent came from northern and western Europe. Thus the quotas heavily favored the English and countries in northern and western Europe, which was precisely what Congress and the president desired. The quota for Great Britain and Northern Ireland was 44 percent of the total, being 65,361. The Republic of Ireland was granted 17,756 places, Germany 25,814, and the Scandinavian countries 6,872. By comparison, Italy received only 5,802, Poland 6,524, Russia 2,784, and Greece 307. Some nations' quotas were so small under this formula that the act permitted them a maximum of 100. Thus countries like Syria, Albania, and Turkey received the lowest allotment. The failure to exclude natives of the Western Hemisphere kept the door open for heavy immigration from Mexico and Canada in the 1920s. Congress did not place limits on countries in this hemisphere until 1965.

The passage of the Johnson-Reed Act marked the end of an era in American history. Asians had already been excluded for the most part, but for Europeans the nation had had an open door. The act ended this virtually free immigration policy. Although the United States did modify its restrictions after World War II, it never again opened its gates to unlimited numbers.

The immigration restrictions of the 1920s, combined with the severe depression of the 1930s, achieved the effect that restrictionists had been clamoring for: drastically reduced numbers of people coming into the United States. The laws, though, did not curtail ethnic conflicts, and the nation experienced tensions over immigration and ethnic relations in every succeeding decade.

Shortly after the final quota system went into effect in 1929, President Herbert Hoover requested the State Department to use its administrative powers for a tight enforcement of the laws. In particular, the public-charge provision of the immigration codes was invoked, for America experienced a deep economic depression during the 1930s and did not want foreign laborers to compete with the growing numbers of unemployed native-born workers seeking jobs. Actually, few from any land wanted to emigrate to America during the early years of the depression. Only 23,068 came in 1933; 28,470 in 1934; and 34,956 in 1935. In several years more persons left the nation than arrived; there were simply not enough jobs to go around, and relief benefits were few and inadequate.

Before the immigration acts and the depression combined to curb the numbers of newcomers, Filipinos moved into Hawaii and California to fill the labor gap created by the restriction on other Orientals. Because the Philippines were then a commonwealth of the United States, there were no legal barriers to population movement; the enormous needs of the sugar planters in Hawaii and the farmers in California provided the spur. The majority of those who came to the United States were of the lower classes and conversed in the Ilocano dialect.

Filipinos had been emigrating to Hawaii to work for the sugar and pineapple planters since the Gentlemen's Agreement of 1907 with Japan had reduced Japanese emigration. In the next quarter century the Hawaiian Islands welcomed 125,000 Filipinos. In the 1920s, however, when California growers feared that Congress might impose quotas on Mexicans, they turned to the Filipinos for labor. Filipinos came to the mainland from Hawaii and directly from the Philippine Islands. According to 1920 census figures, there were only 5,603 Filipinos on the mainland, but 10 years later they numbered 45,208. Other sources estimate that there may have been more than twice that number. Some 90 percent of the Filipinos were single, male, and under 30 years of age. They worked in northern and central California farms and vineyards. Stockton, California, with a concentration of perhaps 4,000 to 8,000 Filipinos, became known at the end of the 1920s as the Manila of California. Other sizable settlements formed in San Francisco, Seattle, and Portland.

The commonwealth status of the Philippines also permitted substantial numbers of Filipinos to be recruited for the United States armed forces, especially the navy. This accounted for the presence of Filipino communities in the San Diego and Los Angeles areas. The majority of these recruits made the military their career and left the service only upon retirement. The armed forces provided them with security and, more important, with the chance to bring their families to the United States. In the navy the Filipinos were usually assigned to mess halls and as personal attendants to high-ranking military personnel.

The depression and American prejudices caused many Filipinos to lose their jobs during the 1930s. A congressional act of 1934, which promised the Philippine Islands their independence in 1946, also established an annual Filipino quota of 50 immigrants. The quota, plus the fact that many Filipinos returned home, cut their numbers in West Coast agriculture; by 1940, 90 percent of those who remained in California were working in such personal domestic service jobs as bellboys, houseboys, cooks, kitchen helpers, and waiters.

As economic conditions improved in the late 1930s, increased numbers of European again began emigrating to America. More important as motivating factors than economics, however, were the triumph of fascism in Germany in 1933 and the coming of war in Europe six years later. As the Germans annexed Austria (1938) and Czechoslovakia (1939) and then crushed Poland (1939) and conquered Norway, Denmark, the Netherlands, Belgium, and France in the spring of 1940, hundreds of thousands fled in terror, and more would have left had they been able to do so.

Many who ran away were opponents of Nazism. University professors, politicians, and church leaders who openly opposed Hitler either escaped nazi-dominated countries or were hounded from their posts and thrown into prison. Eventually, many of those in opposition who did not flee ended up in concentration camps or were executed.

Though millions of political and religious dissenters were persecuted by Hitler's regime, Jews stood out as the major victims of the Nazis. Plagued by legal and other harassments, they sought asylum in other countries. After accepting as many as they thought they could absorb, the nations of the world refused further modification in their immigration policies. Until 1939 Hitler permitted almost all Jews to leave if they chose to do so; unfortunately, most could not find any nation that would accept them. The horrors perpetuated on the Jews by the nazis were legion, but before the mass exterminations in the concentration camps, perhaps the worst single episode occurred on the night of November 9–10, 1938. The government sanctioned a savage assault on German Jews, and throughout the night people were beaten, stores were looted, and homes, hospitals, and old-age institutions were burned; at least 20,000 people were rounded up for deportation to concentration camps. The barbarity of these actions evoked world-wide denunciation. President Franklin D. Roosevelt declared, "I myself could scarcely believe that such things could occur in a twentieth-century civilization."

Nevertheless, U.S. immigration laws remained intact, and the American government made few allowances for the victims of Hitler's terroristic policies. Americans certainly feared economic competition from immigrant workers, for with almost 10 million unemployed in the United States, job prospects for new-comers were dim. The likelihood that additional people in the country would become public charges and swell overburdened relief roles was not discounted either. A few Americans also believed that spies and fifth-column agents would enter as refugees if quotas were eased. But especially important in the opposition to relaxing existing quotas was a strong tinge of anti-Semitism in the United States. Both Protestant and secular newspapers wrote about it but the Catholic church, and Catholics in general, found Jewish support for the Republican cause in Spain particularly galling. Moreover, for Americans of all stripes the word "Jew" was often used synonymously with the word "Communist" and most people in the nation were simply against having any more of them in their midst.

President Roosevelt was aware of American hostility toward Jews, yet he also sympathized with the refugees' plight, as did a number of Americans who urged the nation to assist them. Roosevelt instructed members of the consular service to grant them "the most humane and favorable treatment under the law," which enabled some refugees to come to America; generally the president was willing to let the State Department handle the situation. Unfortunately, anti-Semitism existed in the State Department too, and its influence resulted in a rigid application of the visa policy against Jewish applicants. Typical of this attitude was the assistant secretary of state, Breckenridge Long, who had charge of refugee affairs after 1939. In 1941 he recorded approval, in his diary, of another man's opposition to further immigration. "He said," Long wrote, that "the general type of intending immigrant was just the same as the criminal Jews who crowd our police court dockets in New York. . . . I think he is right. . . ."

The State Department position probably reflected the majority viewpoint in the United States. When, in 1939, Senator Robert F. Wagner of New York and Congresswoman Edith Rogers of Massachusetts proposed a measure to allow 20,000 German refugee children between the ages of 6 and 14 years into the United States above the quota limit, patriotic societies like the American Legion and the Daughters of the American Revolution denounced it. In speaking against the legislation a spokeswoman for the Ladies of the Grand Army of the Republic warned that Congress might "decide to admit 20,000 German-Jewish children!" A year later, however, when mercy ships started bringing children from Great Britain to the United States, patriotic organizations voiced no opposition, and congressional mail ran heavily in approval. Over 15,000 American families each volunteered to take one of the British children, with "a blond English girl, 6 years old" seemingly the most popular choice.

Anti-Semitism reached new heights in the United States in the late 1930s. Groups like the Silver Shirts and the German-American Bund thundered against the Jews. Bigots saw the "hidden hand of international Jewry" around every corner, and patriots organized "Buy Christian" campaigns. The most influential and well-known anti-Semite was the radio priest Father Charles E. Coughlin. Originally a supporter of the New Deal, Coughlin turned against Roosevelt and increasingly used anti-Jewish and anti-communist arguments in his broadcasts and journal, *Social Justice.* This journal reprinted excerpts from the discredited *Protocols of the Elders of Zion* and carried a speech by the German Propaganda Minister Joseph Goebbels. *Social Justice* had an estimated circulation of over 300,000, and millions heard Coughlin's radio voice. In 1940 and 1941 public-opinion polls revealed that 17 to 20 percent of the nation considered Jews "a menace to America." Another 12 to 15 percent admitted that they would support an anti-Semitic campaign, and still others indicated that they would be sympathetic to such a campaign.

Despite the bigotry, though, Jews as well as others who came to America under the quota system received hospitable treatment. A host of organizations, like the National Refugee Service, the Hebrew Immigrant Aid Society, and various ad hoc groups, stood ready to assist the newcomers in finding jobs, housing, and friends.

European arrivals in the 1930s included a number of eminent intellectuals and scientists. Albert Einstein was perhaps the best known of the illustrious immigrants, as they have been called, but other Nobel prizewinners also came during the decade. Among the most noted of these were Thomas Mann, the writer; Bruno Walter and Arturo Toscanini, the conductors; Paul Tillich, the theologian; Béla Bartók, the composer; and Enrico Fermi, the physicist. Several of the scientists who came played key roles in the development of the atomic bomb.

Those who arrived in the 1930s usually adjusted to America more readily than most of the millions who had come before them. For the most part the professionals and refugees were well educated, knew English, and had contacts and skills that they could utilize in the United States. Fleeing in terror from Europe, they were eager to become American citizens and to participate in American society. One such refugee was Henry Kissinger, who would later serve as President Richard Nixon's chief foreign policy adviser and in 1973 would become America's first foreign-born secretary of state.

Not all could adapt as well. Béla Bartók, the composer, never felt at home in America and died in relative obscurity and poverty in New York City in 1945. Some, like Thomas Mann, returned to Europe after the war. Others who lacked the contacts of an Einstein or a Toscanini had to take jobs where they could find them, often beneath their educational levels and skills. The fact that some of them left families and friends behind to an unknown fate added to their anxieties.

Concern that fifth-column agents would enter America if quotas were relaxed may have been one factor blocking a change in immigration laws, but fear of sabotage by enemy aliens already here was even greater during World War II.

Consequently, the federal government interned a few Germans and Italians and carefully watched others during the war. Japanese aliens and American citizens of Japanese ancestry, however, fared quite differently. Most of them on the West Coast were incarcerated in relocation centers that some critics likened to concentration camps.

Certainly, the fear of espionage, heightened by the surprise attack on Pearl Harbor and rumors of attacks to come on the mainland, were real factors in prompting the federal government to intern Japanese Americans. In spite of the fact that no acts of espionage or sabotage by Japanese Americans were uncovered in either Hawaii or California, the boards of supervisors of 11 California counties solemnly declared that "during the attack on Pearl Harbor . . . the Japanese were aided and abetted by fifth columnists of the Japanese." One United States senator insisted

> A Jap born on our soil is a subject of Japan under Japanese law; therefore he owes allegiance to Japan. . . . The Japanese are among our worst enemies. They are cowardly and immoral. They are different from Americans in every conceivable way, and no Japanese . . . should have a right to claim American citizenship. A Jap is a Jap anywhere you find him, and his taking the oath of allegiance to this country would not help, even if he should be permitted to do so. They do not believe in God and have no respect for an oath. They have been plotting for years against the Americans and their democracies.

Even when others pointed out that no espionage had been reported, proponents of internment argued that that merely proved the danger was greater, for the Japanese were tricky, sneaky, and underhanded, plotting for the right moment to subvert America. Ironically, the very absence of overt sabotage was held against them. It was, said General John DeWitt, "a disturbing and confirming indication that such action would be taken[!]"

Behind the discussions of potential disloyalty lay years of racial antagonism toward the Japanese in America. The Oriental Exclusion Act of 1924 slammed the door against Japanese and other Asian immigrants, but it did not end racism. Various California patriotic and nativist groups hated or mistrusted the Japanese in their midst and considered them unassimilable and treacherous. Economic conflicts also influenced attitudes toward the Japanese. Some small businessmen and farmers envied their economic success in agriculture and business. The war clouds gathering in the Far East during the 1930s also added to the fears of Japan and the Japanese.

The attack on Pearl Harbor rekindled the old fears and prejudices and prompted new outbreaks of anti-Japanese hysteria. Responding to demands to remove Japanese Americans from the Pacific Coast, in February 1942 President Roosevelt issued Executive Order 9066, one of the most infamous presidential orders in American history. Under this action, which was later backed by a congressional law, the army rounded up approximately 110,000 West Coast Japanese, most of whom were native-born American citizens, and placed them in ten camps called relocation centers, scattered throughout the western United States. In Hawaii, where prejudice was less intense and the Japanese played a more important role in the economy, only a few were interned.

The hasty removal meant hardship and suffering. Given only five days' notice of the evacuation, those interned could take only what they could carry; the government sequestered all other belongings. In addition to the financial losses the conditions in the relocation centers were miserable. At first the Japanese were placed in temporary quarters, including a hastily converted race track, which lacked basic amenities. Eventually, the government built ten camps, most of them in barren desert country, hot in the summer and cold in the winter. The surroundings were drab and unattractive, complete with barbed wire, military police, and, in some instances, machine guns. One Japanese-American woman wrote of her experience at Camp Minidoka, north of Twin Falls, Idaho.

> When we first arrived here we almost cried and thought that this was a land that God had forgotten. The vast expanse of sagebrush and dust, a landscape so alien to our eyes, and a desolate, woe-begone feeling of being so far removed from home and fireside bogged us down mentally, as well as physically.

Gradually conditions for the internees improved except for those at the Tule Lake, California, camp, who were considered especially disloyal.

One of the sorriest episodes of the Japanese-American internment was the reaction of the United States Supreme Court. Several Japanese Americans challenged the government's policy and took their cases all the way to the highest court. In 1943 in *Hirabayashi* v. *U.S.,* and in 1944 in *Korematsu* v. *U.S.,* the justices upheld military curfews as well as the evacuation. Three dissenting justices—Owen Roberts, Frank Murphy, and Robert Jackson—scored the government's policy and attacked the racial prejudice that supported it. But the majority accepted the argument that internment of these immigrants and their American-born children served the national interest in wartime.

When the government closed the camps in 1945, Japanese Americans were fearful about how they would fare in the United States. Some of the most bitter renounced their American citizenships and returned to Japan. The majority, though, elected to return to California despite federal efforts to relocate them elsewhere. Anti-Japanese groups in California opposed their return. Bumper stickers appeared declaring "No Japs Wanted in California," and a few incidents occurred, especially in the Central Valley of the Golden State. Veterans' groups urged boycotts of reopened Japanese-American businesses, and a few rocks were thrown and shots fired into the homes of Japanese Americans. In Oregon an American Legion post removed the names of local Japanese-American service-men from the public honor roll, and other American Legion posts on the West Coast banned Japanese-American servicemen from membership.

Yet the opposition gradually subsided, and, aided by church and liberal civic groups, Japanese Americans were able to find homes, jobs, and increasing acceptance. They were able to reclaim, however, only about a tenth of their $400 million in forfeited holdings. In 1948 an anti-Japanese proposition on the Califor-nia ballot to make the alien laws harsher was defeated by 59 percent of the voters. Although over 40 percent still favored restrictions against the Japanese, this was the first time in California history that an anti-Japanese referendum had been defeated. In 1952 the California Supreme Court declared the 1913 Alien Land Act unconstitutional, and Congress removed another restriction against the Japa-nese the same year. In 1952 the McCarran-Walter Immigration Act lifted the ban on Asian immigration and the exclusion of Asians from citizenship. Japanese Americans still faced discrimination in the 1950s and 1960s, especially in housing and jobs, but the situation had changed drastically from pre–World War II attitudes and practices. By the 1960s public-opinion polls revealed that most Americans considered Japanese Americans desirable citizens, trustworthy peo-ple, and loyal to the United States. Nevertheless, the trauma for those interned has not been completely overcome. A generation after the camps closed, one Japanese American admitted, "My father still trembles when he talks about this experience." On Memorial Day, 1974, some Japanese Americans, whose children had difficulty in believing the stories of their parents' hardships, made a pilgrim-age to the Tule Lake camp. In Klamath Falls, Oregon, where a few had stopped to pay respects to those who had died at Tule Lake, a woman passing by rolled down her car window and shouted, "You're on the wrong side of the ocean."

Today most Japanese Americans find the same opportunities available to them as do other Americans. The well educated are quickly employed, the affluent can live where they will, and those who choose to marry people of a different heritage are not blocked by miscegenation laws. In other words Japanese Americans are no longer ethnics who are feared; now they are Americans who are respected.

The internment of the Japanese during World War II coincided with the peak of American xenophobia. Measured by public-opinion polls, hostility to-ward American minorities probably reached its greatest intensity during the early 1940s. When the war ended in 1945 the European and Asian worlds had been torn asunder, but few Americans wanted to help any of the survivors begin life anew in the United States. The story of how our immigration policies changed after 1945 is related in the next chapter.

chapter 5

Post–World War II America: A New Wave of Immigrants

When World War II ended in 1945 the Daughters of the American Revolution, the American Legion, the Veterans of Foreign Wars, and several other patriotic groups called for a ban on immigration for five to ten years. Within three years, however, Congress passed legislation to bring 205,000 displaced Europeans to our shores, added another 134,000 to that figure in 1950, and continued to expand the numbers of immigration permits, rather than restrict them, during the next three decades. Despite the essentially narrow McCarran-Walter Immigration Act of 1952, which reiterated American beliefs in the 1924 policies established by the Johnson-Reed Act, special legislation to aid individual groups in dire circumstances characterizes the Congresses of the past four decades. The new policies reflect a more liberal and generous spirit of American society, but they also represent a response to communist expansion and the sense of Christian obligation that many Americans feel requires us to provide a refuge for those escaping from tyranny. Not to be overlooked as an element in bringing about the change is the strength of ethnic lobbying organizations. Unlike the period before World War II, when these groups shied away from opposing the views of the patriotic organizations, in 1946 they recognized that favorable legislation would come about only through petitioning and influencing the Congress. Once the ethnic groups learned this lesson, special-interest legislation, and then a completely revised immigration bill in 1965, worked their way into the statute books.

But before legislation could be passed the temper of the country had to change. Anti-Semitism peaked in 1945–1946, then began to subside. A popular Hollywood film, *The House I Live In,* in which Frank Sinatra made a plea for tolerance in 1945; the publication of books like Laura Z. Hobson's *Gentleman's Agreement* and Carey McWilliams's *A Mask for Privilege,* which exposed the depths of anti-Semitic feelings in this country; the Supreme Court's decision to outlaw restrictive covenants in housing; President Harry S Truman's 1948 proposal for a civil rights program; increased American prosperity—all contributed to the changed perception of minorities.

Postwar public-opinion polls, for example, indicated that fewer Christians believed Jews to be greedy, dishonest, or unscrupulous; and overt anti-Semitism, so common in the 1930s, became less frequent and less respectable. Accompanying the drop in prejudicial attitudes toward Jews was the decline of social and economic discrimination. Universities and professional schools eliminated Jewish quotas, and business firms that had been averse to hiring Jews modified their policies. Changes in major corporations and law firms came slowly. A symbolic landmark was established in December 1973, when E. I du Pont, the world's largest chemical company, chose Irving S. Shapiro, the son of East European Jewish immigrants, as its president and chief executive officer.

Another persistent theme in American history, anti-Catholicism, also subsided after World War II. Conflict between Protestants and Catholics continued over aid to parochial schools, a proposed American ambassador to the Vatican, the relations of church and state, publicly sponsored birth-control clinics, and abortion. But the deep emotional strife of the past declined sharply. The ecumenical movement of the postwar society brought Protestants, Catholics, and Jews together in new areas of cooperation. In this same spirit Pope Paul VI visited the United States in 1965, conducted a prayer service before 70,000 people in New York's Yankee Stadium, and received a warm welcome. In 1979 and 1987 the charismatic Pope John Paul II made similar tours and met with even more enthusiastic receptions.

While decreasing anti-Semitism and anti-Catholicism were essential for the enactment of new immigration legislation, the laws that made possible the admission of so many Asians and blacks from the Caribbean would not have been possible without a decline in racial prejudice. While Chinese and Japanese immigrants had been scorned and were the first ethnic groups to be banned, they soon found growing acceptance in post–World War II America. Educational and employment opportunities began to open up for their children, and by the middle of the 1960s Congress and many state legislatures had outlawed racial discrimination. The most far-reaching of these measures came at the height of the civil rights movement. In 1964 Congress banned discrimination in public accommodations, education, and employment and then passed the Voting Rights Act of 1965 that permitted all adult Americans to register to vote.

The decline of prejudice can be explained by several factors. The fear of divided loyalties that was so potent in World War I and, to a lesser extent, in World War II did not materialize during the cold war. Prejudice is also strongly correlated with levels of income, religious intensity, and education. As incomes and education increased and as religion became less of a commitment and more of a social identification, tolerance grew. Education did not guarantee the end of prejudice, but there is no doubt that the rising levels of education served to dampen the fires of bigotry. A highly educated public seemed more willing to accept ethnic differences. At the same time, minority members absorbed the dominant values of society as they went through the public schools, state colleges, and universities. Finally, as a result of the immigration laws of the 1920s, the nation had achieved a general balance of ethnic groups. Old-stock Americans no longer feared being overrun by hordes of aliens who might undermine their traditions and destroy their institutions. The foreign-born percentage of the population steadily declined from about one-seventh in the 1920s to less than one-twentieth by the 1970s. America was becoming a more homogenized nation as the grandchildren of European immigrants came to be indistinguishable from one another or, indeed, from those whose ancestors came here before the American Revolution.

The abatement of ethnic conflict and the general prosperity of post–World War II America created a climate suitable for the modification of the severe immigration acts. First Congress opened the doors to the families of G.I.s by passing the War Brides Act of 1946, which enabled 120,000 wives, husbands, and children of members of the armed forces to emigrate to the United States. Then it turned its attention to refugees.

The war caused enormous damage to homes and factories in cities and towns throughout Europe, and reshuffling of national boundaries left many persons unable or unwilling to return to their native lands. Some had collaborated with the Nazis during World War II and feared retribution; others scorned the communists; still others could not endure to go back and rebuild their lives amidst the ruins. As a first step in alleviating the problem President Truman issued a directive on December 22, 1945, requiring that, within existing laws, American consulates give preference to the displaced persons in Europe. About 40,000 people benefited from this order before Congress abrogated it with the passage of the Displaced Persons (DP) Act of 1948. The legislation resulted from intensive lobbying on the part of a newly formed Citizens Committee on Displaced Persons, which emphasized that 80 percent of the displaced persons were Christian. The DP Act won approval only after it had been mutilated by opponents of a liberal immigration policy. It was so worded as to favor agriculturists, exiles from the Baltic States, and those of Germanic origin. President Truman signed the bill reluctantly, denouncing the provisions that, as he put it, discriminated "in callous fashion against displaced persons of the Jewish faith." In 1950, after most of the Jewish refugees had gone to Israel, Congress amended the 1948 act and eliminated the offensive stipulations. Ultimately about 400,000 people arrived in the United States as a result of the two DP laws.

These acts only scratched the surface of the immigration problem. Postwar dislocations and the onset of the cold war exacerbated the difficulties of readjustment, and millions more still sought entry into the United States. To cope with the needs of these people, as well as to contain the voices of their friends and relatives in the United States who wanted immigration policies liberalized, in 1947 Congress established a committee to look into the question. Begun in the Republican-controlled 80th Congress but subsequently under the chairmanship of Senator Patrick A. McCarran of Nevada, an avowed opponent of leniency in immigration procedures, a subcommittee carefully studied the old laws and the mass of rules, regulations, and proclamations governing immigration. They gathered data, heard testimony from 400 persons and organizations, and then recommended that the basic national origins system remain intact. While rejecting theories of Nordic supremacy, the committee held, nonetheless, "that the peoples who made the greatest contribution to the development of this country were fully justified in determining that the country was no longer a field for further colonization and, henceforth, further immigration would not only be restricted but directed to admit immigrants considered to be more readily assimilable because of the similarity of their background to those of the principal components of our population." McCarran warned, "We have in the United States today hard-core, indigestible blocs which have not become integrated into the American way of life but which, on the contrary, are our deadly enemies." The proposed legislation became the McCarran-Walter Immigration Act of 1952. It maintained the national origins system, favored skilled workers and relatives, and strengthened security procedures.

The McCarran-Walter Act liberalized immigration in one area: It repealed the ban on Asian citizenship and granted nations in the Far East minimum annual quotas of 100 each. This was not a controversial change in 1952. During World War II, mainly because of foreign policy considerations, Congress repealed the Chinese Exclusion Acts, gave China a token allotment of 105 persons per year, and made Chinese immigrants eligible for citizenship. After the war Congress passed similar bills for natives of the Philippines and of India.

The removal of some restrictions against Asians did not mean the end of racism in immigration policy, for the 1952 act contained other discriminatory provisions. Those of European background born in the Western Hemisphere were eligible to come in from their nations of birth, but Asians in similar circumstances were not. People with one Asian parent were charged to that parent's home country. Thus a person of Italian and English descent who was born in Mexico could enter from Mexico, which was a nonquota nation, whereas a person of French and Japanese descent who was born in Mexico would be charged to the Japanese quota and not to Mexico. The intent of Congress was clear: to admit few people of Asian heritage. The McCarran-Walter Act also cut the number of black West Indians eligible to enter as immigrants. President Truman, who favored broadening the immigration laws and eliminating these provisions and the offensive national origins quotas, rejected the bill, but Congress overrode his veto.

Within a year after the McCarran-Walter Act had become law, efforts were made to modify it. President Eisenhower wanted to admit more refugees, and in 1953 when the Displaced Persons Act expired Congress enacted the Refugee Relief Act. Under it another 200,000 Europeans and a few Asians were admitted. Passed at the height of the cold war, the measure was meant to aid refugees as well as escapees from communist-dominated areas.

Liberals who wanted broad alterations in the law were disappointed, but Congress did make a number of other changes during the 1950s and early 1960s along the lines of the Refugee Relief Act. Soon after the abortive Hungarian Revolution of 1956, Congress passed a law that admitted another 29,000 refugees, chiefly Hungarians, but including Yugoslavians and Chinese. Some 31,000 Dutch-Indonesians, another uprooted group, came in under a law passed the next year. The United Nations declared 1960 World Refugee Year and Congress responded with the Fair Share Law, which opened the doors of this country for a few more immigrants.

In addition to congressional actions, Presidents Dwight D. Eisenhower, John F. Kennedy, and Lyndon B. Johnson used the executive powers they possessed under the existing immigration laws to relax restrictions. Thus 30,000 refugees entered after the 1956 Hungarian Revolution as parolees without visas, ineligible for permanent alien registration until Congress made them eligible. President Kennedy ordered the admission of thousands more, especially the Hong Kong Chinese and the Cubans who sought refuge after Fidel Castro's seizure of power in 1959.

The additions to the basic immigration law made it possible for many to come who did not qualify under the quota system. In the early 1960s most immigrants were of this sort. By then the political climate was more conducive to immigration reform and not simply piecemeal action. In 1963 President Kennedy urged Congress to eliminate ethnic discrimination and the national origins system, which he insisted lacked "basis in either logic or reason. It neither satisfies a national need nor accomplishes an international purpose. In an age of interdependence among nations, such a system . . . discriminates among applicants for admission into the United States on the basis of the accident of birth." After President Kennedy's death, President Johnson called on Congress to enact the Kennedy proposal. Following extensive hearings, a new immigration bill passed overwhelmingly in 1965. Designed to be fully effective in 1968, the act abolished the national origins quota system and made other modifications in immigration policy.

Although the national origins proviso disappeared, an overall limitation remained. Outside of the Western Hemisphere only 170,000 persons, exclusive of parents, spouses, and children of American citizens, were allowed to enter the United States. No nation in the Eastern Hemisphere was permitted to have more than 20,000 of this total, although immediate relatives were not counted as part of the figure. The nation's immigration policy remained selective; but in place of national origins, Congress substituted a preference system admitting immigrants on a first-come, first-served basis. The major preferences were for unification of families, which accounted for 74 percent of the slots. The largest single preference was for brothers and sisters of U.S. citizens, which prompted some observers to call this the brothers and sisters law. In all, 20 percent of the preferences were reserved for those with occupations needed in the United States, but the Labor Department maintained a tight control over certification of eligible applicants. Finally, the 1965 law provided a preference of 6 percent, or 10,200 places, for refugees.

The liberalization of the law for Asians and Europeans accompanied a shift in policy toward Canadians and Latin Americans. For the first time Congress placed a limit—120,000—on immigration from the Western Hemisphere. The administration had not pressed for this restriction but a majority in Congress feared the possibility of a massive increase in Latin Americans, especially Mexicans.

In the 1970s Congress added to the reforms begun in 1965 and shaped a worldwide uniform immigration policy. In 1976 Congress created a preference system for the Western Hemisphere and placed a 20,000 limit on all its nations. This provision affected Mexico, which sent several times that number to the American Southwest annually in the early 1970s. Friends of Mexico said that the United States had a special relationship with its neighbor to the south and should make allowances for a friend. But Congress thought otherwise. The limit on Mexico helped other Latin American nations, however. Whereas Mexico had previously used about a third of the Western Hemisphere's overall total, now other nations could increase their share. In 1978 Congress completed the reforms begun in 1965 when it created a worldwide ceiling of 290,000 quota places annually by combining the Western and Eastern Hemisphere totals; it also established a uniform preference system for all nations. This system reiterated similar clauses from the 1965 act emphasizing family unification, occupation, and refugees.

The concern of Congress for the patchwork manner in which immigration policy was being made prompted another action in 1978. Congress created a Select Commission on Immigration and Refugee Policy, which was to study matters pertaining to immigration and report by March 1981. The establishment of the commission did not preclude other legislation. Still another law, the Refugee Act of 1980, was prompted by the number of refugees who had entered during the 1960s and 1970s, sometimes under emergency executive action. The Refugee Act of 1980 increased the normal annual flow of refugees to 50,000 and the total immigration from 290,000 to 320,000. It also gave the president special powers to deal with the refugee problem.

The changing policies of postwar America led to an increase in immigration compared with the lean depression years. Whereas only 528,000 people arrived in the 1930s, and 120,000 during World War II, the numbers rose in the late 1940s. In the 1950s nearly a quarter of a million arrived annually; in the 1960s the figure reached 320,000; and in the 1970s about 400,000 came each year. In 1978 the figure, swelled by Vietnamese refugees, passed 600,000. In 1980, over 800,000 entered. This included a large number of people from Cuba, Vietnam, and Haiti who later were permitted to become regular immigrants. During the first half of the 1980s immigration averaged about 550,000 annually; and in 1985, more than 570,000 newcomers arrived in the United States. The largest sending nations that year are listed in Table 5.1. Refugees helped account for much of the increase, but immediate family members of United States citizens were not counted as part of the 20,000 per nation limit and they too helped swell the totals. Only one European nation, the United Kingdom, with 13,048, exceeded 10,000 immigrants to the United States in 1985.

Whatever their origins, the post–World War II immigrants, like so many millions before them, faced the task of building a new life in America. Most

Table 5.1 IMMIGRATION TO THE UNITED STATES, 1985
From Ten Leading
Sending Nations

Mexico	61,077
The Philippines	47,978
Korea	35,253
Vietnam	31,895
India	26,026
Mainland China	24,787
Dominican Republic	23,787
Cuba	20,334
Taiwan and Hong Kong	20,066
Jamaica	18,923

Source: Immigration and Naturalization Service, Bulletin (Statistical Analysis Branch, 1986).

coming before the 1965 changes were Europeans, yet they too experienced problems: language barriers, shortages of funds and skills, and the culture shock of a new environment. Often there was discouragement over the chances of finding good jobs. "I knew I would have to start at the bottom of the employment ladder, but I had no idea that the bottom rung was so far underground," lamented one newcomer. Moreover, many of the displaced persons (DPs) had experienced the horrors of concentration-camp life, including malnutrition and physical torture, which made adjustment still more difficult. Those fleeing communism often escaped with only the clothes on their backs.

Yet these people had some advantages. Whether they were fleeing from communism or released from concentration or DP camps, the general climate was probably more friendly to these immigrants than it had been at any other time in modern American history. A host of private organizations and governmental agencies stood ready to assist them. Jewish groups that had actively assisted refugees in the 1930s continued their efforts. The United Service for New Americans, formed in 1946, was especially helpful to Jewish DPs. Various other European ethnic and religious groups also helped the newcomers. The federal government and some local governments assisted still others, and the federal government even airlifted some of those escaping from communism and provided emergency housing for them. In 1957 Hungarians fleeing after the Russian army had crushed the Hungarian Revolution were flown in and quartered temporarily at Camp Kilmer in New Jersey. A federal program begun in 1960 and implemented by the Department of Health, Education, and Welfare aided the Cuban refugees; by 1980 over $1 billion had been spent on them. Later the department helped the Chinese and Vietnamese, among others. Often public and private agencies worked closely together to make the adjustment of the immigrant easier. Moreover, many refugees from communism found America sympathetic to their anti-communist views. By comparison, then, most of the newcomers probably experienced fewer problems than had the nineteenth- and early twentieth-century immigrants. Prior to the 1970s they were fortunate, too, in coming during a period of relative prosperity after World War II when jobs were available.

Although the enactment of special legislation enabled many southern and eastern Europeans to emigrate as refugees, expellees, or displaced persons, many came under the regular immigration laws, especially the 1965 act. American communities of Italians, Portuguese, and Greeks, among others, used the law to bring in their relatives.

Between 1960 and 1975 over 20,000 Italians arrived annually and settled in places where other Italians had gone, such as New York and New Jersey. In the Red Hook section of Brooklyn they found not only friends and relatives who helped them secure jobs and housing but also churches, stores, and community organizations with familiar names. On the streets they heard their native tongue.

Like the Italians, the Portuguese were aided by the 1965 act. They did not emigrate in as large numbers, but a significant community emerged in Newark in the late 1960s and 1970s. Estimates placed the number of Portuguese in New Jersey's largest city in 1980 at 40,000. Most had been long-time residents of Portugal, but a few traced their roots to Angola and Mozambique in Africa. In Newark the newcomers formed a distinct community built around their churches, stores, homes, and social activities.

The Greeks were a third European beneficiary of the 1965 immigration act's provisions. Under the Johnson-Reed Act of 1924 and the McCarran-Walter Act of 1952 Greece received a quota of 307, but from 1966 to 1971 about 15,000 Greeks came annually, mostly under the relative preference provisions. During the 1970s about 100,000 Greeks arrived. Although they settled nearly every-where, most went to Greek communities in Chicago and New York. In the "Big Apple" they generally found homes in the Astoria section, and about 20,000 to 30,000 located in Chicago's Greektown. In New York they were aided by other Greeks; and in 1972 a Hellenic American Neighborhood Action Committee (HANAC) was founded to help Greek-American causes, including those of the newest immigrants. Yet the older Greek communities did not always agree with the newcomers, many of whom were of a higher social status than their predeces-sors. Most of these newcomers took jobs working for others, in factories, restau-rants, and in construction. A few went into business for themselves, including some vendors in the streets of New York City. In the summer of 1980, *Newsweek* reported that the Greeks "have all but taken over the coffee shops" in New York City. By the late 1970s and into the 1980s the backlogs in both Italy and Greece eased and their emigration to America dropped significantly.

By the 1980s American statistics showed conclusively that the 1965 act's most dramatic impact was on Asia. Over 40 percent of the new immigrants in that decade came from the Orient. Not even counting refugees, nations like the Philippines, Korea, China, and India were among the top sending groups.

The more than 8 million immigrants who arrived in the United States between 1970 and 1987, like their predecessors, have settled in every part of the country. The major change is that Los Angeles has replaced New York City as the leading port of entry. New York is the center for much immigration from the Caribbean; but because Los Angeles is closer to Mexico and Asia, that city has now become the first stop for newcomers by the thousands. Mexicans travel north by car, Asians arrive by plane. No longer are there millions coming into New York harbor by ships, passing the Statue of Liberty, and docking at Castle Garden or Ellis Island. The city of Los Angeles had about 2.9 million inhabitants in 1980, almost 40 percent of them Anglo, 30 percent Hispanic, 20 percent black, and 10 percent Asian. Only 20 years earlier 28 percent of the city's population was minorities and 72 percent was Anglo.

Today Hollywood, once a place associated with movie making and glamor, is one of the centers of new immigrant settlement. In the fall of 1980 the principal of Hollywood High School gave a speech to a parents' association meeting; translators then immediately repeated it in Spanish, Korean, and Armenian. Los Angeles's foreign-language television stations also reflect the new wave of immigrants. That city's Spanish station KMEX carried five daily newscasts and live coverage of events of interest to its Hispanic audience. Each December it held a telethon to raise money for Latin immigrants. Although Spanish stations claimed the largest audience, the city's KSCI-TV carried Korean news, Islamic programs, and a costume drama called *Chinese World*.

Aware of the growing Hispanic population in the Los Angeles region, Von's Grocery Company, a large grocery chain, became the first supermarket to court actively the California's Hispanic market. In early 1987, Von's opened its 191st supermarket in Montebello, a city of 58,000 Hispanics in eastern Los Angeles County. The new store had a staff of 300 persons, all of whom were bilingual, and it was stocked with goods that especially catered to Mexican-American tastes.

Like Los Angeles, other cities have had to adjust to the recent waves of foreigners. The thousands of Asians who arrived after 1970 added a distinctive flavor to New York City's more than 7 million residents. Accustomed to huge colonies of Europeans, blacks, and Puerto Ricans, the city is now acclimating itself to Koreans, Vietnamese, Cambodians, Laotians, Indians, Thais, Filipinos, Japanese, and people from the Caribbean. Toledo, Ohio, is home to immigrant communities from the Philippines, India, Korea, and China. Arabs pray five times a day in Dearborn, Michigan, and have transformed streets in their neighborhoods into a Middle Eastern phantasmagoria. Nearby, in Detroit, Chaldeans, an Aramaic-speaking Christian minority from Iraq, own many of the city's grocery stores. Moreover, 125,000 of the 2 million Arabs in the United States live in the Detroit area. Hoboken, New Jersey, houses small colonies from India, many of them well-educated professionals who had limited opportunities for advancement in their native land.

Another post–World War II change in immigration patterns is that so many of the new wave of immigrants are now living in the suburbs. In 1986 a Census Bureau survey reported that almost half of the 4.7 million newcomers arriving between 1975 and 1985 had settled in suburban areas rather than in central cities. Usually Asians, they were the better educated and more prosperous immigrants. And they often lived among other Americans, not in compounds of their own ethnic groups. One such immigrant, college-educated Stephen Yang, remarked of Chinese immigrants in the San Antonio area, "But we don't even have a Chinatown—we just live all over."

While the Asian population of New York City doubled in the 1970s, it tripled in the city's suburbs. In nearby Bergen County, New Jersey, an official suggested that the Asian population in that section was growing even faster in the 1980s. A Japanese journalist who lived in prosperous Scarsdale, New York, remarked that the late-night commuter train from New York City was dubbed " 'the Orient Express,' because there are so many Japanese fathers on it."

Whereas from 1951 to 1960 only 25,201 persons entered the United States from mainland China, Taiwan, and Hong Kong, during the next quarter of a century nearly one-half million Chinese arrived. The impact of such immigration was potentially staggering when one realizes the Chinese-American population in 1960 was less than 250,000. Moreover, these people were generally concentrated in the Chinatowns of a few American cities, such as San Francisco, New York, and Honolulu. The immigrants headed for these cities, substantially swelling the population already there. San Francisco's Chinatown more than doubled its population from 1952 to 1972 and New York City's Chinese population grew from 33,000 in 1960 to over 100,000 in 1980, about half of whom were living in the city's old Chinatown. By 1980 New York City's Chinese population had become the nation's largest. The rapid influx of immigrants strained housing. In the mid-1980s some experts estimated that nearly 2,000 new immigrants were searching monthly for apartments in New York City's Chinatown. In addition, restaurants and garment shops also sought Chinatown locations. The old Chinatown spread north into "Little Italy" and east into the famed Lower East Side, the home for tens of thousands of Europeans decades before. Capital to purchase housing for people and businesses came from Hong Kong, where uneasy investors feared the transfer of that colony's control from Great Britain to China, scheduled to take place in 1997. As a result, commercial rents were higher in Chinatown than in most areas of the city.

Not only did the new Chinese immigrants have to face high priced and crowded housing, but community facilities were also strained. In the 1970s and 1980s newspapers carried stories of conflicts between the old and new Chinese, including violent gang and street fights. The nation's Chinatown had won a reputation for their low crime rates, but were now threatened by the new violence.

Like earlier immigrants without language and labor skills, Chinese immigrants could be exploited. Even when they had mastered English, they had trouble finding work. One Chinese described his parents' situation in a garment factory: "There [are] no vacations, no pensions; they just work and work all their lives. We're willing to work, but can't find [good] jobs." In 1972 an estimated 7,500 Chinese, most of them immigrants and many of them women, worked in 250 garment factories—virtual sweatshops in New York City's Chinatown—for wages as low as 65 and 75 cents an hour. A Labor Department administrator said these "employees in Chinatown are one of the worst exploited groups in the metropolitan area."

As new migrants poured into San Francisco and New York, the garment industry expanded. Wages improved somewhat as the number of shops grew. New York's 250 shops of 1972 numbered 550 by 1987 and employed 22,000, mostly unionized, workers. The city's old garment district gave way to the new center in Chinatown.

Filipino immigration to the United States has also increased both to the mainland and to Hawaii. Over 47,000 came in 1985. In 1980 the Filipino community in Honolulu and environs was the largest in the world outside of the Philippine Islands, numbering more than 60,000. Like other Asians, many of these recent immigrants have been professional workers. A large contingent found itself stigmatized on the West Coast but not on the East Coast. As a result, many of the better-educated Filipinos have come to New York. In the late 1970s it was estimated that more than 9,000 Filipino doctors lived in America compared to about 13,000 in the Philippines. There is hardly a hospital in San Francisco, Los Angeles, or Chicago without Filipino nurses. Medical and nursing schools in the Philippines train their students in American methods, and the students find a ready market for their skills in the United States. This is indicative of the U.S. impact on Philippine culture and the attractiveness of the United States to many people there.

More striking than the Filipinos are the Koreans. The number of Koreans in America before 1950 was not large. Then came a few students, a few businessmen, and—after the Korean War ended in 1953—wives of American servicemen. The Korean War also had an impact on Korean society, for now Koreans learned about opportunities in the United States. The penetration of American culture triggered immigration, especially after the 1965 Immigration Act. In the nineteenth century, Europeans had learned about America from letters, newspapers, guide books, and the stories of those who had already emigrated. This was also true for Koreans, who learned of our country from the wives of American servicemen and from students, many of whom stayed after their period of study ended. Korean newspapers also told of life here; in 1976 one series of articles was published as a book, *Day and Night of Komericans,* which became a best-seller. Knowledge was one thing, the law was another; and not until the 1965 reform was it possible for many Koreans to emigrate. First came doctors and nurses, and once they were settled they sent for their relatives.

The 1980 census reported 357,393 Koreans in the United States, and population experts put the figure at 542,400 in 1985, most of whom are recent arrivals. Los Angeles, with more than 150,000, houses the largest contingent, but there are sizable numbers in New York City and Chicago. Koreans in Los Angeles mixed with other people, including Samoans, Mexicans, and Chinese, but had their own community life and neighborhoods. For Koreans, an important institution was the church. Because so many were Protestants they affiliated with Presbyterian and Methodist congregations, and began to hold separate services in Korean. In some cases this meant that Koreans gave new life to declining Protestant churches. In 1985 the First United Methodist Church of Flushing, in Queens, New York City, had only 30 members in its English-speaking congregation but over 450 in its Korean congregation.

These new Koreans are particularly successful in running small businesses, especially grocery and vegetable stores, and in 1980 it was estimated that they controlled about 6,000 enterprises in Los Angeles. In New York City the most prosperous Koreans were the health professionals, but in traditional immigrant fashion, they have also taken over businesses that had been run by those who came before them. They have just about replaced Italians and Jews in the fruit and vegetable stores in the nation's largest city. In 1987 Koreans ran about 80 percent of the greengroceries in New York City.

Their entrepreneurial activities were not confined to Los Angeles, New York City, or Chicago. They also moved into declining neighborhoods in cities like Newark, New Jersey. In El Paso, Texas, only one Korean store existed in 1982, but 30 were reported there three years later. Many of the newcomers at first had lived and worked in California before moving to El Paso. In that Texas city, as elsewhere, they quickly earned a reputation for successful merchandising. As one El Paso merchant put it, "They're moving in like crazy—it seems every space that's available, they take it. They're very hard-working and industrious."

As striking as the growth of the Korean community was that of people from India. Few Indians had emigrated to the United States before the 1965 immigration changes. After that many engineers, doctors, and scientists came to the United States to take advantage of opportunities in the nation's businesses, hospitals, and universities. Although they settled in most regions of the country, the largest contingent of Indians could be found in the New York City area and California. A majority of the first immigrants were men who soon afterwards began to send for their wives and families.

The 1980 census reported 387,223 Asian Indians, but some experts thought the figure was over a half million by 1985. Of the nation's newcomers, these Indians had the highest incomes and even earned more than the national average. The educated elite did well economically in professional positions, as did others who went into business, especially those running newsstands and motels. Perhaps the largest successful business was founded by two brothers, Suesh and Bawnesh Kapor, who arrived in the early 1970s. In 1983 they won the contract to operate 143 of New York City's Transit Authority newsstands, and they ran others along the railroad lines to the suburbs.

In California, another center of Indian settlement, these new immigrants bought and ran many inexpensive motels. The first Indian immigrant to purchase one was Nanlal Patel, who bought a motel in Sacramento in the 1940s. He was followed by many others, frequently with the surname Patel, and by 1985 an estimated 80 percent of the state's independent motels were operated by Indians. Branching out from the West Coast, they began to buy motels across the country. One owner observed, "You can travel from San Francisco to New York, and there's not a town where an Indian, a Patel, is not there." In Tucson, children of these Indian immigrants ranked among the city's elite students. Many of them arrived after IBM shifted some of its operations from Boulder, Colorado, to Arizona.

While Chinese, Filipinos, Koreans, and Asian Indians comprised the largest numbers from Asia, they were by no means the only ones to benefit from the 1965 immigration act. The numbers emigrating from Pakistan and Thailand also grew, as did those from the Middle East. After the 1979 revolution in Iran, many Iranians fled to the United States. Some were students already here who managed to change their status to immigrants. In the first half of the 1980s, over 11,000 Iranians annually became American immigrants, a fourfold increase over the average for the 1970s.

Iranians, like so many of the other new immigrants, settled in California, Texas, and New York. Not a few of these newcomers had been prosperous in Iran. In their new homes they also ventured into business, especially real estate and the construction of housing and shopping centers. The Ersa Grae firm, headed by Iranian All Ebrahimi, built five subdivisions in Texas and two in Nashville, Tennessee.

The situation in Iran typified the Middle East, plagued by instability and war. Conflicts between Israel and her Arab neighboring states prompted many Palestinians, Lebanese, Jordanians, and Syrians to evacuate from the area. Just as the Chaldeans ran grocery stores in Detroit, Christian Palestinians purchased and operated similar shops in California. One Palestinian estimated that in the mid-1980s Palestinians ran nearly half of San Francisco's small grocery stores. Mostly, these were family business affairs. Said one owner, "The wife, the little kid can work behind the cash register. You use your family. How else are you going to make it?"

Israel, a nation of immigrants, began to watch more people leaving than entering in the early 1980s, a movement that worried the Israeli government. But the lure, or the "magic of America," was strong. As one migrant put it, "I don't think there is so much 'push' pushing people out of Israel as there is 'pull' or magnet drawing them to the West—mostly to America." Israelis, like other Middle-Eastern peoples, were thoroughly familiar with the United States, through the buying of American goods, watching American television programs, reading American magazines, and drinking in the wonders of America from letters sent by those who were already settled there. And with modern air travel it was easy to get to the United States.

While the number of immigrants from Asia rose in the 20 years after enactment of the 1965 immigration reforms, significant increases in Africans coming to our shores were also recorded in the last decade. Egypt and Ethiopia, which experienced a Marxist revolution in the 1970s, witnessed an exodus of their people, many of whom chose to go to the United States. The explosive situation in South Africa also prompted a small emigration to the United States in the early 1980s. In 1975, 586 South Africans, usually English by background and highly educated and skilled, came to America; a decade later the figure was 1,246. One South African family member who had moved to New Jersey said of his native land, "It's a beautiful country, but it is burning underneath . . . ; after the riots in 1976, you knew it was going to blow up."

After 1965 residents of the Caribbean also emigrated to the United States. Many Hispanics, who will be treated in the next chapter, came from the area, as did other non-Hispanics. The new law made it possible for substantial increases in migration from English-speaking nations in the region as well. Jamaica became one of the largest sending nations of people north to America. It was not unusual for Jamaican women to begin the migration process, arriving to work as nurses or maids. In New York City, which housed the largest contingent of West Indians, Jamaicans and other English-speaking immigrants mixed with a variety of other newcomers as well as American blacks. Although the Jamaicans participated in existing activities, they also had their own cultural institutions. Cricket, a popular game in Jamaica, was now played in Brooklyn, Philadelphia, and other cities by these newcomers.

From Haiti French- and Creole-speaking migrants fled the dictatorial regime of François Duvalier and a severely depressed economy. At first a number of relatively well-educated Haitians emigrated, followed by those with fewer skills. Once in the United States, they took whatever jobs they could get, often being paid poorly. They suffered because they were black as well as immigrants. Like other newcomers before them, they congregated together; one Haitian colony in the Crown Heights section of Brooklyn already had about 75,000 people by the 1980s. In the late 1970s some Haitians, who could not qualify as immigrants under American laws, were so desperate to leave that they sailed in boats for hundreds of miles to the Florida coast. Once in the United States, they were arrested by immigration authorities, who insisted that they were illegal immigrants and not entitled to remain here. Their cause was taken up by some religious groups and fought in the courts in an attempt to win permission for them to stay. This issue will be taken up in Chapter 7 dealing with recent refugees.

Among many who came for economic reasons, whether from Europe, Asia, Africa, or Latin America, were a striking number of highly skilled and educated people—especially scientists, engineers, physicians, and other health professionals. These were the so-called brain drain to America.

Most of the immigrants, however, were not among the elite of their societies. Nor, as had been customary in an earlier era, did males constitute a majority of those coming after World War II. The War Brides Act, the refugee laws, and the provisions for uniting families helped tip the sex ratio in favor of women. Many immigrants were young children coming with their parents. Thus the bulk of post–World War II entrants was not admitted under the category of general occupations. But of those who did have training a larger proportion than ever before was professional. In fact, by the 1960s professionals made up a plurality of those ranked occupationally; and of 167,241 immigrants with skills who came in 1972, 48,887 (28 percent) were listed as professional, technical, and kindred workers.

From the end of the war until the 1960s Great Britain and Canada, especially, sent scientists and engineers to the United States, and Germany was not far behind. Most immigrant scientists and engineers found jobs in private industry, but a considerable number taught and did research in American universities. Many of those emigrating had originally come with a temporary visa or as students, but elected to remain in this country. The number of doctors emigrating to the United States also increased steadily. In 1949, 1,145 of them came; but in 1972 that figure was topped by physicians from India alone. By 1987 it was reported that 28,000 Indian doctors were in the United States, and they comprised 10 percent of the nation's anesthesiologists. In the mid-1970s the 9,000 Filipino physicians here outnumbered the native-born black physicians. Over 70,000 doctors emigrated to the United States between 1945 and 1976 when Congress amended the immigration laws to cut their numbers.

The scientific community of America was disproportionately foreign-born. In 1961 the foreign-born made up about 5 percent of the American population but 24 percent of the members of the National Academy of Sciences. The National Register of Scientific and Technical Personnel estimated in 1970 that 8 percent of the nation's professional scientists were born and had received their secondary educations abroad. Of the 43 American holders of Nobel prizes in physics and chemistry through 1964, 16 were of foreign origin. Of the 28 Americans receiving Nobel prizes in medicine and physiology, 8 were foreign-born.

The situation in medicine was similar as American hospitals increasingly became dependent upon immigrant physicians for their staffs. In 1950 only 5 percent of the new medical licenses were granted to foreign graduates, but by 1961 this figure reached 18 percent. Most, but not all, of these foreign-trained doctors were immigrants. Ten years later, more immigrant doctors came to America than were graduated that year by half the nation's 120 medical schools. In New York City, where nearly 30 percent of the foreign-born doctors settled, 70 to 80 percent of the residents and interns of some hospitals were immigrants. After the changes in the law in 1976 the proportions in some hospitals began to decline.

While the immigration laws and procedures favored the admission of scientists, engineers, and doctors from abroad, attractive conditions in America were also essential to lure them. A study done by the National Science Foundation in mid-1970 revealed several reasons for the emigration to America. Many, such as the Cubans, disliked their political situations at home, and others were curious about life in America. Insufficient opportunities for research at home also drove some out. But, above all, existing opportunities made the United States seem like the land of golden opportunity. Most of the newcomers cited a higher standard of living in America, lower taxes, and higher salaries as major factors inducing emigration. About one-half said that their American salaries were at least twice what they would have been at home.

The brain drain to the New World prompted uneasiness in several European nations and especially in Great Britain. A committee of the Royal Society concluded in 1963, "We have not been able to arrive at a reliable figure for the cost of educating these scientists. We regard as much more serious the economic consequences of the loss to this country of the leadership and the creative contributions to science and technology which they would have made in the course of their working lives." Although the number coming from Great Britain was the largest from any one country, the drain was just as serious from the Netherlands, Norway, and Sweden. By 1968, however, partly because of improved conditions in Europe and the changes in the immigration laws, the brain drain from Europe to America declined, while the numbers of Asian and Latin-American scientists and engineers arriving in the United States multiplied.

The increase in the number of professionals from the developing nations was part of a general shift in immigration patterns largely prompted by the new immigration act of 1965. Twenty years afterward it was clear that a new era in immigration had begun, a period marked by large-scale emigration from the Third World and away from the traditional influx from Europe. In 1965 the Immigration and Naturalization Service recorded 296,697 entrants to the United States, but by 1985 the figure almost doubled to 570,009. Marked shifts occurred, as can be seen from Table 5.2. The numbers coming from Europe dropped from 113,424 in 1965 to 63,043 in 1985. By the 1980s Europeans accounted for only about 10 percent of the total. In North America, Mexico replaced Canada as the leading source of new migrants and people from the Caribbean and South America also made substantial dents in the statistics. But the biggest increases were from Asia. In 1965 about 20,000 immigrants, 5 percent of the total, arrived from the Far East. By the mid-1980s Asians accounted for nearly half of the new immigrants.

In the immediate future these trends will probably continue. Knowledge about the United States is plentiful in Third World countries and so is the desire to emigrate. Commenting on the situation in Israel one scholar noted, "Com-

**Table 5.2   IMMIGRANTS ADMITTED BY SELECTED
COUNTRY OR REGION OF BIRTH**
Fiscal Years ended June 30, 1965 and
September 30, 1985

Country of birth	1965	1985
Europe	**113,424**	**63,043**
Germany	24,045	7,109
Ireland	5,463	1,397
Italy	10,821	3,214
United Kingdom	27,358	13,408
Asia	**20,683**	**264,208**
China and Taiwan	4,057	29,682
India	712	26,026
Iran	582	16,071
Korea	2,165	35,253
Pakistan	187	5,744
The Philippines	3,130	47,978
Vietnam	226	31,895
North America	**126,729**	**182,045**
Canada	38,327	11,385
Central America	12,423	26,302
Mexico	37,969	61,077
West Indies	37,583	83,281
Dominican Republic	9,054	23,787
Jamaica	1,837	18,923
Trinidad and Tobago	485	2,831
South America	**11,084**	**39,058**
Colombia	10,885	11,982
Africa	**3,383**	**17,117**

Source: Immigration and Naturalization Service, *Statistical Yearbooks,* and *Bulletin* (Statistical Analysis Branch, 1986).

munications are dominated by the 'big eye' of television where the American
influence is large, indeed almost inescapable." He noted that in nations throughout the globe, "Millions share sleepless nights pondering the machinations and
incredible complexities of the Ewings of 'Dallas'—in about as many tongues and
accents as one could care to conjure. Blue jeans are the great leveller of the
twentieth century, popular as much in Leningrad as in Louisville. Everyman's
dreams and expectations tend somehow to be spun out in Hollywood and on
Madison Avenue rather than in centers closer to home." In 1986 the State
Department announced that the countries with the largest backlogs of those
awaiting visas to this country were as shown in Table 5.3. Because each nation
is allowed only 20,000 visas annually, excluding refugees and immediate family
members of U.S. citizens, the wait could be for an indefinite period for the people
from Mexico, the Philippines, India, Korea, and China.

In retrospect the decades since World War II have witnessed major trans-

**Table 5.3 PERSONS AWAITING VISAS BY
COUNTRY, 1986**

Country	Awaiting visas
Mexico	366,820
The Philippines	362,695
India	142,734
Korea	134,778
China (Mainland-born)	112,843
Vietnam	97,539
China (Taiwan-born)	69,397
Jamaica	52,909
Dominican Republic	37,332
Guyana	37,133
Hong Kong	34,059
Pakistan	30,234

Source: U.S. Department of State: Bureau of Consular
Affairs, *Bulletin,* Vol. V, No. 86.

formations in American immigration policies and in the sources of American immigration. When the war ended, special efforts were made to bring European refugees to this country beyond established quotas. In 1965 Congress threw out the McCarran-Walter Act of 1952 and completely rewrote American immigration policies, giving preferences to relatives of Americans as well as to those whose skills were needed in our labor market. Since then greater consideration has also been given to the needs of political refugees. As a result, Asians and Latin Americans account for the vast majority of immigrants.

Americans have viewed these changes with mixed feelings. Though the nation became more tolerant toward racial and ethnic minorities after the 1940s, prejudice by no means disappeared. In the 1980s a growing number of violent incidents occurred against Asians, especially Indochinese refugees. These will be discussed in Chapter 7. In addition, debates over bilingualism sometimes exposed opposition to Hispanics. Public-opinion polls in recent decades indicated that members of the dominant American culture did not wish to see immigration increased.

Of all the issues prompting debate none emerged so lively as the concern over illegal immigration. Because the undocumented could not satisfy legal entry requirements or chose not to wait for years, many migrants entered the United States illegally or arrived on student or visitors' visas and then remained when their visas expired. No one knew how many undocumented immigrants lived and worked in the United States in the 1980s; estimates ranged from 2 to 12 million. Most experts put the figure around 3 million or so in the mid-1980s.

One thing was clear: Growing numbers were trying to come to the United States without proper immigration papers. Table 5.4 indicates the trend up to 1985. The figure for 1986 was even higher, topping 1.8 million.

**Table 5.4   DEPORTABLE
IMMIGRANTS
Selected Years,
1966–1985**

Year	Number deportable
1966	89,751
1967	108,327
1970	277,377
1973	542,934
1980	910,361
1985	1,348,749

Source: Immigration and Naturalization Service, *Statistical Yearbooks,* and *The Woodlands Forum,* Vol. 3, No. 3 (1986).

The growth of this undocumented population prompted much debate and finally led to the passage of a new immigration law in 1986. These aliens were said to cause unemployment because they reportedly took jobs at low pay from American resident aliens and citizens. President Jimmy Carter's Secretary of Labor Ray Marshall told a reporter in 1979, "It is false to say American workers cannot be found for all of the jobs filled by undocumented workers. . . . The truth is that there are millions of American workers in all of these low-paying occupations already." Some insisted they caused crime and were a public burden because they used schools, hospitals, and the welfare system.

Defenders of undocumented aliens claimed that these charges were exaggerated or absurd. Furthermore, critics insisted these aliens were good for the American economy because they took jobs that Americans did not want and because they paid more in taxes than they used in benefits. One avocado grower told of American workers, "We tried, but they don't want the jobs. Picking avocados is damn hard work. Americans work a day or two and drift away, it's easier to go on welfare. The illegals are really good workers."

In 1972 and again in 1973 the House of Representatives voted to make it unlawful knowingly to employ undocumented aliens, but the Senate took no action. A decade later the situation was reversed as the Senate twice passed a similar bill, but the House did not.

By then political alliances had been formed. Hispanic and black organizations and representatives, along with large agricultural producers, many employers, civil liberties groups, and religious leaders, opposed such measures. Employers of undocumented aliens claimed they could not get Americans to work for them while Hispanic and civil liberties groups argued that an employer sanction measure would lead to discrimination against Hispanics in the labor market. They feared that to avoid prosecution employers would not hire "foreign-looking" people or those with Hispanic names.

Unions and immigration restriction groups like the Federation of Americans for Immigration Reform said the nation ought to gain control of its borders and that undocumented immigration caused too many problems in the United States. They were joined by environmental groups who feared the adverse effects of increased population. One such environmentalist warned about the "continued degradation of the environment," in part caused by the "swelling stream of immigrants landing on our shores and crossing our borders, and an immigration policy incapable of coping with this invasion."

In 1984 the House and the Senate passed different versions of the employer sanctions bill, but as Congress moved toward adjournment, the two bodies could not agree on a compromise. By 1985 and early 1986 it appeared the measure was dead. In the last days of the congressional session ending in the fall of 1986, the two bodies finally agreed and enacted the Immigration Reform and Control Act of 1986.

The employer sanctions provision proved to be the center of the bill, but other sections were necessary for a compromise. The law gave growers permission to bring in temporary alien farm workers if sufficient Americans could not be found to work on their large farms. To counter the employer sanctions, an amnesty was granted to those undocumented who could prove that they had lived in the United States since 1982; if they could show this proof, they were eligible to become resident aliens. The law went into effect in 1987.

Even some Hispanics favored this measure because of the amnesty provision that would grant many illegal aliens the privilege of becoming resident aliens and eventually citizens. Moreover, some feared a more restrictive measure might emerge in the future. The act also appeared to contain provisions protecting them against discrimination. It made it unlawful for employers to discriminate against persons because of their national origins. Of course, agribusiness was pleased with the section providing for temporary farm workers. Some of those who worried about the effects of illegal immigration did not like the amnesty, which they said was unfair. One member of Congress asked, "How about all the people who waited all these years to come in legally?" Enough legislators believed that employer sanctions would check illegal migration that they supported the bill.

How would this new immigration legislation affect future illegal immigration? While some politicians hailed the new law as enacting a far-reaching program to halt such immigration, others were skeptical. One observer put it, "After the initial shock it will be business as usual on the border." Many undocumented persons already in the country were reported searching for bogus papers to prove they had arrived before 1982 and had lived here since that date.

Quite obviously the future of the entry of newcomers without appropriate papers would depend on whether Congress voted necessary funds for adequate enforcement and whether the border authorities could prove themselves efficient in enforcing the law. Too often the Immigration and Naturalization Service had been unable to enforce existing laws, and it clearly needed more personnel and funds to modernize. Perhaps the future was best predicted by one of the bill's staunchest supporters, Representative Charles E. Schumer of New York, who said, "The bill is a gamble, a riverboat gamble. There is no guarantee that employer sanctions will work or that amnesty will work. We are headed into uncharted waters."

chapter 6

The Hispanics

The era that began with World War II has witnessed Hispanic presence in this country whose importance is revealed in the immigration figures. Starting with the bracero movement during World War II, the Puerto Rican migrations to New York City and other East Coast places after the war, and the migration north from Mexico in the late 1940s and 1950s, Spanish-speaking people have carved a niche for themselves that rivals, or perhaps exceeds, that of the Germans during the nineteenth century.

Since 1968 Mexico has been the source of more newcomers to the United States than any other country. Mexicans and other Hispanic immigrants account for more than one-fourth of all legal entrants to this country since about 1965. If illegals were incorporated into the official figures, the percentage would probably be higher. No one knows how many undocumented individuals arrive in the United States every year, but experts estimate that at least 50 percent are Mexican.

The census records of early 1980 revealed that there were more than 14 million people of Mexican, Puerto Rican, Cuban, and other Latin-American origins in this country. Between 1980 and 1985 the nation's population grew 3.3 percent; however, the Hispanic population grew 16 percent and totaled over 17 million. Because so many Hispanics who arrived illegally had never been counted by the federal government, the figures no doubt understated the actual number. The Hispanics are, after black Americans, the nation's largest minority. Population experts point out that with a high birth rate and substantial immigration, the numbers of Hispanics will continue to grow at a rapid rate. "The implications for this country are enormous," one former federal official observed. "Not too far in the future," he predicted, "many areas will have Spanish-speaking majorities, and Latin American culture will make a very deep impression on the mainstream of U.S. society." Acknowledging the reality of this statement, President Jimmy Carter established an Office of Hispanic Affairs in the White House in 1977.

The signs of Hispanic vitality are evident almost everywhere in America and not only in utterances of governmental officials and census data. More than a hundred television and radio stations broadcast in Spanish; Pacific Telephone puts out a Spanish-language supplement for its telephone directories; Chicago bus notices and Philadelphia civil service examinations appear in both languages; and shops from California to New York display *Aqui se habla español* placards in their windows. By 1970 Spanish had replaced Italian as the nation's most frequently spoken foreign language, and in 1978 *Variety* estimated that millions of people in this country used Spanish as their native tongue. From 1973 to 1980 Dade County, Florida, which contains Miami, officially was bilingual.

Although large Hispanic communities exist in practically every major city in the country, different groups predominate in different areas. The Puerto Ricans are most significant in New York, Philadelphia, and Cleveland; the Cubans in Miami and New Orleans; the Mexicans in Los Angeles, San Antonio, San Francisco, Seattle, Detroit, Denver, and throughout smaller southwestern communities. Experts estimate that 700,000 Hispanics, or about 20 percent of the city's population, live in Chicago; southern Florida has a majority of the nation's more than 800,000 Cubans, including a large percentage of the 124,000 who arrived in this country in the spring and summer of 1980. On the East Coast, New York houses the widest variety of Hispanics, with Puerto Rican, Dominican, Cuban, Colombian, and Ecuadorian communities.

Of all the Hispanic groups the Mexican Americans are the largest and most prominent, with perhaps 12 million or more in this country; some 80 percent live in the Southwest, the majority in urban areas. They constitute approximately 20 percent of the population in California and Arizona, 25 percent in Texas and Colorado, and nearly 40 percent in New Mexico. The Los Angeles area alone has nearly 2 million people of Mexican ancestry. Until about 1965 they were an almost forgotten minority, but in more recent times historians, sociologists, journalists, politicians, and federal officials have become increasingly aware of their presence.

Some Mexicans in the United States, especially those in New Mexico and southern Colorado, can trace their ancestry back many centuries. The city of Santa Fe, New Mexico, was founded in 1609, a generation before the Puritans set foot in New England. Most of what is now the heartland of Mexican-

American country in the five states of the Southwest belonged to Spain and then to Mexico; the United States did not annex it until the signing of the Treaty of Guadalupe Hidalgo in 1848. At that time Mexico recognized the American annexation of Texas and also ceded all or part of what is now Colorado, New Mexico, Nevada, Arizona, and California. Aside from Nevada all these states have important Mexican-American communities. In the Treaty of Guadalupe Hidalgo the United States guaranteed that all Mexican citizens in the newly acquired territories would be able to retain their property and traditions. Those who chose not to leave within a year were accorded American citizenship with all its rights and privileges. It is estimated that the Mexican population of the Southwest at that time was about 75,000, with most of them in what is now New Mexico and California.

Ever since, the history of the Mexicans in the United States has been tied to the history of the Southwest. As the region grew, so did the influx of Mexicans—legal and illegal, permanent and temporary, daily and seasonal, commuter, student, and tourist. The beginning of the twentieth century witnessed the completion of the great southwestern railroads, the expansion of cotton planting in Texas, Arizona, and California, and the irrigation of farmlands in the Imperial and San Joaquin valleys in California. All these industries needed cheap labor, and the Mexican worker provided it. As the century progressed, Mexicans made up more than 60 percent of the common laborers on the railroad track gangs, in the mines of Arizona and New Mexico, for the fruit and truck crops of Texas and California, and in the numerous packing plants on the West Coast. They also dominated the labor supply in the sugar-beet fields of Colorado and cultivated sugar beets in states as far north as Montana and Michigan and as far east as Ohio.

The coming of Mexican laborers coincided not only with the rapid growth and development of the Southwest but also with the curbing of immigration from China and Japan and later from Europe and with the revolutionary upheavals in Mexico beginning in 1910. Mexican workers, cowboys, shepherds, and ranch hands had crossed the Mexican-American border frequently and easily between 1850 and 1910, just as others had moved north and south or east and west in the United States. There was no border patrol, and American immigration officials were more concerned with keeping out Orientals than with tracking down small numbers of Mexicans. But as agriculture grew it demanded hundreds of thousands of cheap, mobile laborers who could pick the crops quickly in one area and then perhaps move on to other areas and harvest whatever else was ripe. In Texas the migratory farm workers usually started in the southern part of the state in June, then moved eastward and eventually westward for the later harvest in the central part of the state. In California, on the other hand (where more than 200 crops are cultivated), the growing season ranges from 240 to 365 days, thereby keeping workers busy all year. Today that state's agricultural income alone exceeds $10 billion annually.

Before 1910 most of the Mexican migrants were temporary laborers, but after the upheaval caused by the Mexican Revolution many permanent settlers arrived. Although the overwhelming number were lower-class agrarian workers, the migration also included artisans, professionals, and businessmen whose property was destroyed by the violence accompanying the revolutionary chaos.

The Mexican Revolution spurred movement, but so too did a number of other factors. From 1877 to 1910 Mexico's population increased from 9.4 million to 15 million without a commensurate increase in the means of subsistence. A small percentage of *haciendados* (feudal barons) controlled most of the country's land, which was tilled by the agricultural proletariat. There existed between hacienda owners and their laborers a patron–peon relationship, and each role was well defined. As the economy boomed, though, prices rose while daily wages remained constant or even declined to an amount well below that needed to care for a family. At the beginning of the twentieth century the construction of the Mexican Central and Mexican National railroads, as well as the opening of mines in northern Mexico, encouraged movement.

Once the exodus from central and eastern Mexico began, many workers saw no need to stop at the border. Wages in the United States were at least five times as much as in Mexico, and American businessmen avidly sought the foreign peon. As two scholars who have studied the Mexican migration have pointed out, the inability of the Mexicans "to speak English, their ignorance of personal rights under American law, and their recent experience as virtual serfs under the exploitative dictatorship of Porfirio Díaz made them ideal workers from the growers' viewpoint." The northward migration brought about 10 percent of Mexico's population to the southwestern borderlands.

The first Mexican migrants in the twentieth century were overwhelmingly males, mostly transient, who found work on the railroad track gangs. They lived in boxcars and moved from place to place with the Southern Pacific or the Santa Fe or the Chicago, Rock Island, and Pacific. By 1910 they could be found from Chicago to California and as far north as Wyoming. They were cheap laborers who worked for $1 to $1.25 a day, less than their predecessors—the Greeks, the Italians, and the Japanese. Employers found Mexicans desirable because of their tractability and their willingness to work at more arduous jobs for longer hours at lower wages and in worse living conditions than the Europeans or Asians. Many of today's Mexican-American *colonias* (settlements) originated as railroad labor camps.

With the influx of Mexicans, El Paso, Texas, became a major placement center and assembly point for workers in an arc reaching from Louisiana to the state of Washington. Three major railroads passed through this border city, and not only were railroad, mine, and seasonal agricultural workers recruited here, but representatives from labor-contracting companies also took thousands of immigrants to distributing centers in Kansas City, Missouri, Los Angeles, and San Antonio.

After 1910 more and more Mexican newcomers found work in agriculture rather than on the railroads. This was true despite the fact that the major southwestern railroad employed more than 50,000 Mexicans. During World War I, European immigration fell drastically, American residents went off to war, and the expanding agricultural acres needed hands. As a result the laws governing contract labor were temporarily suspended in 1917, and Mexicans, otherwise ineligible for immigration visas, were brought in to cultivate the crops and work the harvest. The depression of 1921–1922 left many of them unemployed, but then the resumption of prosperity and the immigration restriction acts of 1921 and 1924 stimulated a further demand for Mexican labor. Large southwestern agricultural growers put great pressure on Congress to exempt Mexicans from the quota area, and their intensive efforts succeeded. Before 1965, though, to be legally admitted to the United States, Mexicans had to pay fees for visas and medical examinations, show that they were literate and not likely to become public charges, and prove that they had not been guilty of violating the contract labor laws. These reasons, plus an inadequately patrolled border (not until 1924, in fact, was money appropriated for border wardens), made it easier for Mexican agricultural workers to enter illegally than to go through the rigmarole of formal application. Scholars estimate that in the 1920s there were at least as many illegal immigrants as there were legal ones—about 500,000. The 1920s immigrants worked primarily in the agricultural areas of California and Texas but also in the Michigan sugar-beet fields and in the industrial areas in and around Chicago, Detroit, Milwaukee, and western Pennsylvania. Chicago's Mexican population, in fact, shot up from 3,854 in 1920 to 19,362 ten years later, and the city claimed the largest Mexican population east of Denver.

Not only did the depression of the 1930s curtail Mexican immigration, but many Mexicans and their American-born children were encouraged—even forced—by local government officials to return to Mexico, which was not seriously affected by the depression. The Mexican government helped many repatriates return; in cities like Los Angeles, welfare agencies paid for the return passage. It is estimated that almost half a million, or more than one-third of the Mexican-American population in 1930, were removed between 1929 and 1940. About half these people were American-born.

The Mexicans who remained in the United States experienced severe deprivations. In Gary, Indiana, social workers found them living without furniture and with only boxes for tables, and the floor for beds. Moreover, they fell victim to tuberculosis and rickets, and malnutrition was common among their children.

One report, noting the poor housing, the large numbers of unemployed, and the deteriorating health, observed, "The agony and suffering that all of these people endure is beyond comprehension of any who have not experienced it." Southwestern agricultural wages fell from 35 cents to 15 cents an hour. In Texas, Mexican cotton pickers, working from sunrise to sunset, were lucky to earn 80 cents a day; other Mexican farm workers had to be content with 60 cents a day. In California by the late 1930s migratory Mexican families averaged $254 a year, and even there American whites were given preferential treatment. By 1939, in fact, more than 90 percent of the Golden State's field workers were dust-bowl refugees who had replaced the minority group members. In 1940 one investigator found that most of the Mexican agricultural workers in Hidalgo County, Texas, earned less than $400 a year. In the same year it was found that a quarter of the Mexican children between 6 and 9 years of age worked in the fields with their parents; 80 percent of those in the 10–14-year age group did so as well.

The coming of World War II opened up new opportunities for Mexican laborers in the Southwest. Many of those in California and Texas moved out of rural areas to urban centers, where they found jobs in airplane plants, shipyards, and other war-related industries. In the Midwest, steel mills, foundries, and automobile factories (which were now manufacturing for military needs) could not fill their job vacancies fast enough as those eligible for military service went off to war. The southwestern agricultural fields were also starved for workers.

At this juncture the governments of Mexico and the United States inaugurated an entirely new program: the importation of contract laborers, known as braceros, to work in the fields and on the railroads. According to the bracero agreement, Mexicans came into the United States for temporary seasonal jobs, then returned to Mexico when their tasks were completed. From 1942 to 1947, when the initial program ended, the United States received about 220,000 braceros. The program was administered by the Department of Agriculture, and the agreement stipulated that there would be a guaranteed minimum number of working days, adequate wages, and suitable living accommodations. Braceros worked in 21 states, more than half going to California. The Mexican government would not allow any of its nationals to work in Texas, though, because of the intense discrimination in the Lone Star State.

From the braceros' point of view the program was a good one. Most of the workers were men who could not provide adequately for their families at home, and the jobs in the United States offered what they considered good wages. Although they earned only 30 cents an hour and less than $500 a year, this amount still provided them with enough to send money back to their families.

Although protective provisions had been written into the law, many observers were later appalled to find the braceros living in converted chicken coops, abandoned railroad cars, and rickety wooden structures that were on the verge

Table 6.1 BRACEROS ENTERING THE UNITED STATES UNDER CONTRACT, 1942–1964

1942	4,203	1950	67,500	1958	432,857
1943	52,098	1951	192,000	1959	437,643
1944	62,170	1952	197,100	1960	315,846
1945	49,454	1953	201,388	1961	291,420
1946	32,043	1954	309,033	1962	194,978
1947	19,632	1955	398,650	1963	186,865
1948	35,345	1956	445,197	1964	177,736
1949	107,000	1957	436,049		

Source: U.S. Congress, Senate, Committee on the Judiciary, *Temporary Worker Programs: Background and Issues,* 96th Congress, 1st Session (1980).

of collapse. The braceros themselves, however, were attracted by the wages and kept returning whenever they could. Their acceptance of conditions that others would consider deplorable and degrading has been explained by Richard B. Craig in *The Bracero Program.* The Mexican laborer, Craig noted, is "accustomed to living, and indeed thriving, in a virtual state of physical and mental peonage. The Mexican . . . bracero or wetback* probably found little except language (and not always that) to distinguish between the *patron* and the strawboss. It would appear, in sum, that the sociopsychological milieu in which the average Mexican peasant was reared prepared him ideally for his role as the servile, hard-working, seldom complaining, perpetually polite bracero."

The original bracero program ended in 1947, but there were temporary extensions until 1951 when the clamorings from southwestern growers and the impact of the Korean War combined to induce Congress to reestablish it. The second time it lasted until 1964. Table 6.1 shows the numbers of braceros entering the United States during the 22-year program. The apparently bottomless reservoir of cheap labor from south of the border helped build up the multibillion-dollar agricultural concerns from California through Texas, which, unlike the wartime years, were now included in the revised program. One appreciative and callous grower acknowledged: "We used to own slaves but now we rent them from the government."

In the 1950s braceros earned 50 cents an hour (30 cents for cotton chopping in Arkansas) and undercut American laborers. The Mexican Americans in the Southwest were particularly resentful. They did the same work as the braceros, often side by side, but for lower wages, worse housing and facilities, and no transportation. The humiliation and bitterness that these citizens felt when they compared their situations to that of the imported foreign laborers eventually reached the ears of liberal politicians in Congress and prominent labor officials.

*The term "wetback" *(mojado),* which designates an illegal immigrant, originated because many Mexicans swam across the Rio Grande River, which separates Mexico from Texas, and waded across during relatively dry periods when the water was shallow.

Both groups protested the continuation of the bracero program, but they lacked the numbers or the influence to prevail in the 1950s. In the 1960s the Kennedy administration proved more sympathetic and helped bring the program to a close.

Other factors also militated against the program. The southwestern growers had already begun to increase mechanization and thereby decreased their need for more hands; in 1962 Secretary of Labor Arthur Goldberg imposed a $1-an-hour minimum wage; and at about the same time, labor shortages below the Rio Grande made the Mexican government eager to end the agreements. These factors combined to kill the bracero program. During the 22 years of its existence, from 1942 to 1964, almost 5 million braceros came into the country, and they were viewed as indispensable to the southwestern economy. Moreover, their earnings contributed to the Mexican economy as well, because they sent more than $200 million to their relatives at home.

Besides braceros, whose wages and living conditions were stipulated by agreement, the southwestern farmers also employed an untold number of illegal immigrants. For the most part, they were not selected by the Mexican government for the bracero program but had backgrounds and needs similar to those who were admitted. The conditions these aliens were willing to accept in the United States—wages of 20 to 30 cents an hour, housing without plumbing or electricity, washing in irrigation ditches—hint at what life must have been like in Mexico. Certainly, the inhumanity and cruelty that they experienced here must have been an improvement over what they left behind; otherwise they would not have struggled to enter the United States. A more plausible explanation, however, might be that with wages double or triple those in Mexico, workers might be willing to endure great hardships in exchange for economic gain. The growers, of course, found them ideal laborers. Fearing disclosure of their illegal status, the Mexicans performed their tasks well; they neither argued nor complained, and they cost practically nothing. In fact, some unscrupulous southwestern agricultural entrepreneurs turned these undocumented aliens in to immigration officials before payday, thereby saving themselves the cost of the workers' meager wages. Between 1947 and 1954, when the Immigration Service inaugurated a major campaign to round up and deport illegal aliens, more than 4 million of them were apprehended in the United States, but no one knows how many escaped detection. From 1946 to 1954, however, illegal Mexican entrants were the most important source of southwestern farm labor.

Although a great many undocumented migrants were deported to Mexico, the number of legal Mexican immigrants began to rise in the 1950s. Since then, except for refugees, Mexico annually has sent the largest number of immigrants to this country. From 1950 to 1986 almost 2 million Mexicans emigrated to the United States, averaging about 60,000 annually in the 1970s and 1980s. And in 1986 another 350,000 awaited visas in Mexico. Beginning in 1957 the American government stopped counting those who returned; some experts believe, however, that Mexicans return home at a fairly high rate. Hispanics from the Caribbean also returned frequently in a circulatory migration pattern.

Mexicans looked north because their nation's economy did not develop fast enough to absorb its rapidly growing population. The devaluation of the peso in 1976, and again in the early 1980s following the collapse of the oil market, only served to worsen the economic situation and stimulate further emigration. Valued at 24 pesos to the dollar in 1982, the rate fell to 750 to the dollar in 1986, and to 948 in January 1987. Predictions were also made that the peso might drop to 1,548 to the dollar by the end of 1987.

Many Mexicans who could not obtain visas crossed the border illegally. Like the braceros, a large number of these newcomers to the United States labored in agriculture, but most worked in urban service, construction, or industrial jobs. They undertook tasks shunned by American citizens. In 1977 an estimated 10 percent of California's 9.7-million labor pool consisted of undocumented immigrants. "You couldn't eat at a hotel in this town," a Los Angeles resident told a *Newsweek* reporter in 1978, "if a vacuum cleaner scooped up all the illegal aliens."

While undocumented aliens from Mexico had previously been single males with few skills and little education, the situation in Mexico deteriorated so drastically in the 1980s that border agents reported catching new types of illegal entrants: skilled workers and highly educated professionals. An immigration official in Washington, D.C., observed, "There is a perception on the border that there are more people with higher-level skills coming in. We seem to be running into more middle-class people and family units than we did before the big influx that began with the start of their economic crisis."

That Mexicans and Mexican Americans were victimized and exploited there can be no doubt. But why they endured such abuse for so many decades with few protests until the 1960s requires a deeper inquiry into their backgrounds. A majority of them in the Southwest were products of several centuries of intermixture between Spaniards and Indians (there was also a "rica" class of landowners and ranchers) and they came from a culture of poverty. In the United States discrimination against them added to their woes. For generations, in both Mexico and in this country, they had been forced to assume the lowest position in the social order. The Roman Catholic church, which in Mexico combines traditional doctrine with native folk practices, preached a certain fatalism about life, and the relationship of the rural poor to the major landowners or *patrons* reinforced these teachings in Mexico and in the United States. Education for the peons in Mexico prior to 1930 was practically nonexistent, and they came to regard it as a luxury for the upper classes. The immigrants brought such attitudes with them to the United States, and this, combined with the prejudices and inadequacies of schoolteachers and administrators ill prepared to handle Spanish-speaking children, has prevented Mexican children from exploiting educational opportunities in the ways that Jewish, German, Greek, Armenian, and Oriental children have done. Finally, it must be noted that many Mexican workers looked upon their years in the United States as a temporary expedient. They expected to return home; their sojourn north of the border more likely than not gave them an improved status in their home communities. As one Mexican newspaper explained it, in the United States these workers "learn many good things, to be temperate, to dress well, to earn good wages, to live properly, to eat properly, to speak English and much of modern agriculture. That is, they become cultured and when they return to Mexico, they progress rapidly."

The Mexican peasants who moved to the United States may have crossed an international boundary, but, for the most part, they continued to dwell in a land whose physical characteristics were familiar and among people who might easily have been their neighbors at home. The Mexican communities in the Southwest, for example, were so well developed that the newcomer did not have to relinquish his faith, his language, or his cultural ties in order to be accepted. Continued migrations sustained these Mexican *colonias* in the United States and to a considerable extent retarded assimilation and acculturation.

In this country the large farmers and industrialists welcomed the Mexicans for the labor they provided. Lack of familiarity with Mexican customs allowed the Americans to misinterpret good manners and respect for authority as docility, illiteracy as ignorance, and a lack of the Puritan work ethic as laziness. Moreover, the fact that good jobs were scarce and that illegal entry compromised a migrant's position also kept Mexican resentment and anger from surfacing at the wrong moments. The Mexicans' willingness to work has sometimes been misrepresented in a paternalistic and prejudicial manner. A brochure to entice large employers to Tucson in 1977 stipulated, "Employers who have established plants in Tucson say that our Mexican Americans are easy to train, will follow instructions, are more loyal, and equal or exceed the productivity of workers in other parts of the country." The advertisement created a good deal of controversy within the city; Mexican-American inhabitants resented the tone of the piece as well as the characteristics they were alleged to possess.

That Mexicans are docile is belied by their history in the past century. In Mexico the revolution of 1910 was at least in part a peasant movement, and in the United States too there were enough incidents of labor strife to call for a reexamination of careless characterizations. Mexicans led strikes in the Texas Panhandle in 1883 and on the Pacific Railways in Los Angeles 20 years later. To protest labor conditions thousands of Mexican workers walked away from sugar-beet, onion, celery, berry, and citrus crops in California, Texas, Idaho, Colorado, Washington, and Michigan in the 1920s and 1930s. That these protests produced few permanent advances does not reflect defects in the Mexican character. Instead, it reflects the harshness of reprisals, the intense competition for jobs, the shifting nature of the migrant work force, the mechanization of agriculture, and the movement of the more prosperous and accomplished to urban areas where industrial jobs promised greater remuneration.

In more recent times about 10 percent of Mexicans were members of trade unions whereas the figure for all Americans topped 25 percent. Some critics have charged that this low union membership proved that the Mexicans are uninterested in unions, but it is more accurate to say that unions have traditionally been uninterested in organizing Mexican Americans, and this union indifference and even hostility accounts for the low rate of membership. In the late 1970s, however, some unions, the International Ladies Garment Workers' Union among them, demonstrated more interest in organizing Mexicans, even illegal immigrants.

Another problem that Mexicans as well as other minorities have had in the United States is that Americans could not or would not understand why any group was reluctant to part with its own heritage and to embrace the values of the dominant society. But the fact was that Mexican peons struggled from day to day merely to provide the essentials of life for their families. They often did not see the long-range benefits that might accrue to their children from a good education. Even when they did, they may have been shrewd enough to recognize that American education would undermine traditional values and lead their children away from the family and its culture and into the outstretched arms of the dominant culture. Even in rural Mexico in the 1930s schools were built faster than students could be found to occupy them. Peasants were not enthusiastic about educating their children, for they cherished family life, in which everyone had a prescribed role. The status quo provided too much comfort and security for them to sacrifice it for another culture whose values they had difficulty in comprehending.

Given Mexican-American resistance to acculturation, which was reinforced by the physical proximity of the Mexican border, and given the continued influx of newcomers from the old country, it is not surprising that as late as 1940 most Mexican-American families still spoke Spanish at home. Many of these families also looked upon their stays in the United States as temporary and expected to return to Mexico someday. With this pervasive frame of reference it is understandable why few broke away from their cultural patterns to seek a new way of life in the Anglo world. For those who attempted to do so, the intense societal prejudices formed an almost insuperable barrier.

Although discrimination against Mexicans existed throughout the American Southwest, it was not uniform in either emotional tone or effect. For example, Mexicans were expected to live in their own barrios (ghettos), were restricted from using many public recreational facilities, could obtain mostly menial and relatively unskilled jobs, and in general were expected to accept a subordinate role in society. In New Mexico, however, there was a tradition of Hispanic participation in government, and the upper-class Americans of Mexican background moved easily throughout society. In New Mexico, also, those of Mexican descent, regardless of class, have been active in local politics, and their numbers (until recently almost half the population) have determined where and when they could hold office. In Colorado, Mexican *colonias* date back to the 1850s, and there, too, prejudice existed but was not intense. Nor was Arizona, despite its segregated schools and movie theaters, a particularly harsh place for Mexicans. But in California, and especially in Texas, bigotry toward Mexicans has been extreme. In the Lone Star State, with its strong Southern heritage, Mexicans encountered more overt discrimination than anywhere else in the country. Food shops routinely refused to serve them; kindergarten teachers called their children greasers; churches held separate services "For Colored and Mexicans." Typical was this statement from a Texas farmer. "You can't mix with a Mexican and hold his respect," he told an interviewer. "It's like the nigger; as long as you keep him in his place he is all right." And during World War II, when the Mexican government, incensed at the treatment those of Mexican ancestry received in Texas, refused to allow braceros to work in the state, one Mexican-American weekly noted: "The Nazis of Texas are not political partners of the Führer of Germany but indeed they are slaves to the same prejudices and superstitions."

It was also during World War II when two particularly heinous events involving Mexican Americans took place in Los Angeles. One, in 1942, involved the arrest and conviction of a gang of teenage boys for murder although the prosecution presented no evidence at the trial to justify their conviction. Existing community prejudices, combined with the unkempt and disheveled appearances of the youths (the prosecuting attorney refused to allow them to bathe or change their clothes during the first week of the trial) sufficed to bring forth a guilty verdict. Similar miscarriages of justice reflecting community prejudices have been rendered in other sections of the country toward other minority group members at different times, but few have been marked by such gross disregard of evidence. Inability to raise bail forced the defendants to spend two years in San Quentin prison before an appeals court unanimously reversed the lower court's decision "for lack of evidence" and reprimanded the trial judge for his injudicious behavior during the proceedings.

The other event that won national attention and pitted Mexican-American youths against Anglos took place in June 1943. The Zoot Suit Riots involved Mexican-American youth sporting the then faddish zoot suit of baggy trousers with high waists and tight cuffs, long coats with wide shoulders and loose backs, and broad-brimmed flat hats. On the evening of June 3, 1943, a group of sailors was assaulted while walking in a slum area surrounded by the Mexican barrio. The sailors claimed that their assailants were Mexicans. They reported the incident to the police, who returned to the area but could find no one to arrest. The following night 200 sailors took the law into their own hands, went into the Mexican district of Los Angeles, and beat up every zoot suiter they could find. One naval officer explained their mission: "We're out to do what the police have failed to do, we're going to clean up this situation. . . ." Not surprisingly, the Los Angeles police at the time did nothing to deter the servicemen from their course. For the next few nights sailors, soldiers, and marines paraded the streets of Los Angeles indiscriminately attacking Mexicans in what *Time* magazine called "the ugliest brand of mob action since the coolie race riots of the 1870s." It took the intervention of the Mexican government through the U.S. Department of State to curb military leaves in the Los Angeles area, which put an end to this mob action. The Zoot Suit Riots led to the formation of the Los Angeles Commission on Human Rights in 1944, but the new organization could do little to alter established prejudices.

In retrospect it is difficult to imagine positive effects emerging from a miscarriage of justice or from a bloody riot; yet the two events did at least focus attention upon the Mexican Americans in an urban setting. Most writing about Mexican Americans portrayed them as living in rural areas and as being exploited by money-hungry large-scale growers. Although this picture is not totally unfounded, after World War II only the Mexican-American minority, not the majority, was still tied to the land. In 1950 two-thirds of those of Mexican ancestry lived in urban areas; and today about 90 percent live in cities.

In an urban setting Mexican Americans have come to resemble other immigrants and minorities in American history. The second and third generations are beginning to break away from familiar traditions and place more emphasis on American values. The extended family has been gradually replaced by the more typically American nuclear family, and work horizons have expanded. During World War II, when opportunities developed in airplane plants and shipyards, the urbanized Mexican did not have to leave at harvest time to earn more money in the field. After the war there were additional opportunities. By the 1950s California's Mexican Americans made up 20 percent of auto workers, half the members of the building-trades union, and a majority of those working in the garment factories.

Semiskilled and skilled jobs had opened up opportunities for advancement and assimilation for many minorities, and they did so for the Mexicans as well. By 1970 more than 30,000 people of Mexican ancestry held professional positions, and their enrollment in colleges and universities was still small but growing. In the early 1980s Mexican Americans made up 1 to 2 percent of California's lawyers and health professionals. While the group comprised about 20 percent of the state's population, it made up only about 5 percent of the University of California's enrollment.

Two key problems that most recent immigrants faced were lack of ability to speak English and low levels of skills. Mexicans are among the poorest-educated immigrants. In 1980 the Census Bureau reported that about three-fourths of them in California had not gone beyond the eighth grade; among other newcomers, 36.2 percent of the Latin Americans, 18.1 percent of the Asians, and 9.5 percent of U.S.-born California residents fell into this category. About half of the Mexican immigrants reported difficulty with English. Hence they took lower-level jobs in textile, food service, machinery, and apparel industries. While these new workers helped the economy grow, the futures of their children rested heavily on educational achievement. On the other hand, these same pressures for assimilation and mobility will also force the relinquishment of some traditional Mexican-American values. For example, women have usually stayed home, but in recent years, like the Anglo Americans, they have found jobs outside their homes. In 1980 about 44 percent of Mexican-American women worked in paid employment, which was almost equal to the national figure of 48 percent.

Given the problems of Mexicans and their children it is not surprising that although they are comparatively well-off in the urban California of the 1980s, they still constitute one-third of those below the poverty level in Texas and New Mexico and one-fourth of the poor in Arizona and Colorado. In 1984, 11.5 percent of non-Hispanic whites lived below the poverty line, and the percentage for Mexicans was over twice that figure. The following year the median family income of Mexicans was $19,785, higher than that of blacks and another Hispanic group, the Puerto Ricans, but below that of the national median family income of $26,433. While low levels of education and inability to speak English explain much of the gap, another reason was, as a Mexican American bitterly acknowledged to a Dallas reporter in 1980, " 'Mexicans' get only 'Mexican jobs,' " by which he meant menial, low-paying, dead-end employment.

Rural Mexican-American families, such as those in much of New Mexico and southern Texas, however, have yearly incomes considerably less than their urban counterparts and still live in the most modest dwellings, sometimes without plumbing or electricity. In such isolated communities they have inadequate opportunities to improve their lives.

While too many Mexican-American families lived in poverty or struggled with low incomes, a growing number succeeded in business. In 1986 *Money* magazine told its readers of Jose de Santiago. At age 17 he crossed the border illegally. "I came here with nothing to lose and everything to gain," he later recalled. Beginning with a low-wage job so common to undocumented aliens, he found better employment, became a citizen, and eventually formed his own business in Houston, Texas. By 1986 he was running a $2 million-a-year enterprise and he had been awarded the 1985 Minority Small Business Person award by President Ronald Reagan.

Another Mexican immigrant, María Elba Molina emigrated with her family to Arizona when she was 8 years old. Through education and hard work she became a vice-president of Home Federal Savings and Loan in Tucson, a high position for an immigrant woman. Dissatisfied, she began her own company, the J. Elba Corp. Inc., to sell products in the Hispanic community. "I decided I would incorporate my own firm, do what I had always wanted, which was to be on my own; I would try it," she recalled. Her successful firm not only sold to small clients but television stations and banking institutions as well.

These individual successful Mexican Americans have won the admiration of other Americans. However, because Anglos have been willing to overlook existing deprivations or ascribe them to defects inherent in those of Mexican descent, recent years have witnessed the rise of an activist Chicano movement dedicated to improving the economic lot of the group while fostering a self-conscious nationalism. The Chicano movement took shape in the late 1960s at a time when other frustrated groups—blacks, Indians, women—were also vigorously protesting. The Chicanos want to retain their ethnic identity while raising the standard of living of all Mexican Americans. Although they cherish the traditional values of their culture, including a respect and affection for the family, the cult of masculinity *(machismo),* and a sense of obligation to others in the community, their demands for equal education, training, and job opportunities will eventually produce Americans of Mexican descent and the Chicano movement will probably fade out.

Reflecting the goals of this emerging group were four prominent Mexican-American leaders—César Chávez, Reies López Tijerina, Rudolpho (Corky) González, and José Angel Guitiérrez—whose commitment was to end the existing inequalities. The best known of the four is César Chávez, who, along with 600 Filipinos and Filipino organizer Larry Itliong, led California's grape pickers on a five-year strike that ended with the strikers' receiving higher wages and improved working conditions in 1970. Chávez's union lost contracts and workers to the Teamsters Union in 1973 and 1974, only to win most of them back later when California passed a law permitting agricultural workers to unionize. Organization among Mexican-American farm workers has been successful during a period of increased use of farm machinery, which has meant a loss of jobs in agriculture. Hence the Chávez goals for California farm workers appear to be the most limited of those of the four activists, but he was the first Chicano leader to achieve national prominence, and he has become a symbol and a unifying force for Chicano aspirations.

In New Mexico Reies López Tijerina inaugurated the *Alianza Federal de Mercedes* (the Federal Alliance of Land Grants) in 1963 to regain for Mexican

Americans the lands that he charged Anglos stole from the ancestors of Mexican Americans in violation of the 1848 Treaty of Guadalupe Hidalgo. In this goal he has been unsuccessful, but like Chávez he has been able to use this forum to focus on the state's rural poverty and also to rally support for the Chicano movement. The zeal of Tijerina and some of his followers has led them to massive acts of civil disobedience and a two-year prison term for the *Alianza* leader. Tijerina was released from jail in 1971 on condition that he hold no formal position in the *Alianza* movement.

In Denver, Colorado, and Crystal City in southeast Texas two other Chicano leaders have used more orthodox methods to rally their followers. Both started new political parties. In Denver in 1965 Corky González organized a civil rights group, the Crusade for Justice, which he hoped would develop into a new political party. The organization dedicated itself to protecting individual Chicanos from police brutality and judicial bigotry while improving educational, occupational, and social conditions. In Texas, José Angel Guitiérrez, following along the lines of González's Crusade for Justice, founded *La Raza Unida* party, which he hoped would result in Chicano control of some 20 counties where Mexican Americans constitute a majority in south Texas. Guitiérrez believed that Chicanos could never control their own destinies or achieve political power by working within this country's major political parties, but a few years later he changed his views and became a judge in Zavala County, Texas. Today most Mexican Americans support the Democratic party. The four leaders who called for significant change in the 1960s, however, gave their followers specific goals to strive for along with renewed hope for the future.

Since the 1960s a flock of new organizations and groups have developed— the Brown Berets, the Mexican American Youth Organization (MAYO), the League of United Latin American Citizens, the Mexican American Legal Defense and Educational Fund, and a Congress of Mexican American Unity representing 200 Chicano organizations, all dedicated to fostering the goals that the four leaders articulated so well. These groups have now become quite sophisticated in their abilities to exercise political influence. One of the most important groups is a coalition of 26 Hispanic organizations founded in 1968 as the Southwest Council of La Raza and renamed the National Council of La Raza in 1973. The council moved to Washington, D.C., in 1970, reflecting its national orientation. It published a journal, called *Agenda: A Journal of Issues,* and did research and was active on behalf of all Hispanics, not just Mexican Americans. The existence of these various organizations suggests that the future for Americans of Mexican descent will be considerably different from the past.

Politicians have responded to the growing power of Hispanics. Whereas Richard Nixon appointed fewer than 10 of them to presidential and policy positions in the federal government, and Gerald Ford fewer than 25, by mid-1979

Jimmy Carter had appointed nearly 200 Hispanics to important managerial and judicial posts. President Ronald Reagan has not ignored the Hispanic community in making appointments, but he has not been particularly zealous about seeking out their members either.

But in general, most politicians did respond to the steady political growth of Mexican Americans and Hispanics generally. In 1986 the National Association of Latino Elected and Appointed officials reported that 3,202 Hispanics were serving in public office. This number had grown by 100 percent in a decade. The officials included 183 mayors, 117 state legislators, 1,048 municipal elected officials, and 1,188 school board members. Among the emerging Hispanic leaders was Harvard-educated Henry Cisneros, mayor of San Antonio, the largest city to be headed by a Hispanic. At the state level Arizona and New Mexico for the first time were electing men with Spanish surnames as their chief executives. In Congress the Hispanic bloc exerted considerable pressure to defeat the Simpson-Mazzoli Immigration Reform and Control bills in the early 1980s, and used their collective influence to win some changes when the bill finally became law in 1986.

As impressive as the political growth of Hispanics—including Mexican Americans—has been in the last decade or so, they are nonetheless underrepresented politically. In Los Angeles Richard Alatorre became the first Hispanic elected to the City Council and that was in 1985. The following year Alatorre still remained the only Hispanic on the 15-member City Council even though Mexican Americans made up nearly 30 percent of the city's population. Since Hispanics were the nation's fastest growing minority, numbering over 17 million in 1987, or over 7 percent of the nation's population, they needed to increase the 3,202 officials several times to be proportionately represented. In California, for example, in the 1980s Hispanics make up nearly 20 percent of the population but less than 10 percent of the elected officials.

One reason for this lack of political prominence is that Mexican Americans, along with Canadians, have the lowest rate among immigrants in applying for citizenship. Among the reasons for this was perhaps that Mexicans, like Canadians to the north, could return home easily and were not yet committed to becoming American citizens. Then, too, groups at the lower levels of the economic scale tend to have low rates of voting.

Yet economics and citizenship alone do not explain the faint impact of voter turnout and number of elected officials. Hispanics represented a great number of cultures and countries, and although growing were still a minority in most cities. Political power required effective coalitions. In New York City's borough of Queens the 1980 Census counted 262,422 Spanish-speaking individuals, about 14 percent of that borough's population. One-third were Puerto Ricans, who were American citizens, along with Cubans, Dominicans, Colombians, Ecuadorans, Uruguayans, and Argentines. The borough had a vibrant variety of ethnic cultures, but no Hispanic elected officials appeared, except on some local boards. Haydee Vambrana, the Puerto Rican leader of the Concerned Citizens of Queens, summarized the problem, "The Hispanic community, from top to bottom, needs an education on how to use the American political system."

Also on the East Coast the major Spanish-speaking groups—Puerto Ricans in the New York area and Cubans in southern Florida—made their major impact on the mainland after World War II. Aside from their common language, though, the differences between the two groups overshadow their similarities.

The United States acquired Puerto Rico from Spain at the end of the Spanish-American War in 1898, and in 1917 Puerto Ricans were granted American citizenship. Ever since, Puerto Ricans have been moving to the mainland. In 1910 the census recorded 1,500 of them; by 1930 there were 53,000. Like members of other groups, those who came were escaping from a land with too many people and too few jobs. The Great Depression and World War II cut the flow to the mainland, but beginning in 1945 the flow swelled to a torrent. Relatively cheap air transportation and an abundance of skilled and semiskilled jobs in New York City served as the magnets. As late as 1940 New York City had slightly more than 60,000 Puerto Ricans; in a decade the figure had quadrupled. Today there are over 2 million Puerto Ricans scattered throughout the continental United States, with perhaps two-thirds of these in the New York area. In 1987 the other major centers for Puerto Ricans were Chicago, with a colony of about 100,000, and Philadelphia, with more than 30,000, but the official figures probably underestimate the actual totals. There are also Puerto Rican communities in Bridgeport, Connecticut; Rochester, New York; Dayton, Ohio; Boston, Massachusetts; Miami, Florida; Milwaukee, Wisconsin; and numerous cities in New Jersey.

By the mid-1970s the exodus from Puerto Rico was slowing down and it appeared that the number of Puerto Ricans leaving the mainland was greater than those arriving. No one knew the exact figures but some experts suggested that the net flow back to Puerto Rico was around 200,000 in the late 1970s. The severe recession and inflation of that period accounted for much of the move. Some Puerto Ricans found that the skills they picked up in New York City, Chicago, and other cities, including mastery of English, enabled them to get ahead in Puerto Rico. But they were not always welcome in Puerto Rico and were sometimes called "Newyoricans," a pejorative term meaning pushy, aggressive, and out of touch with life in Puerto Rico.

The Puerto Rican experience in New York and other major cities on the continent is probably closer to that of the European immigrants who landed on the East Coast and settled in urban areas than to that of the Mexicans in the West. Although there are Puerto Rican migrant workers who move up and down the East Coast according to the seasons, essentially they are an urban people with the problems of the city's poor.

In New York they replaced the European immigrants in lower-level factory jobs—especially the Jews and Italians in the garment district—and in the city's worst slums. Like the Europeans, they spoke a foreign language but, unlike them, they encountered a color problem. Many Puerto Ricans are the products of centuries of racial mixing between the island's white and black populations. Although higher status is afforded those of lighter complexions, darker skin does not have quite the impact in Puerto Rico that it has in the United States. On the mainland, though, Puerto Ricans learned that the darker one's skin the greater the difficulty in gaining acceptance and being able to adjust to the dominant culture. One social worker reported that in her dealings with Puerto Rican drug addicts, inevitably the darkest member of the family was the one affected. Piri Thomas in his moving *Down These Mean Streets,* an autobiographical account of growing up in New York City's East Harlem ghetto, recalled his own difficulties as the darkest member of his family and how bitter he felt toward his father for passing along such pigmentation to him.

To read the social and economic statistics of Puerto Ricans in New York City and elsewhere is to recall the plight of minorities in the past. In 1985 Puerto Ricans had the lowest median family incomes of any Hispanic group: $12,371, less than half the national average of $26,433. A distressing number of families, nearly half, were headed by women with small earnings. In that year roughly 42 percent of the Puerto Ricans lived below the government's poverty line. The group's unemployment rate was double that of other segments of the population. Prospects for the current generation are not bright. The Puerto Rican Association for Community Affairs reported in 1983 that the group's high school dropout rates ran as high as 80 percent in New York City and that many of those in school were reading below grade level. A 1987 New York State report put the figure lower, but still over 60 percent. The report concluded with this statement about New York's Hispanics: "The dropout rates and low school achievement levels of a staggering number of Hispanic high school students have a direct, devastating effect on their communities. The damage inflicted on young Hispanics today threatens society tomorrow."

In addition Puerto Ricans have a higher incidence of juvenile delinquency and more drug addicts, and are particularly susceptible to ailments like tuberculosis and venereal diseases. There are also greater incidents of police brutality toward them. In a word, they are plagued with the disabilities historically associated with lower-class, poorly educated immigrants. Until American society decides to be more humane and more concerned with these people their plight will be precarious at best.

Whether Puerto Ricans will follow along the paths established by the European immigrants is not certain. They are concentrated in the New York City area where job prospects are only fair, and they do not seem to be making as much progress as other Hispanics. Still, there are some signs that Puerto Ricans will move up the ladder. In 1969 Joseph Montserrat, who later became the first Puerto Rican president of the New York City Board of Education, pointed out that most of the group's members had been in New York for fewer than 15 years, that half of them were under 21 years of age, and that 84 percent of those of Puerto Rican ancestry born on the mainland were under 14 years old. Nevertheless, by 1960 only 25 percent of the Puerto Ricans were classified as unskilled or service workers; the rest were rated as semiskilled, clerical and sales, craftsmen and foremen, engaged in professional, managerial, or technical occupations, or working as proprietors. By 1964 Puerto Ricans owned more than 6,000 small businesses in New York City, including groceries, barber shops, and dry-cleaning stores. Since 1969 there has also been an open enrollment policy at the City University of New York, mandating admission to any resident high school graduate seeking entry. This policy alone opened an avenue for Puerto Ricans that had been closed to members of ethnic groups in the past. Earlier groups had been forced to fight quotas and had been challenged to meet standards that only a minority of the older immigrants or their children ever attained.

Besides poverty, language, and their concomitant difficulties, Puerto Ricans have lacked political organizations with power and visible leaders. Joseph Montserrat, Herman Badillo—a Bronx congressman who resigned to become a deputy mayor of New York—and Congressman Robert Garcia serve as models of achievement through diligence and hard work, but they are examples of individual prowess more than of group accomplishment. The Puerto Rican caucus that emerged in the New York state legislature in the 1970s won some gains for its people but was still relatively weak. Moreover, there are no unifying organizations comparable to the German turnverein, the Irish Catholic church, or the Jewish mutual-assistance societies that help members of their respective ethnic groups. The Young Lords, a militant body of teenagers, have demonstrated for free food and Puerto Rican studies programs in the colleges, and the Puerto Rican Association for Community Affairs inaugurated ASPIRA to encourage Puerto Rican youth to exploit their talents to the fullest, but they deal with relatively few people and lack the resources for mobilizing an ethnic community. The Roman Catholic church cannot do it because the Puerto Rican attachment to Catholicism is too slight, and besides, many Puerto Ricans in New York have found the Protestant pentecostal churches more to their liking. The only institutions that have extensive contact with the Puerto Ricans are city agencies that minister to the poor—and they are much too rigid and impersonal to provide the warmth and succor needed during the transition period in a new society.

The other Hispanic minority that has made a major impact on the East Coast, and the first immigrant group to change the complexion of a southern city in the twentieth century, is the Cubans. They came in several waves. The first began in 1959 and lasted until the Cuban Missile Crisis of 1962 brought it to a halt. Another exodus began in the fall of 1965 and lasted into the early 1970s. The third migration came in 1980 when over 120,000 landed in Key West, Florida. As a group the Cubans are considerably different from most other immigrants into this country. First of all, the bulk of them are political refugees who left their homes because of the policies inaugurated by Fidel Castro after he led a successful revolution against the regime of Fulgencio Batista in 1958. Secondly, many Cuban refugees came from the elite of their society. According to one study, in the first wave about 70 percent were professional, skilled, or white-collar workers; almost 40 percent had some college education; and 80 percent of those who came had yearly incomes above those earned by the average Cuban.

The exodus of 1980 was somewhat different. Social and economic problems in Cuba and the reports coming from America by visiting Cuban Americans in the late 1970s set the stage for the dramatic exodus. When Castro decided to permit the dissatisfied to leave, a vast flotilla of ships, large and small, set sail from Florida to pick up refugees in Cuba. Relatives and friends of the Cubans and those eager to make money out of providing transportation were involved in the movement, as were voluntary agencies helping the newcomers settle. The Carter administration was uncertain how to handle the situation, but for the most part permitted hundreds of boats to land their passengers. Using the camps inhabited by the Vietnamese refugees in the mid-1970s, the immigration authorities worked with voluntary agencies to settle the Cubans and reunite them with their families in America. Not all the refugees were settled easily, however, and some of the single males without family connections in the United States were detained in the camps. The exodus of 1980 was a migration primarily of young adult males in their prime working years. However, among them were some criminals and mental patients who were neither wanted by this nation nor by the immigration authorities. Because they were inadmissible under existing laws, several thousand found themselves imprisoned in the United States. At first Cuba refused to take them back, but finally agreed to do so. In 1985, the accord was suspended by the Cuban government because it objected to the United States sending Voice of America Radio Marti transmissions to Cuba. After further negotiations the two nations reached an agreement in 1986. Cuba was to accept some 2,700 prisoners and the United States in turn agreed to admit several thousand political prisoners in Cuban jails. The two nations also negotiated terms for allowing eligible Cubans to emigrate to the United States.

Since Miami, Florida, is the city closest to Havana in both distance and culture, most of the 1960s refugees went there. The U.S. government assisted them in the move from Cuba by waiving immigration requirements, providing plans for an airlift, and establishing agencies to help the newcomers adjust to this country. They have made an impressive impact in the city since they left Cuba a generation ago and have moved up the economic ladder to achieve middle-class and upper-middle-class status in this country faster than any other ethnic group since the Huguenots of colonial times.

The 700,000 or so Cubans have in fact revitalized a sleepy southern town and transformed it into a major international hub. Miami is now regarded as the capital of Latin America because it attracts business people and financiers from the entire Western Hemisphere, not to mention those looking for fun. Argentine ranchers, Ecuadoran manufacturers, and Colombian drug peddlers find the city enticing and exciting. Nightclubs, resorts, and hotels abound. It is perhaps the most comfortable place in the country for Latin Americans because Spanish is not merely a second language but is in many places the language of communication. Business people are finding themselves at a severe competitive disadvantage if they know only English. Enterprising Cubans have taken over or established thousands of businesses. Whereas in 1970 there were fewer than 1,000 establishments owned by Cubans, a decade later the figure hovered around 10,000—banks, construction companies, radio and television stations, and so forth. No significant area of business in Miami has been immune to the Hispanic presence. The city now has more international and out-of-state banks than any other in the country save New York City. These banks and financial institutions attract money from every Latin-American nation. In addition, an enterprising Cuban thought up the now established Trade Fair of the Americas, an annual event in which practically all Latin-American nations participate.

Individual success stories about Cubans abound. Carlos Arboleya was chief auditor of Cuba's largest bank when he fled his native land. Beginning anew with little money, he worked as a clerk in a shoe factory before finding his place in banking again. By 1968 he had become president of the Fidelity Bank and a U.S. citizen. He later assumed the vice-chairmanship of the Barnett Bank of South Florida, a bank with assets of $3.5 billion. While banking was attractive to Cubans, so was Miami's garment industry, formerly run by Italians and Jews. "The Cubans really put some zing into this industry. Almost 100 percent of the small manufacturers are Cuban, almost 100 percent of the contractors, big and small, are Cuban and almost all the top management is Cuban," noted one businessman. He no doubt had in mind Cubans like Antonio Acosta, owner of Tony and Toni Fashions, a $500,000 a year business.

Another Cuban immigrant, Yvonne Santa Maria, never held a job before leaving for Miami in 1963. She arrived with no funds. "No money. No jewels. We were not even allowed to take out phone numbers," she recalled. She found employment in several of the city's banks, and at age 57 was president of the Ponce de Leon Federal Savings and Loan Association in Coral Gables, Florida.

Many Cubans at first did not think of themselves as Americans, but looked instead to the day when Fidel Castro's government would be overthrown and they could return home. But after the failure of a CIA-sponsored invasion to overturn the Castro regime in 1961 and the Cuban Missile Crisis the next year, they began to think of themselves as permanent residents of America. Subsequently they made rapid economic progress, began to become American citizens, and began to become involved in politics. In 1985, Miami elected Harvard-educated lawyer Xavier Suarez as its first Cuban-American mayor. He defeated another Cuban, Raul Masvidal. Both men were born in Cuba and had come to America 25 years ago. The following year, Richard Martinez, another Hispanic, won the governorship of Florida.

While these individual stories illustrate the economic success of Cubans and their emergence politically, not all Cubans have been able to make the adjustment to a new life so easily. For some the move to America was too abrupt and they were unable to start their careers anew. They found themselves taking low-paying jobs. In 1985 the Census Bureau reported that Cubans had a median family income of $22,587. This was less than the national midpoint of $26,433, but higher than other Hispanic groups. Moreover, it might be considered high when one realizes that Cubans have been here for only about one generation.

Because of the economic success of the Cubans and because of their known hostility to communism, one read and heard mostly praise for those who arrived in the United States during the 1960s. They have settled in almost every part of the country in addition to southern Florida (New York City has the second largest Cuban settlement, over 100,000) and alone among urban immigrant groups of the past 150 years have avoided the decades of squalor usually associated with newcomers. As a result, they have avoided most of the bigotry and discrimination that the others have experienced. The magazine stories about the Cuban émigrés refer to them as resourceful, aggressive, energetic—characteristics that most Americans have been taught to respect.

Next to Mexicans, Puerto Ricans, and Cubans, Dominicans are the largest group to have come from Latin America. Because some enter illegally and many go back, the precise number living here is not known, but from the late 1960s into the 1980s about 12,000 annually were leaving the Dominican Republic. From 1983 through 1985 they averaged over 20,000 annually, placing them near the top of immigrants to the United States in those years. Their total number in the United States exceeds 350,000 in 1987. Most have settled in the New York City area, especially in Manhattan's Upper West Side, making it the second largest "Dominican" city in the world. Though not prosperous by American measuring rods, the migrants are well off by Dominican standards and have achieved a lower-middle-class status. Yet even these migrants have been affected by a high unemployment rate. The lack of opportunities in their own land, however, stimulates emigration to America where they join friends and families.

Many Dominicans hope to make money and return home; like turn-of-the-century immigrants, some have done so. However, it has not always been easy to find a high-paying job in America. Many found employment in New York's reviving garment industry, working in small shops at low pay. Others worked in the city's service industries. As New York's Hispanic population grew, many Dominicans found new opportunities. The city's 8,000 bodegas, small grocery stores originally run by Puerto Ricans, became increasingly managed by Dominicans. These stores, described by some observers as combination mom-and-pop groceries, drugstores, and neighborhood social clubs, carried a variety of products desired by Hispanics. One Puerto Rican owner of a chain of bodegas explained their appeal, "The supermarkets, with all their advanced sales techniques, will never wipe out the bodegas because they are part of the community."

Another Hispanic group settling in New York is the Colombians. In the 1950s, political turmoil forced many to emigrate, including some professionals; and in the next two decades economic problems pushed many out. Like so many other immigrants the Colombians seek new opportunities. One scholar estimates that over half the Colombian women who have arrived here have gone to work; this is a higher percentage than the national average. In New York City they have earned a reputation as hard workers, which helps them get jobs, but also opens them up to exploitation. Colombians tend to be conservative and many send their children to parochial schools, which they believe have better discipline than public schools, despite the fact that they resent the non-Hispanic, and especially Irish-American, control of the Catholic church. In recent years, however, the hierarchy in the Northeast has made special efforts to reach out to the Hispanics. Spanish-speaking priests have been appointed to head parishes and to preach in the language of the parishioners.

Mexicans, Puerto Ricans, Cubans, and to a lesser extent Dominicans and Colombians, made up the largest Hispanic groups in the late 1980s, but they were by no means the only ones. In the mid-1980s, the census takers found another 1.7 million from Central and South America, in addition to a large number who identified themselves as Hispanic but did not reveal their precise origins.

These Central and South Americans usually settled where Cubans, Puerto Ricans, and Mexicans had gone: in cities like New York, Miami, Los Angeles, San Antonio, Chicago, San Diego, New Orleans, and Houston. In New Orleans, for example, a settlement of Hondurans had originally begun when they entered on the banana boats, found jobs, opened shops, and sent for their compatriots.

One center of this migration was the nation's capital, Washington, D.C. Small numbers lived there before this population increased in the 1970s. The census found 93,000 Hispanics in the Washington area, about 19,000 in Washington proper and the rest equally divided between the Virginia and Maryland suburbs. Their numbers increased rapidly in the 1980s when violence in Central

America prompted many persons to seek safety elsewhere. A Hispanic marketing firm estimated that 20,000 Central Americans arrived in the Washington area in 1980 and 1981 alone.

Many took jobs in the city's restaurants as dishwashers, busboys, and eventually waiters. A Hispanic leader told the *Washington Post,* "There's a top-notch French restaurant in Washington where the maitre d' speaks with a French accent and the waiter who comes up and takes your order is from El Salvador. He's one of the top waiters there. I asked him, 'How do you get a job like this?' He said, 'You come in at the lowest possible rung and demonstrate you are a hard worker and you go up.' " Symbolic of the growing Hispanic presence in the area was the construction of a new mall called Plaza International.

San Francisco also attracted a growing number of Central Americans. The 1980 census reported 83,000 persons or over 12 percent of the city's population to be Hispanics. The largest groups were Nicaraguans, then Salvadorans and Mexicans. The newcomers gave the Mission District of that city a distinct Latin flavor. Spanish movie houses provided an alternative to television in English, and one could hear Spanish spoken in churches and on the streets.

The new Hispanic immigrants included highly educated professionals such as physicians, who found employment in city hospitals as residents and interns. They also number thousands of others escaping poverty, unemployment, or underemployment, who believed what they had heard about America and its need for their labor, even if this meant washing dishes, cleaning cars, and scrubbing floors. The violence in El Salvador, Guatemala, and Nicaragua in the 1980s prompted tens of thousands of people to seek a better life in the United States. And if they could not get proper immigrant papers, they entered illegally, first by going to Mexico and then crossing the southern border of the United States. They are important enough to be discussed in the chapter on refugees.

The rapid growth of the Hispanic population in the 1970s and 1980s prompted uneasiness among many Americans. Two issues in particular seem to cause the most debate: language and undocumented immigration. Because many Hispanics, like Germans, Scandinavians, and countless immigrants before them, were reluctant to give up quickly their cultures and language, some Americans believed that they would remain an undigested mass within the United States. In 1981 U.S. Senator Alan Simpson (R–Wyoming) argued, "A substantial proportion of these new persons and their descendants do not assimilate satisfactorily into our society." And he concluded that they "may well create in America some of the same social, political, and economic problems that exist in the countries from which they have chosen to depart. Furthermore, if language and cultural separation rise above a certain level, the unity and political stability of our nation will—in time—be seriously eroded."

The concern over the maintenance of ethnic cultures was reflected in the debates over bilingual voting and educational programs. Under the terms of the amended Voting Rights Act of 1965, the United States government required many election districts to print bilingual ballots. Hispanic and civil rights groups supported these ballots, but critics said they fostered separatism and hindered assimilation.

A similar controversy erupted around bilingual education and public services, especially in California. In 1974 the United States Supreme Court in a case involving San Francisco's Chinese schoolchildren ruled that children must be educated in a language that they can understand. How this policy would be implemented was left unstated, and states and school districts adopted different programs.

In 1973 California passed a law requiring the state to employ bilingual staff members or interpreters when 5 percent or more of the clientele did not speak English. As a result over 3,000 positions required bilingual proficiency. The state employed an additional 2,600 employees to help people who did not speak English with the state's labor and vehicle services, and ran an elaborate bilingual program in the schools. In 1986 nearly 600,000 schoolchildren, mostly Hispanic, attended bilingual classes of one kind or another. Like the debate over voting, critics insisted such education fostered ethnic division, but Hispanic and other ethnic organizations defended them as necessary.

Out of the debates over bilingual program, U.S. English emerged in 1983, an organization that aimed to promote English as the official national language. U.S. English managed to be placed on California's 1986 ballot as Proposition 63, declaring English to be the state's official language and ordering the legislature to "make no law which diminishes or ignores the role of English." Charles Kamasaki of the National Council of La Raza claimed that English-only proposals were "fundamentally racist in character," and he said they "help promote an anti-immigrant, anti-ethnic atmosphere." The voters adopted Proposition 63 by a two-to-one majority.

Because of the vagueness of Proposition 63 what its victory in California meant was left unclear. Some California proponents of U.S. English thought it would weaken bilingualism, while proponents elsewhere were heartened by the strong California showing. They promised action in other states. Opponents insisted that the battle was not over, but merely shifted to the courts. Antonia Hernandaz, president and general counsel of the Mexican American Legal Defense and Educational Fund, promised to "work vigorously to defend the rights and services threatened by English-only."

The second issue prompting uneasiness about the growing Hispanic presence in the United States was undocumented immigration. While 90 percent of those apprehended were Mexicans, most experts believe that this figure inflated the number of Mexican undocumented aliens because the Immigration and Naturalization Service concentrated its enforcement efforts along the southwestern U.S. border. Yet Mexicans were probably the largest single group to seek illegal entry into the United States, and they were joined by substantial numbers of other Hispanics, from the Dominican Republic, El Salvador, and Guatemala among other countries. In the public mind, the vast bulk of undocumented immigrants were thought to be Hispanic.

Certainly the pressures to enter without papers were great in Mexico, the Caribbean, and Central America. In those regions poverty was common, unemployment frequent, and violence not unknown. Jobs paying much better than those at home were available in the United States. And the immigration agents were unable to plug the Mexican border, even though the border patrol halted a growing number seeking entry. The reality of the situation is that a 1,900-mile border runs between Brownsville, Texas, and San Diego, California, and only about 80 miles of this stretch is barricaded. Only the regions around main entry points like San Diego, Nogales, Arizona, and El Paso, Texas, are well covered. Furthermore, smugglers stood ready—for a price—to assist persons seeking to cross the border.

Once in the United States, jobs, usually unskilled, were readily available. And if social security cards, driver's licenses, birth certificates, and even resident alien cards were required, fraudulent ones could be purchased. Because the Immigration and Naturalization Service lacked the personnel needed to track down undocumented aliens once in the United States, these people could usually avoid capture.

Undocumented aliens' problems do not end once they enter the United States. Evidence suggests that the vast bulk of them come to work, but because they often lack education and skills, do not speak English, and have an illegal status, they are usually forced to accept jobs Americans do not want. They sometimes accept wages below the legal minimum; sanitary and health standards are not always maintained by their employers; and benefits most citizens expect are not even offered to them. What effect the 1986 Immigration Reform and Control Act would have on the flow of undocumented immigration is not yet known.

Not all undocumented entrants came solely in search of a better economic life. Some fled the violence and political turmoil plaguing Central America in the 1980s. Many of these persons considered themselves to be political refugees, perhaps entitled to asylum in the United States. Their plight will be considered in the next chapter.

chapter 7

The New Refugees

During the immediate post–World War II period the response of the United States to the problems of European refugees, displaced persons, and Holocaust survivors indicated that the nation had embarked on a new and more generous refugee policy. Few refugees had gained entry during the 1930s and the American government had made practically no effort to rescue Jews from Hitler's gas chambers during the war. By way of contrast, the United States admitted about 700,000 refugees and other displaced persons between 1945 and 1960. These were mostly Europeans, but included some Asians and a few persons from the Middle East. Beginning in 1959, and lasting into the 1980s, about 800,000 Cubans found a new home in America. Following the collapse of the American-backed government in South Vietnam, the nation began to admit large numbers of Indochinese refugees. By the late 1980s their total was approaching 1 million, mostly from Vietnam but also including tens of thousands of Laotians and Cambodians.

The numbers arriving from Castro's Cuba began to decline in the early 1970s, but a major crisis occurred in the spring of 1975 when communist armies conquered South Vietnam. In the last days before the fall of Saigon, thousands of Vietnamese who feared for their futures in a communist Vietnam desperately tried to escape on American planes arriving at the Tan Son Nhut airport. When shelling closed the airport, the United States began landing helicopters on the roof of the American Embassy. In eight days 65,000 people were airlifted to American vessels, then removed to Guam, and finally housed temporarily in American military bases in the United States. Another 65,000 persons found their own means of escape. Some stole or bought ships, while others piloted military and civilian planes to American bases in Thailand. For the next two years a steady trickle found its way out of Vietnam. Altogether about 170,000 Vietnamese refugees came to the United States between 1975 and 1978.

In 1978 a new crisis developed in Indochina. In Vietnam, hundreds of thousands of people began to flee as the communists tightened their hold on the country and drove out members of the business class. These included Vietnam's ethnic Chinese who fled to Thailand and China, as well as thousands of others fleeing by boat to South and East Asian nations. In addition, the refugee crisis spread to Laos as the communists took control there. Among those endangered in Laos were Hmong hill tribesmen who had fought against the communists with the financial backing of the U.S. Central Intelligence Agency (CIA). Many of these people, along with other Laotian refugees, crossed over into the growing refugee camps of Thailand.

While the situation deteriorated in both Vietnam and Laos, the bloodbath of Pol Pot's Cambodian Khmer Rouge government sent shock waves throughout the world. This regime had established itself in 1975, but was overthrown by an invading army from Vietnam three years later. Then the world learned of the mass executions and saw films of the mass graves. As the radical Pol Pot regime collapsed in the face of the Vietnamese invasion, thousands of Cambodians crossed the border into Thailand.

While a multitude of people poured into refugee camps in Thailand, others, including the so-called boat people, headed by sea for Hong Kong, Thailand, the Philippines, or Malaysia. Neighboring Asian states were wary of these newcomers, and claimed they lacked the resources to care for them; some countries turned the boats away. At sea, pirates preyed on them, raping the women, killing the resisters, and taking their possessions. Amid horror stories reporting such events, the Carter administration decided to take in thousands of new refugees; at peak time 14,000 Indochinese were being admitted monthly.

The crisis lasted from 1978 into the years of the Reagan administration. The Refugee Act of 1980 fixed the "normal flow" of refugees at 50,000 annually, but allowed the administration, to admit a larger number after consultation with Congress. In the early 1980s, the flow was several times greater, reaching a total of 700,000 Indochinese by 1985. In the mid-1980s these numbers decreased to about 40,000 annually.

Immigrants still came from the refugee camps, but others entered directly from Vietnam under the Orderly Departure Program. They emigrated through an arrangement with the Vietnamese government to process directly relatives of Vietnamese already in the United States. Also through this program the United States agreed to admit persons of the old regime held as political prisoners in

Vietnam. Finally, the two nations began a program for the emigration to the United States of the children fathered by American servicemen and from Vietnamese mothers. Thousands of these Amerasian children lived in Vietnam after the American withdrawal in 1973, most with no knowledge of their fathers; some were abandoned by their mothers.

The 1975 wave was temporarily housed in army bases in the United States. There government officials and voluntary workers began a program to help them adjust to their new lives in America. They were instructed in English and given a crash course in American mores. Even after they left the refugee camps, they received financial aid from the United States government, instruction in English, and job training. Working through state agencies and voluntary religious and ethnic groups, the federal government sought to scatter the Vietnamese throughout the United States. Federal officials feared that if too many settled in one state or region, opposition would arise and the entire program would be endangered. This was not a casual fear, for public opinion polls taken in 1975 revealed considerable opposition to these latest immigrants. Outside Camp Chafee, Arkansas, one of the military posts housing the Asians, pickets appeared carrying signs with slogans like "Let's start helping Americans first."

Attempts to disperse the refugees were partially successful. Vietnamese found homes from Maine to Oregon and from California to Virginia; they settled in the cold of Minnesota and the heat of Texas. Yet nearly one-third of them ended up in California, with Texas being the second most popular state. Voluntary agencies had found homes and jobs outside California, but many then relocated to the Golden State, especially in the southern half. The camps were closed in December 1975, and the groups coming after the first wave were settled directly into American communities.

Who were these latest refugees to America and how did they fare in their new land? In the first wave arriving in 1975, many were urban, well educated, knew English, and had had close ties to the United States' efforts in South Vietnam by reason of working with American armed forces or for American corporations. Some had been officials in the South Vietnam government or military officers.

Among the second wave coming during the large exodus from Indochina in 1978 to the early 1980s were ethnic Chinese who frequently owned small businesses in the cities. These middle-class persons often settled in America's Chinatowns rather than near other Vietnamese. Included too in this influx were Vietnamese business people and individuals who had worked for the United States and the government of South Vietnam before 1975. Although a predicted bloodbath did not take place when the communists took over, these people found themselves harassed by the new regime and their old ways of livelihood were destroyed. Others in this wave were the many desperate people from Laos and

Cambodia; not a few had been peasants uprooted by the constant fighting. Hmong tribesmen frequently were illiterate farmers, lacking urban skills and experience.

Regardless of their backgrounds, all Indochinese refugees faced problems in their new land, including racism that erupted into public hostility and even violence. In Philadelphia, Denver, New Orleans, New York, and Seadrift, Texas, the refugees encountered chilly receptions. The most newsworthy violent episode pitted Vietnamese fishermen against white Texans. Some refugees who entered in 1975 settled along the Texas Gulf Coast to engage in shellfishing. Unfamiliar with American regulations and customs about fishing for shrimp and crabs, the immigrants used smaller boats than did Americans and they did not always follow the established rules and procedures. Tempers flared as prices for shrimp and crabs remained low and fuel prices were high in 1978 and 1979. One American complained, "There's too many gooks and too few blue crabs. The government gives them loans and houses but doesn't care about us. Who's gonna protect our rights? The Vietnamese are gonna take over, it just isn't right." In the summer of 1979, an American trapper was killed during a fight between native whites and refugees. Although the Vietnamese were arrested and indicted, tensions remained high when they were acquitted of murder charges.

Ugly episodes of racism and violence during the 1980s victimized other groups too. In Washington, D.C., arsonists fire-bombed 11 Korean stores in a two-year period and in one incident a Korean woman was killed. In Philadelphia, Koreans reported a rise in thefts committed openly. In a Detroit bar, unemployed and angry automobile workers beat Vincent Chin, a Chinese American, to death. Asian Americans were incensed when the defendants were sentenced to only three years probation and a $3,780 fine. These occurrences were by no means isolated. The U.S. Commission on Civil Rights reported in 1986 that there was a 62-percent increase in anti-Asian incidents from 1984 to 1985. In Los Angeles County in 1986 violence against Asians accounted for half of the racial incidents, compared to only 15 percent the year before.

While the rapid growth of racial violence was troubling, most refugees did not experience it. Their most acute problems included lack of English, lack of familiarity with American ways, and little or no capital. Federal government programs along with aid from church and community groups helped many of the newcomers become self-sufficient, and by the late 1980s some of the first wave of refugees was on the way to becoming successful in a new land. In Chicago, Vietnamese immigrants revived the once economically depressed Argyle Street. Within 10 years of their arrival they operated 50 shops in this "Little Saigon." A city alderman remarked of their success, "The change has been astronomical. No one used to dare go there after 5 P.M. and now there is a real night life."

Ten years after appearing on the scene, these refugees also began to make their marks academically. The media publicized stories of Vietnamese arriving penniless with no knowledge of English and winning academic awards a short time later. In 1984 one such refugee, Chi Luu, became the valedictorian of his graduating class at The City College of the City University of New York. Two years after that, Hoang Nhu Tran became the second Vietnamese immigrant to graduate from the Air Force Academy and the first to be named a Rhodes Scholar for two years study at Oxford University, England. The son of a high-ranking Vietnamese air force officer, he fled in 1975 to the United States.

For the boat people and others who arrived in the 1980s the picture was not as bright. Many had survived horrendous conditions at sea and malnutrition in refugee camps. Moreover, many were poorly educated; some of the Laotians were not even literate in their own language. Uprooted by constant fighting and emotionally drained by refugee camp living, they lacked the knowledge and means to adapt readily to American ways. The cultural gap was deep. An official working with the Hmong people relocated in Montana observed that they had never encountered freeways, food stamps, checkbooks, or birth-control pills. He explained, "This is like Disneyland to them. It's like us going to Mars and starting over again."

Social workers and government officials reported that immigrant women had an especially difficult time in adjusting to life in the United States. Learning English was hard: "I could not learn English because I missed my country very much," reported one Vietnamese woman. She said during her first year in America, "I never go out unless I am with my sponsor. I cried all the time." Some had been raped and sexually abused on the boats by pirates and then suffered further in the refugee camps. In Vietnam they were unaccustomed to working for wages, but in America their families needed their income. (One social worker in California noted that when the women worked the man lost face.) Yet a desire to work was not sufficient. A California refugee explained that she had not sought a job because "When I go out, some people ask me lots of questions and I can't answer enough."

The difficulties of the newest Indochinese refugees worried some government officials who feared they would become a permanent dependent class. Governmental surveys in the 1980s did report high rates of welfare dependency, but at the same time noted that the longer the refugees remained here, the more likely they were to learn English, find jobs, and become self-sufficient. No doubt the first wave with their higher status would adjust more easily, but a decade was too soon to draw firm conclusions about these latest immigrants.

In the past two decades the United States welcomed other refugees fleeing communism. Following the Russian invasion of Czechoslovakia in 1968, the United States permitted several thousand Czechs to enter under the refugee provisions of the 1965 immigration act. In the late 1960s and early 1970s several thousand Soviet Jews obtained permission to leave the Soviet Union. Congress voted to tie increased trade with Russia to a relaxation of Soviet emigration policy. The Soviet government responded by tightening its restrictions. Only 13,000 people were permitted to leave in 1975, about one-third the number of two years before. After that, Soviet policy varied greatly. In 1979 the figure reached 50,000, two-thirds of whom settled in the United States. Then following the 1979 Russian invasion of Afghanistan and the cooling of relations between the two superpowers, the Soviets cut the flow drastically with only a few thousand receiving permission to leave. The number was less than 1,000 in 1986, but it began to increase again in 1987.

Altogether about 80,000 Soviet Jews emigrated to the United States during the 1970s and coupled with those coming in the 1960s and 1980s, the total surpassed 100,000. Often emigrating as families, the working adults were usually well educated professionals, engineers, and technicians. Soviet Jews settled in Los Angeles, Philadelphia, Baltimore, and Chicago, but the largest group resided in Brooklyn, New York, in an area called Brighton Beach. There a small but thriving Russian culture emerged as Russian-language newspapers appeared on the newsstands and restaurants specializing in Russian cuisine were established. So noticeable was this influence that commentators labeled Brighton Beach "Odessa by the Sea."

In the 1980s the federal government also welcomed other persons from communist nations. Following the Soviet invasion of Afghanistan and the subsequent growth of a large Afghan refugee population in neighboring Pakistan, the United States began to accept several thousand of these people annually. When the trade union Solidarity movement collapsed in Poland, America admitted several thousand Poles. Indeed, the federal government always seemed willing to accept some persons fleeing communism. Table 7.1 indicates refugee admissions for 1984.

Table 7.1   REFUGEE ADMISSIONS BY COUNTRY, 1984

Nationality	Refugee arrivals
Afghanistan	2,231
Czechoslovakia	773
El Salvador	67
Ethiopia	2,347
Iran	2,812
Kampuchea (Cambodia)	17,875
Laos	7,423
Poland	3,794
Rumania	4,281
Vietnam	23,172
All others	2,975
Total	67,750

Source: Immigration and Naturalization Service, *Statistical Yearbook,* 1984.

Not all refugees were offered a friendly reception in the United States. During the early 1970s the government demonstrated practically no eagerness to welcome those fleeing right-wing Latin-American governments that the United States supported, and only a few hundred were admitted. When an American-backed coup toppled the socialist regime of Chile's Salvador Allende in 1973, we accepted only a handful of fleeing Chileans. After 1977 the Carter administration did take a few more along with a thousand or so Argentines imprisoned by its military regime. While these efforts demonstrated some willingness to receive refugees from right-wing military dictatorships, the numbers involved stand in striking contrast to the hundreds of thousands of Cubans and Indochinese the nation has taken.

The most glaring difference in response to political refugees was revealed in the attempt of Haitians to win asylum in the United States. Haiti was governed by a brutal dictatorship, but American government officials refused to acknowledge that persons in Haiti were being persecuted and hence would not admit them as refugees. There was another way for these unfortunate people to find safety in the United States. If they were able to enter the country illegally or as visitors, they could then ask for political asylum. In 1968 the United States Senate had acceded to the United Nations Protocol on Refugees, which committed the nation to grant asylum to persons who could prove they had a well-founded fear of persecution if they returned to their homelands. During the 1970s and early 1980s a growing number of Haitians, usually poor and arriving by boat on the coast of Florida, requested asylum, but only a few received it.

Regulations governing asylum were imprecise and exactly what each individual had to prove was not clear. Moreover, the United States supported the Haitian regime of François ("Papa Doc") Duvalier and later that of his son, Jean-Claude ("Baby Doc") because that regime backed American foreign policy in Latin America. For the Immigration and Naturalization Service (INS) to grant asylum to Haitians would be an admission that the United States government befriended a government that persecuted its citizens. INS and the State Department insisted that Haitians came here to better themselves economically and were not political refugees.

Congress seemed to resolve this problem when it enacted the Refugee Act of 1980. Whereas the Immigration Act of 1965 defined refugees as those fleeing communism, the new act declared refugees to be persons who had a well-founded fear of persecution on the grounds of race, religion, nationality, or politics. The law thus seemed to cover groups like the Haitians, and not simply persons escaping communism like Soviets, Poles, or Indochinese. Moreover, one provision of the act set aside 5,000 places each year to grant asylum for those already in the United States if they could satisfactorily prove their cases.

The 1980 legislation did not lead to a new policy. The Carter administration still refused to admit Haitians as refugees and turned down the overwhelming number of asylum requests. Carter officials insisted that the criteria for asylum "must be a narrow and carefully focused standard" that required individuals to prove that they would be subject to death or harsh persecution if they returned home.

The Reagan administration went even further to discourage these refugees. When authorities caught Haitians without proper immigration papers, they threw these unfortunate migrants in jail while their requests for asylum were being heard. Haitians were promised release but only if they returned home. In addition, the president ordered the coast guard to intercept and turn around boats suspected of bringing undocumented Haitians into the United States. While controversial, the interdiction and detention policies led to a sharp drop in the number of Haitians trying to enter the United States illegally. Court appeals led to the freeing of many of those in detention while their cases were being heard, but few Haitians won asylum under President Ronald Reagan's administration. Under the 1986 Immigration Reform and Control Act, Haitians residing in the country before 1982 became eligible for resident aliens status, but those who entered after still faced an uphill battle in trying to win asylum.

Nor were Haitians the only persons having difficulty gaining asylum. As civil war and violence spread in El Salvador, Nicaragua, and Guatemala, thousands of Central Americans fled their homes. Many sought safety in nearby Honduras and Mexico. Some then headed for the Mexican-U.S. border and joined hundreds of thousands of other persons trying to enter the United States illegally. No one knew how many Central Americans managed to elude the border patrol, but some estimates in the late 1980s put the number of undocumented Central Americans in the United States as high as one-half million.

Many Salvadorans settled with other Central Americans in Washington, D.C., while others located among Hispanic communities in cities such as Los Angeles, Miami, New York, San Francisco, and towns along the Mexican-Texas border. Once there, friends, relatives, and refugee groups helped them find jobs and housing. The largest contingent of Nicaraguans, most of whom had migrated to the United States after the Marxist-led Sandinistas had seized power in 1979, resided in Florida. Immigration officials estimated that 70,000 Nicaraguans lived in Florida with southern California and San Francisco containing the next largest groups.

If caught, Central Americans, like Haitians, could request political asylum. But Salvadorans, Nicaraguans, and Guatemalans were no more successful than Haitians in winning the right to stay in the United States. In the early 1980s only a few of the requests were successful. A Government Accounting Office study of asylum requests in 1984 reported 2 percent of Salvadorans and 7 percent of Nicaraguans were successful in winning asylum, compared to a rate of 24 percent for all requests. Two-thirds of the requests from Iran and

**Table 7.2   NUMBER OF
            PERSONS
            GRANTED
            ASYLUM BY
            COUNTRY,
            1984**

Country	Total
Afghanistan	327
Cuba	82
El Salvador	105
Ethiopia	243
Guatemala	17
Haiti	19
Iran	3,294
Nicaragua	305
Poland	413
Rumania	106
All others	796
Total	5,607

Source: Immigration and
Naturalization Service, *Statistical
Yearbook,* 1984.

one-half of those from Poland were granted. Table 7.2 indicates asylum granted
by country in 1984. Iran accounted for over 60 percent of those persons who
obtained asylum.

In early 1986, Haitians, Guatemalans, and Salvadorans did slightly better
but still fared poorly compared to a success rate of 59 percent for Poles, 64 percent
for Iranians, and 72 percent for Rumanians. Critics insisted that the government
was pursuing a double standard, that anti-communists like the Cubans could
easily become refugees while Salvadorans could not.

Defenders of administration policy pointed to the fact that most asylum
requests from Iran were granted, but what that government was ruled by was an
Islamic elite, not communists. Furthermore, the administration answered that
few persons fleeing the alleged communist Sandinista regime in Nicaragua were
granted asylum either, and that most Central Americans who entered the United
States did so for economic and not political reasons.

Spokespersons for the Central Intelligence Agency and immigration officials suggested another reason for rejecting these requests: the concern that a
generous asylum policy would lead to increased illegal immigration. Government
officials feared that allowing these persons to stay in America might encourage
still others to enter in the hope that they too would be given political asylum. The
commissioner of the Immigration and Naturalization Service warned that if the
United States failed to deport Salvadorans there could be "an invasion of 'feet

people' magnifying the migration of that region, making what we already see as a stream become a torrent."

In early 1986 a federal judge in Florida, where three-quarters of all Nicaraguan asylum appeals originated, announced that he would no longer order the deportation of Nicaraguans. The Immigration and Naturalization Service also shifted policy and in 1986 granted asylum for half of the Nicaraguans requesting it.

Angered by what they charged was a politically motivated asylum policy, friends of Salvadoran and Guatemalan refugees suggested another way to halt deportations. They urged that Salvadorans and Guatemalans be given extended voluntary departure status (EVD). In the past, Ugandans, Afghans, Poles, Nicaraguans, Ethiopians, Iranians, and others had been granted EVD for various lengths of time. Under EVD the United States recognized that conditions in the aliens' homelands had changed, and that for INS to deport persons to these homelands, even if here illegally or with expired visas, would expose these persons to danger or even death. EVD was for a temporary period, usually six months, and was not meant to be a way for people to stay in the United States indefinitely. Friends of Salvadorans argued that conditions were so bad there that the United States should halt all deportations of Salvadorans for up to two years and give them a temporary safe haven in the United States. Bills were introduced to effect this change, but they failed to pass.

Unable to gain EVD for Salvadorans or win many cases of asylum, a number of religious leaders stepped forward to offer undocumented Central Americans sanctuary in homes and churches. Largely a grass-roots movement, in the early 1980s dozens of individual congregations declared themselves to be sanctuaries for refugees. By 1987 about 300 congregations had made such declarations, though only a few actually harbored such persons.

Though a centuries-old tradition, sanctuary had no legal status in the United States. Nonetheless, the government at first said it would not take action against these churches, but in 1984 and 1985 it moved against several congregations and sanctuary leaders. In Texas several Roman Catholic leaders were arrested and brought to trial, and one, Jack Elder, was sentenced to one year in prison. The most sensational trial involved the Southside United Presbyterian Church of Tucson, Arizona. For the first time, the government used an informer and undercover agent to attend meetings at the church. Drawing upon evidence obtained by these methods, the government arrested church leaders and brought them to trial. After weeks of trial, the jury found the defendants, including Southside's minister John Fife and several nuns, guilty of conspiracy to smuggle Salvadorans and Guatemalans into the United States. Judge Earl Carroll placed the convicted sanctuary leaders on probation.

While at first limited to churches, the sanctuary movement spread in the mid-1980s to encompass cities and state entities. City officials in Berkeley, California, and Cambridge, Massachusetts, and San Francisco, among others, voted to make their communities sanctuaries. In early 1986 New Mexico's Governor Toney Anaya formally declared his state a sanctuary and said he hoped the action would start "a snowball effect" throughout the nation. The state of Massachusetts went even further in 1986. Armed with a budget of $250,000, the state's Legal Assistance Corporation began to aid Central Americans in their attempts to stay in America and to challenge federal immigration policy in the courts. These declarations of sanctuary were not uncontroversial. In several communities voters overturned previous sanctuary positions, and in New Mexico a new governor, Garrey Carruthers, rescinded his state's previous sanctuary proclamation.

Most of the world's 15 million or so refugees no doubt want to return to their own homes. But if the evidence of refugee flows since World War II is an indicator of future trends, tens of thousands of these people continue to look to the United States as a political haven. In recent years most persons either admitted to the United States as refugees or granted asylum came from nations whose governments the United States disapproves of—Vietnam, Poland, the Soviet Union, Iran, and Afghanistan to name a few. But because the nation's refugee and asylum policies are so closely tied to foreign policy and because the religious and ethnic groups sympathetic to all refugees are well organized, the debate and legal conflict concerning these policies will surely continue in the years ahead.

chapter 8

Pilgrims' Progress: Ethnic Mobility in Modern America

The grim living conditions facing the old and new immigrants confronted their children and sometimes their grandchildren. Oftentimes, the newcomers moved slowly out of poverty and the ghetto, and gains witnessed by the second and third generations were lost. Yet the striking fact of American history is that of social mobility, an improvement in the status and living conditions of the descendants of the millions who flocked to the United States. Progress was by no means even from group to group or from generation to generation.

Of the old immigrants who were Europeans, the Irish probably had the most difficult time, but a few made spectacular progress and became veritable personifications of the rags-to-riches story. Robert Joseph Cuddihy began as an office boy in Funk & Wagnalls publishing house in New York City at the age of 16. Working his way up through the publishing world, he became a wealthy and powerful publisher. Joseph P. Kennedy, the son of a Boston immigrant saloon keeper and father of President John F. Kennedy, made his fortune on Wall Street and in the motion picture business and later served as ambassador to Great Britain. John Buckley, the founder of one of America's leading conservative families, emigrated to America without much money. After a mixture of success and failure in Texas, his son, William F. Buckley, arrived in New York City nearly penniless in 1922 but soon thereafter became a millionaire. Peter McDonnell began his career as a bondsman in New York City and laid the foundation of a major Wall Street brokerage house.

But most of America's Irish moved up the social scale slowly. Working in unskilled occupations provided few opportunities for advancement. The growth of canals and railroads offered low-paying, backbreaking jobs that left the workers unemployed and practically destitute whenever and wherever each project ended. As a result, Irish settlements developed all over the country but usually at or near canal and railroad depots. The opening of mill towns in New England also created opportunities for those willing to work long and hard.

The Irish did manage to improve their lot during the nineteenth century. By the 1870s in Boston they had already come to dominate the police and fire departments. Throughout the nation young Irishwomen staffed urban elementary schools. They constituted 25 percent of the teachers in Boston and New York City in the 1880s and a generation later gained a foothold in the teaching ranks of Buffalo, Chicago, and San Francisco. The most thrifty of the workers saved money to buy houses. This was possible in part because many persisted at one job and in one place year after year. The Irish also tended to marry late, thereby enabling young workers to save enough for down payments on modest homes. If these schemes for property accumulation proved insufficient, wives and children worked and contributed to the family coffers. Putting children to work added to the family's income, of course, but it also hurt the younger generation's chances for future mobility.

Accomplishments in many businesses were achieved at a time when education was not as necessary as it would later become. The construction industry boomed as urban America grew. The Irish, using the influence of friends in city hall, became contractors and builders. By 1890 there were twice as many of them in these occupations as of other immigrant groups. In Philadelphia Edward J. Lafferty constructed the city's waterworks, and James P. (Sunny Jim) McNichol, another Irish politician-contractor, helped build the city's subways, sewers, and water filtration plant.

During the twentieth century, and especially after World War II, the Irish progressed rapidly to middle- and upper-middle-class status. They ran businesses, worked in banks and insurance companies, and became doctors, lawyers, professors, civil servants, and technicians. The occupational distribution of the American Irish in 1980 resembled that of the northern urban Anglo-Saxon Protestants. Among the white Catholics in America, the Irish usually had more education, better jobs, and higher incomes. Few could claim the fabulous wealth of America's most famous Irish family, the Kennedys, but not many were poor, either. The American Irish had at long last arrived.

To consider the Irish experience solely in terms of the move from shanties to suburban homes and from ditch diggers to lawyers is to look at an incomplete picture. In two special vocational areas—the Roman Catholic church and politics—the Irish had experiences that were unique, not because they were so lucrative but because the ethnic group valued these positions. To have a son become a lawyer or doctor was of course a sign of success, but the Irish also considered it important to give a son and a daughter to the Church.

That the Irish dominated the Catholic church in America is not surprising. In Ireland the Church was the carrier of the faith and a source of comfort in the face of English oppression. It served a similar function in America. The hostility of native Protestant Americans to the Irish and to Catholicism only made the Church more important, for it provided the embattled Irish immigrant with a bulwark of security.

Shortly after the Irish arrived in the 1840s, they became the dominant group in the American Catholic hierarchy. From Archbishop John Hughes of New York to Baltimore's James Cardinal Gibbons, the first American cardinal, and on to New York's Francis Cardinal Spellman, the leading American Catholics have usually been of Irish origin. They supported the parochial schools, sent their sons and daughters to do God's work, and gave what they could from their meager incomes for religious activities. When non-Irish Catholics, such as the Italians, arrived in large numbers, they often resented Irish control of the Church and demanded their own clergy and parishes. The Church disapproved of nationality or ethnic parishes in principle, but, nonetheless, the practice existed among Germans, Poles, and French Canadians. In the twentieth century, Irish control of the Church hierarchy gradually lessened but never disappeared. In the 1980s the Irish constituted fewer than one-fifth of the Catholics in the United States but about one-third of the clergy and one-half of the hierarchy.

Irish domination of urban politics was not so complete as that of the Church, but it was impressive. New York City elected a Roman Catholic mayor in 1880, and Boston followed suit four years later. Before the end of the century Irish "bosses" dominated local politics in New York, Jersey City, Hoboken, Boston, Chicago, Buffalo, Albany and Troy (New York), Pittsburgh, St. Paul, St. Louis, Kansas City (Missouri), Omaha, New Orleans, and San Francisco. New York City's famed Tammany Hall passed into Irish hands when "Honest John" (his enemies called him crooked as a ram's horn) Kelly succeeded Protestant boss William M. Tweed in 1874, and it remained under Irish control for the next 80 years. Bosses Frank Hague of Jersey City and Tom Pendergast of Kansas City, Missouri, were legends in their day, as was Mayor Richard Daley of Chicago in his.

No other Irish urban politician was so extraordinary as James Michael Curley of Boston. He served in local offices before becoming U.S. congressman, mayor of the city, and then governor of Massachusetts. Curley symbolized many aspects of the Irish style in politics. He maintained his contacts with the Church and the Irish community and was a skillful showman. He played upon the Irish resentment of Boston's Yankees and Brahmins to build a personal following, and he provided jobs and social services for the poor. He also knew how to appeal to his followers: "My mother was obliged to work . . . as a scrubwoman toiling nights in office buildings downtown. I thought of her one night while leaving City Hall during my first term as Mayor. I told the scrubwomen cleaning the corridors to get up; 'The only time a woman should go down on her knees is when she is praying to Almighty God,' I said. Next morning I ordered longhandled mops and issued an order that scrubwomen were never again to get down on their knees in City Hall." Critics attacked Curley for corruption, but no matter—he won an election even while in jail.

The Irish reach for the presidency began in 1928 when Al Smith from the Lower East Side of New York City became a candidate. He rose swiftly through New York City's Democratic organization (Tammany Hall) and served as state legislator and governor before grasping for the big prize. Smith epitomized the Irish Catholic politician, a factor that worked both for and against him in 1928. He opposed prohibition, attacked the immigration restriction laws, and was a devout Catholic. As a result, he won the Catholic and immigrant vote in many places and reversed Democratic fortunes of the 1920s by capturing a dozen or so of the nation's largest cities. The Democratic presidential candidate amassed more popular votes than any of his predecessors ever had. (Part of the explanation for this, no doubt, was that a larger percentage of women voted in 1928 than in 1920 or 1924.) Nevertheless, many Protestants feared that the Roman Catholic church would exert a strong influence on a Catholic in the White House and voted Republican for the first time in their lives.

After Smith's defeat no Irish Catholic and no other member of an ethnic minority group made the bid for the presidency until John F. Kennedy's triumph in 1960. Keenly aware that politicos still regarded his Roman Catholic faith as a severe handicap, Kennedy faced the religious issue squarely. His primary victory in West Virginia proved he could win Protestant votes, and his smooth political machine achieved a first-ballot victory at the Democratic convention. Yet the religious issue would not die, and Kennedy had to make several strong statements about his belief in the separation of church and state. In the election Kennedy lost some votes because of his Catholicism, but he ran strongly in the heavily Catholic Northeast and slipped into the presidency by the narrowest margin of any victorious candidate since Woodrow Wilson in 1916.

Kennedy's election, culminating a century of Irish political activity, was built on the earlier victories of Irish politicians in city wards. His religious commitments were public knowledge, as were his ties to the Irish community. Some even said an "Irish Mafia" had won him the nomination. A few Catholics went to the other extreme and insisted that Kennedy was not Catholic enough. Kennedy was clearly different from both Al Smith and James Curley. Born into a wealthy family, educated at Choate and Harvard, he was assimilated, cosmopolitan, and intellectual, and he did not seem particularly Irish—except for political purposes. Whether another type of Irish politician could have won in 1960 is debatable, but the old ward boss was a thing of the past by then. The Irish had arrived in politics as they had in business and the Church.

Another Irish Democrat, New York's Senator Daniel Patrick Moynihan, later pointed out that on the day that Kennedy died the Speaker of the House of Representatives, the majority leader of the U.S. Senate, and the chairman of the Democratic National Committee were all Irish Catholic Democrats. Moynihan suggested that perhaps such Irish domination will not occur again, but Thomas (Tip) O'Neill, former Speaker of the House, was one of the most prominent Democrats to oppose President Ronald Reagan, also of Irish descent, during his tenure in the White House. Irish Catholic ancestry is obviously no longer a handicap for any candidate making a bid for the presidency.

The largest of the old immigrant groups, the Germans, generally rose faster than the Irish. They had certain advantages over the Irish: They were not so poor when they arrived and they had more education. Unlike the Irish, many Germans farmed successfully, but most lived in or later moved to the cities. Those without skills or education took laboring jobs, but many became skilled workers in America's growing industries. They were also cabinetmakers, bakers, tailors, bookbinders, and furniture makers, and often they were the leaders in the craft unions. For example, the bakers' unions in the 1870s and 1880s were solidly German. Some German workers even veered off into radical politics.

German immigrants and their children did well in business and were an established minority by the time of World War I. They brought with them their love of beer drinking and their beer-making skills, and they founded breweries that became virtually a German monopoly in the early twentieth century. St. Louis and Milwaukee are centers of the beer business, and names like Pabst, Miller, Schlitz, Schaefer, and Anheuser-Busch became household words in twentieth-century America. Germans also ran beer gardens, hotels, and restaurants like Mader's in Milwaukee and Luchow's in New York City. An observer said of the beer gardens: "The commencement of one of these establishments appears to be very simple. A German obtains a cellar, a cask of beer, a cheese, a loaf of bread, and some pretzels—puts out a sign and the business is started." Although breweries and beer gardens were the most notable German connections to the liquor business, a few Germans, such as Paul Krug, developed vineyards in California.

Germans also excelled in other areas of business. George Westinghouse, a poor farm boy from upstate New York, patented the air brake for trains and then founded a major corporation. Another inventor, Charles Steinmetz, who became known as the wizard of Schenectady, was the dynamic force behind the huge General Electric Company. Although Steinmetz had a European education, he arrived at Ellis Island from Germany without funds or a job. Indeed, he was almost deported. His mastery of electricity led him to fame and fortune. John A. Roebling, another innovator, put his ideas about steel cables to use in building suspension bridges. Roebling died while supervising the construction of his most famous bridge, the Brooklyn Bridge.

Other Germans used their talents in the ethnic community as clergymen and editors of German periodicals and newspapers, which were numerous on the eve of World War I, or operated small businesses that catered to the German-American community. A few branched out into politics, among them Robert Wagner of New York and the socialist Victor Berger of Milwaukee. These politicians, like the Irish, built their strength on the ethnic vote and service to the ethnic communities. Earlier, Germans had elected congressmen and senators regularly after the Civil War and governors in Illinois and Kentucky in the 1890s.

Germans also excelled in music. City orchestras in the nineteenth century were heavily German, and German singers were popular in America, as were German singing societies. Besides playing musical instruments, Germans also made them. Steinway and Sons was the most famous of the German piano makers, but others such as Knabe, Weber, and Wurlitzer were well known too.

Although World War I was a shattering experience for many German Americans and caused many of their institutions to decline, it did not impede their socioeconomic progress. They prospered in practically every key area of American business, in the professions—as doctors, lawyers, engineers—in government, and in science. They were well represented among the American corporate elite, had high educational levels and solid incomes. Not many were poor. So much were the descendants of German immigrants a part of American life that few Americans conceived of them as a distinct ethnic group. Nevertheless, President Richard Nixon's chief White House assistants from 1969 to 1973, H. R. Haldeman and John Ehrlichman, were known to a number of Washingtonians as the German shepherds.

Like the Germans, the Swedes have also prospered. The children and grandchildren of many of those who tilled the soil in the Upper Midwest sought their opportunities in burgeoning cities like Minneapolis and Chicago. In the urban areas they became skilled workers and clerks and gradually moved into better jobs. As a group the Swedes prospered about as well as the Germans; in the twentieth century they were second only to the British in their proportion of skilled workers in America. A few even advanced into the business elite; Swedish-born Rudolph A. Peterson, for example, became president of the giant Bank of America in 1961. A minority remained farmers and prospered on the land.

The Norwegians were similar to the Swedes in their immigration patterns, migrating into the Upper Midwest to become farmers and farm laborers. But the Norwegians were also sailors and found jobs as seamen in American ports; they were especially important on the West Coast. Like the Swedes, Norwegians became increasingly urbanized after 1900, and many came to America with skills that they could use in the expanding industrial society. By the 1980s Norwegian Americans had done well and had generally moved into the middle class, with many becoming successful businessmen, skilled workers, and professionals. Of course, politics was open in areas where the Norwegians and Swedes were numerous. In 1892 Knute Nelson, with the aid of his fellow Norwegians, won the governorship of Minnesota, and Swedish and Norwegian names have been prominent in the politics of Minnesota, Wisconsin, and the adjacent states since then.

The Finns in America were slower to move up the occupational ladder compared to their Swedish and Norwegian neighbors. Of the Protestant groups immigrating after 1880 the Finns were the least skilled, and this no doubt accounts for some of their difficulties in achieving occupational mobility. They generally settled in the Midwest but were not inclined to become farmers. They moved frequently in search of work and were especially numerous in the mining regions of the Upper Midwest. They often worked in company towns, where opportunities for mobility were not abundant for those beginning without skills. Finns also tried to found their own businesses but were not notably successful. Thus they were more like the new immigrants than the old. Later generations did finally move out of the unskilled ranks and compete more successfully, but they usually lagged behind the Swedes and Norwegians.

None of the old immigrants, not even the Irish, were so scorned as the Chinese. After they had been forced out of mines and had helped build the railroads and raise crops in California, the Chinese drifted to the cities in search of employment. A few were successful merchants, but most found urban life harsh and jobs limited. They worked as domestics, as cigar makers, or in other low-paying industries. Most important to the livelihood of Chinese Americans was the laundry. The proverbial laundry developed largely because the Chinese could find little else to do. The shortage of women on the frontier left this domestic service, considered woman's work, open to the Chinese. A laundry required little skill and practically no capital, only soap, a scrub board, an iron, an ironing board, and long hours of hard labor. Laundries were usually one-man or family enterprises. As the Chinese moved into the cities or to the East, they took their laundries with them. By 1880 over 7,000 Chinese made their livings in laundries in San Francisco alone, and in 1920 the U.S. Census Bureau reported that nearly a third of employed Chinese were engaged in laundry work.

In addition to the laundries, restaurants and groceries were important to the Chinese community. Chinese restaurants originated in the mining camps along the railroads, where the Chinese prepared their own food. They preferred their own food, and the bosses agreed that it was cheaper than furnishing an American diet. The Chinese discovered that others liked their cuisine too; chop suey and chow mein became staples of Chinese restaurants. Restaurants required some capital, hence they were not as numerous as laundries. But like the laundries, they were often family businesses and served as an outlet for entrepreneurs blocked from other jobs.

Groceries were the third main small business of the Chinese but were not so important as the restaurants and laundries. Nevertheless, enterprising businessmen found outlets for their skills and energies. In the South and West, Chinese groceries thrived, and a few later expanded into supermarkets.

Until World War II the Chinese-American community had many service workers, small proprietors and operatives, and few professional and technical workers. But a strong family system, a commitment to education, and hard work led to changing patterns after 1945. Declining prejudice, especially during World War II when America was an ally of China, also helped. Prior to the war Chinese Americans serving in the United States navy had been limited to becoming messmen and stewards, but during the war they were admitted as apprentice seamen. Shipyards, aircraft factories, and other defense industries experiencing labor shortages began to employ workers of Chinese ancestry. These were modest changes, but they marked the beginning of improved employment opportunities for Chinese Americans.

The Chinese-American community of the 1980s was different from that of a century before. By 1960 many Chinese had moved into the middle class. Jobs in laundries and other undesirable forms of employment were shunned, while larger numbers engaged in technical and professional work. Particularly in mathematics and science the Chinese made a name for themselves; several won Nobel prizes, among them Chen Ning Yang and Yzyng Dao Lee. Veneration for learning and scholarship was revealed by the fact that by the 1960s proportionately more Chinese than Caucasians had completed college.

In business, while laundries were declining, restaurants thrived, and Chinese Americans found new opportunities in finance, trade, architecture, and computing. Perhaps most well-known of the Chinese immigrants was I. M. Pei, who achieved an international reputation as an architect. Pei arrived in the United States in 1935 to study engineering at the Massachusetts Institute of Technology. He later switched to architecture and decided to remain in the United States, becoming an American citizen in 1954. He has been asked to design major projects, including the John Hancock Building in Boston and the East Wing of the National Gallery in Washington, D.C. A similar story of fame and success could be told of An Wang, founder of the Massachusetts computing firm that bears his name.

Chinese women, like American women generally, have moved into the professional and managerial labor market, and some have become successful in spite of the discrimination against their sex. One of San Francisco's most well-known restaurants was run by Cecilia Chiang, who entered the United States in 1958. Of her success, she said, "I have confidence. I love people, I love food, and about Chinese food, I think I know better than all the people I know." While running restaurants was a traditional Chinese occupation, it was unusual for women to operate them. By 1986 Chiang owned four restaurants in California. On a national level, in 1983 Connie Chung became a high-paid and leading television news personality for NBC.

With a small population to build a political base upon, politics was not a common way up the social ladder; but in Hawaii, with its large Chinese population, the chances were better. Hiram Fong made his political career there. He began as deputy attorney for the city and county of Honolulu, then moved into the legislature, and finally ended in the United States Senate.

Fong's career in some ways symbolizes the rise of Chinese Americans. Born into a large and poor family, he began work as a farm laborer. But he was an enterprising young man and worked his way through the University of Hawaii and Harvard Law School. He became a successful lawyer and businessman before he launched his political career.

Outside of Hawaii it has been more difficult for Chinese Americans, and Asians generally, to win political office. But in California, New York, and elsewhere, they emerged victorious in the 1980s. When the people of Delaware chose Shien Biau Woo lieutenant governor of Delaware in 1984, he won national recognition. In 1985 Los Angeles elected its first Chinese American to the City Council, and Mayor Dianne Feinstein of San Francisco appointed a Chinese American to the Board of Supervisors.

As successful as Chinese Americans were after World War II, the picture was not uniformly bright. Some were still poor and jammed into overcrowded Chinatowns. Many were aged members of the old bachelor society or families that had not shared in the advantages of the younger generation. Still others were recent immigrants who had come when the quotas were loosened after 1965. As we have noted, some of these immigrants made low wages as waiters or in sweatshops reminiscent of the old immigrant neighborhoods. These immigrants, who suffered from lack of education and language skills, simply could not get better jobs. In New York City, for example, the 1970 census revealed that the median family income in Chinatown was lower than the national averages for all groups, for the Chinese nationally, and for the Chinese in the metropolitan area. Clearly New York's more prosperous Chinese Americans had moved to less crowded areas, like the borough of Queens, or to the surrounding suburbs. Thus the pattern of success for the Chinese was spotty, but if the latest newcomers could improve their positions the future would be more optimistic.

Of the millions of immigrants coming after 1880, the so-called new immigrants, no group experienced such startling success as the Jews. Sephardic Jews,

who came in the colonial period, were already solidly middle class by the time
the German Jews arrived before the Civil War. Many German Jews had been
traders in Germany, and they took up peddling and storekeeping in the New
World. Spreading out over the nation, they made rapid progress in commerce and
trade. The Lehmans and Seligmans achieved prominence in finance and banking,
while Benjamin Altman and Adam Gimbel became major department-store owners. A study made in 1889 of 18,000 gainfully employed Jews, most of whom were
from German-speaking countries, found that approximately one-third were re-
tailers; 15 percent were bankers; 17 percent were accountants, bookkeepers,
clerks, and copyists; and 12 percent were salesmen, commercial travelers, and
agents.

The bulk of the eastern European Jews, coming after 1880, was poor, but
they too succeeded in America in the twentieth century. In 1980 family incomes
of America's Jews were higher than those of any other ethnic group, including
the elite white Protestant Episcopalians. And their educational levels were also
high. Almost 90 percent of the Jews of college age were attending institutions of
higher education in the 1970s, and a high proportion was in graduate and professional schools.

Of the first generation from eastern Europe, a majority worked in the
garment industry and in trade, with only a few in the professions. Jews were
involved in the formation—and in their early years made up most of the members—of both the ILGWU and the Amalgamated Clothing Workers Union,
founded in 1910 and 1914, respectively. The children of these union members
more often than not acquired college educations and sought higher-status occupations. Anti-Semitism in the professions, including discriminatory quotas in medical schools, made it harder to achieve professional mobility, but it was accomplished nonetheless. Statistics of the late 1960s indicated that about half of all
gainfully employed adult Jews engaged in a professional activity, more than
double the figure for Protestants and Catholics. And by the early 1970s yearly
incomes for a majority of Jewish families, whose head was typically between 30
and 59 years of age, averaged over $16,000, compared to a national average for
all families of under $11,000. In the 1980s scholars estimate that Jews earn almost
50 percent more than non-Jews.

Second-generation Jews usually chose professions in which they could be
independently employed and not subject to the bigotry of prejudiced employers.
As a result many became physicians, lawyers, accountants, pharmacists, and
dentists. In the 1930s and even in the 1960s, Jews made up more than half of New
York City's dentists, physicians, and lawyers. The third generation of Jews still
found law and medicine attractive, but the decline of discriminatory hiring practices in the business and academic worlds opened opportunities not available to
their parents and grandparents. Irving S. Shapiro—mentioned earlier as the chief

executive of du Pont—is one example of how far Jews have been able to rise when the sole criteria have been performance and potential. Other such Jewish chief executives include Gerald Greenwald of Chrysler Motors and Sidney Kirschner of National Service Industries.

On Wall Street, except for Jewish firms, large investment houses, law firms, and major banks rarely hired Jews, Italians, and other persons of Southern and Eastern European origins. In the 1970s and 1980s, however, the need for talent was great, a more tolerant atmosphere emerged, and the sharp division between Jewish and Gentile investment houses began to blur. In 1987 the top executive of the nation's fourth-largest bank—the Manufacturers Trust Company—was Edward Miller, the son of Lithuanian immigrants. Miller had not gone to an Ivy League school, but had attended Brooklyn College in New York City. In 1983 another Jewish banker, Boris S. Berkovitch, became vice-chairman of an old firm run by old-stock Americans, Morgan Guaranty Trust Company. A study completed in 1986 revealed that 58 percent of the nation's 4,350 senior executives just below the chief executive level were Protestant, but seven years before the figure had been 68 percent. The percentage of Jews had grown from 5.6 percent to 7.4 percent in the same period. An examination of Chicago's top business leaders revealed similar findings. Among those under age 40, non-Protestants made even larger gains.

The careers of Henry Kissinger in academia and in politics and of Harold T. Shapiro in academia are indicative of trends in these fields. Kissinger excelled as a professor at Harvard, a university that for several decades limited the number of Jewish students it would admit. He later served as the first Jewish secretary of state under Presidents Richard M. Nixon and Gerald Ford. The State Department was another outpost that has long had a reputation for anti-Semitism within its ranks.

After earning his Ph.D. in economics at Princeton University, Shapiro took a teaching position at the University of Michigan. He then turned his hand to administration and became the first Jewish president of that distinguished state university. In 1987 he accepted the presidency of Princeton University, which had a reputation of being the symbol of white Protestant elitism. Until the 1960s Princeton had restricted its Jewish enrollment. Upon hearing of Shapiro's appointment as Princeton's first Jewish president, a member of the Hillel Foundation said, "This shows that Princeton has come a long way. If you would have asked Jewish students at Princeton in the 1960s if they could picture Princeton with a Jewish president, I'm sure they would have said no."

Although individual Jews can be found in almost every line of business and professional endeavor, as a group the East Europeans have made their greatest impact in the clothing, entertainment, and intellectual worlds of American society. By the earliest years of the twentieth century the manufacture of ready-to-wear clothing was in the hands of Jewish owners. In 1950 more than 85 percent of American-made clothes were manufactured in Jewish-owned shops. In the entertainment field both the theater and the movies provided avenues of mobility for Jewish actors, actresses, writers, tunesmiths, directors, and producers. Two Jews of Russian ancestry, David Sarnoff and William Paley, developed what one financial publication called "perhaps the world's two greatest broadcasting empires," the Radio Corporation of America (now part of General Electric) and the Columbia Broadcasting System (CBS), respectively. In the intellectual community leading journals such as *Commentary,* since 1945, and *The New York Review of Books,* for the past decade or so, have relied on Jewish sponsors and/or editors. Authors like Norman Mailer, Philip Roth, Saul Bellow, Bernard Malamud, and Meyer Levin have been among the major figures in American literature in the past three decades. And in academia prominent scholars like historian Oscar Handlin, social scientist Seymour Martin Lipset, and economist and Nobel Prize winner Milton Friedman are a credit to the nation's leading universities. Artist Ben Shahn, discoverer of polio vaccine Jonas Salk, filmmaker Stanley Kubrick, violinist Yehudi Menuhin, musician Leonard Bernstein, and former Supreme Court justice and ambassador to the United Nations Arthur Goldberg—these are only a few of the Jews of East European descent who have distinguished themselves in American society. Not all Jews are as prominent and accomplished as the aforementioned group, but it is worth noting that no twentieth-century European minority has risen as fast, in terms of social and economic mobility, as the descendants of Jews who arrived from eastern Europe at the turn of the century.

The remarkable success of Jews was undoubtedly the consequence of hard work, skill, and an arduous struggle in an expanding economy. Their traditional respect for learning facilitated advancement because education was an important vehicle for social mobility. To what extent American public schools really served the immigrants is a subject of debate and in need of study, but in the case of Jewish immigrants they were of great advantage. Parents pushed their children to achieve, and they themselves, eager for an education, attended the public evening schools. As journalist Abraham Cahan, chronicler of the Lower East Side of New York City, put it, "The ghetto rang with a clamor for knowledge."

In addition to their respect for education, Jews brought with them an urban living experience and skills that could be used in commercial and industrial America. Though Jews faced tensions and problems common to all immigrant groups, their families were relatively stable, providing a sense of security as well as a springboard for their children. The older German-Jewish community, another extraordinarily accomplished group, with its many welfare agencies, was sometimes suspicious of and hostile to the greenhorns from eastern Europe with their different dress, language, and ideas; but on the whole it was a source of strength to the newcomers. Inadvertently, anti-Semitism united and strengthened the entire Jewish community and prompted many of the more successful to help their less fortunate kin.

Also to be reckoned with are the intangibles, such as the culture of the immigrant group, which cannot be precisely measured. Certainly, there was a clash between Protestantism and Judaism, but in many ways there was an agreement over key values. Jews found it easier than did some others to accept the American stress upon achievement and mobility. The differences over religion did not lead to the rejection of these broader American values. On the contrary, more than one analyst has observed how readily Jewish Americans accepted the Protestant ethic of hard work and material accomplishment.

Perhaps the reasons for Jewish emigration also had something to do with their success in the United States. Like so many others, they came in search of a better life, but, unlike many others, they could not return to the Old World. The pogroms that had driven them away dimmed most hopes for returning. Because they had to make it here—not in the Old World—Jews came with a determination to make America truly the Promised Land.

As we have seen, the Italians had a somewhat different experience. They were probably poorer than the Jews and, coming from a rural background, were unfamiliar with city life. A large number were interested only in collecting a bit of cash in order to return to Italy. For many Italians success meant returning home with something, not achieving status in the United States. Often they moved from job to job and finally back to Italy. Consequently, they did not experience the rapid social mobility that Jews did, but they gradually prospered nonetheless.

Although most Italians lived in cities, a few succeeded on the land. On both the East and West coasts Italians became skillful truck farmers and supplied the growing urban areas with food. The di Giorgio orchards eventually covered 40,000 acres in California. More famous were the wineries of California, like Italian-Swiss Colony and Gallo Brothers. In 1971 the Gallo Winery had revenues of a quarter of a billion dollars. Along with German wines, Italian-American wines became the best known in American stores. A few Italians also became successful in the South, raising cotton, sugar cane, and other crops.

Like all other ethnic groups, the Italian have their notable success stories. Among northern Italians the career of Amadeo P. Giannini, founder of the Bank of America, is outstanding. Giannini began as a banker for immigrants but expanded his operations in the early twentieth century. When the San Francisco earthquake struck in 1906, he rescued his bank's gold, hidden in a produce wagon, and was quickly ready to open for business again. Expanding from San Francisco's North Beach Italian colony, he branched out and became a major factor in the state's growing economy. He saw the future in branch banking and expanded from real estate to industrial financing. When he retired in 1945, the Bank of America had become the largest private bank in the world, with $5.5 billion in deposits and over 3 million depositors.

Other Italians ran groceries and opened restaurants. Some were importers of products such as olive oil, macaroni, and ravioli; others were producers of ethnic goods in demand by Italian Americans and later by other Americans as well. One such family ethnic enterprise was begun by Joseph Pellegrino. As a boy he arrived in America from Sicily with $13. After shining shoes and buying and selling cooking oils for a living, he went into the pasta business. He eventually took over the Prince Company and made it the largest pasta maker in America, employing 1,000 persons in the 1980s.

For most, however, success came gradually and not spectacularly. Beginning as garment workers in New York City, day laborers or miners in Pennsylvania, or in other unskilled or semiskilled jobs, Italian Americans found the path upward difficult. Although some individuals made giant leaps, the second generation improved itself over the first modestly, becoming construction workers and foremen, small businessmen, and lesser white-collar workers rather than unskilled laborers, factory workers, and miners. After World War II the third generation made greater progress. As job opportunities expanded with the decline of prejudice, some Italian Americans even found new chances in large businesses, finance, and the professions. In the early 1970s the presidents of the Ford Motor Company and the Chrysler Corporation were Lee A. Iacocca and John Riccardo, both of Italian descent. When Riccardo left the failing Chrysler Corporation, Iacocca replaced him to have a try at putting the company on its feet. His dynamic leadership and the revival of the Chrysler Corporation made Iacocca something of a folk hero and made his autobiography, *Iacocca,* a best-seller in the mid-1980s.

The rise of these two men in business was both symbolic and representative of the upward mobility of ethnic Americans into the nation's business elite. As banks and corporations began to hire Jews so they hired men and women of Italian, Irish, and other ancestries as well. In 1985 Anthony P. Terracciano, the grandson of Italian immigrants, became vice-chairman of New York City's Chase Manhattan Bank, the same position that Peter C. Palmieri obtained at the Irving Trust Company the year before.

It is not difficult to explain the reasons these opportunities recently became available in the formerly restricted field of investment banking. A *New York Times* article in June 1986 pinpointed the need for change: "Deregulation has forced large commercial banks to engage in new activities that require skilled, aggressive executives. To fill the posts, the banks are tossing aside old barriers and converting their upper managements increasingly into meritocracies. As Barry M. Allen, first vice president of the Bank of Boston, put it: 'We can't afford to keep out any talented person.'" Therefore old school ties, family connections, and a "gentleman's C" in college grades are less important factors in the banking world of today. And ethnic names, which were once the kiss of death, have become less significant.

Part of the change has also occurred because of changed values among members of minority groups that had formerly shunned higher education. After World War II, and especially since the 1960s, people of almost every background have come to realize that greater opportunities exist in this society for those who have attended college, graduate, or professional schools, and who have marketable skills of a rather sophisticated level when they complete their educations.

One such group was those of southern Italian ancestry. Until 1945 most Italian Americans who attended college were of northern Italian descent, but this changed. Even so, the general education level of Italian Americans was lower than the average for other whites. In the 1950s, for instance, fewer than 5 percent of native-born Italian Americans were completing college, a figure well below the national average. Yet the Italians began to catch up in college attendance after 1960, the rates from then on resembling those of other white Americans. For those with an education, prestige jobs were opening and with them the possibility of higher incomes. In general, Italian Americans were achieving middle-class status, not the equal of Jews or even the Irish, but ahead of recent immigrant groups like the Puerto Ricans (who are of course American citizens by birth) and the Mexicans.

Settling in large numbers in urban areas and being Catholic opened other possibilities to Italians for broader participation and achievement, in particular with regard to the Catholic church and politics. However, the Irish controlled the Church and played a large role in urban politics. Not until after World War II did Italian Americans begin to break into the hierarchy of American Catholicism. In 1967 the grandson of an Italian immigrant became bishop of the diocese embracing Mississippi, and a year later another Italian American became bishop of Brooklyn, the largest diocese in the United States. Although Italians were moving up in the Church by the 1980s, they were still underrepresented in the hierarchy.

Once Italians began to register and vote in American elections, they began to rise politically. But in this case too the move upward was slow. Before World War II the most successful Italian-American politician was congressman and later mayor of New York Fiorello La Guardia. La Guardia was something of an anomaly. He was Protestant, not Catholic; he had a Jewish mother; and he could speak several languages. He also tried to appeal to many groups, not merely to Italian Americans. San Francisco with its large Italian population also had an Italian mayor in the 1930s, but not until after the war did Italian Americans make many breakthroughs politically. In 1946 in Rhode Island John O. Pastore became the first man of Italian background to be elected governor of a state. Rhode Island later sent Pastore to the U.S. Senate, the first Italian American elected to the upper house of Congress. Increasingly, in the 1950s and 1960s Italians were elected to important political offices as congressmen, state legislators, and mayors of big cities. In the 1970s Connecticut voters twice elected Ella Grasso governor of the state; this was the highest political office ever held by an Italian-American woman. In 1982 in neighboring New York, Mario Cuomo became the first Italian American to be elected governor, and he won a landslide reelection four years later. When Walter Mondale, the Democratic candidate for the presidency in 1984, picked his running mate he chose Congresswoman Geraldine Ferraro of New York. Most comment centered on her being the first woman from a major party to run for vice-president, but she was also the first Italian American, man or woman, to run for such a high office.

Perhaps symbolic of the political arrival of Italian Americans was Carmine G. De Sapio's takeover of the leadership of New York's Tammany Hall in 1949. Irish hegemony was clearly on the wane in big cities, and Italians were one of the groups benefiting from it. By 1974 two men of Italian descent, Meade H. Esposito, a Brooklyn Democrat, and Assemblyman Joseph M. Margiotta, a Nassau County Republican, were regarded as among the most powerful political bosses in New York State. Esposito headed a typically urban enclave of mixed ethnic groups, while Margiotta, who symbolizes what *The New York Times* called "the coming of age, politically, of the suburbs," controlled "the most effective political machine east of Chicago." He presided over a prosperous and predominantly white, Americanized homogeneous group more akin to the white Anglo-Saxon Protestant (WASP) critics of urban bossism of yesteryear than to the greenhorns of another era, who depended on their local politicians to ease the adjustment to the New World. Esposito, like the bosses of old, ran his domain "as a series of fiefdoms to be placated, appeased and sometimes bossed." Margiotta, on the other hand, handled his organization "like the million-dollar corporation it is." One of his outstanding triumphs occurred in 1980 when Nassau County Executive Alfonse M. D'Amato ousted the venerable Jacob Javits and won the Republican primary nomination for the U.S. Senate. D'Amato then won election to the Senate. New York's voters overwhelmingly reelected him in 1986 for a second term.

For a long period of time Italians had received a good deal of negative publicity because some of them had participated in organized criminal activities. In the 1950s Senator Estes Kefauver of Tennessee conducted hearings about crime in America and paraded Italian-American gangsters before the committee and a national television audience. Kefauver said that the Mafia was controlled by Italian Americans and Italians in Italy, and it was "the shadowy international organization that lurks behind much of organized criminal activity." The charge that Italians in America were involved with the Mafia was not new. As early as

1891 the New York *Tribune* had insisted that "in large cities throughout the country, Italians of criminal antecedents and propensities are more or less closely affiliated for the purpose of requiring injuries and gratifying animosities by secret vengeances. These organizations in common speech and belief are connected with the *Mafia,* and that designation fairly indicates their character and motives. Through their agency the most infernal crimes have been committed and have gone unpunished."

Certainly some Italian Americans have been involved in organized crime. As Humbert Nelli, historian of Italians in Chicago, put it:

Crime, one means of economic advancement independent of education, social background or political connections, provided for all classes of Italians opportunities for quick and substantial monetary gain and sometimes for social and political advancement as well. Within the colony bankers and padroni, blackhanders and other lawbreakers all realized small but important profits by swindling or terrorizing compatriots. The "syndicate," a business operation reaping vast profits from the American community, offered almost limitless opportunities for promotion within its hierarchy. Thus for some, crime offered means of advancement within the ethnic community and for others, opportunities outside it.

How many or what percentage of Italians and their children engaged in such work is impossible to determine. Popular accounts and later stereotypes about the Black Hand, the Mafia, and members of *La Cosa Nostra* emphasized unduly this type of endeavor among Italians and Italian Americans.

Al Capone, the Italian-American leader of crime in Chicago during the violent and colorful days of prohibition in the 1920s, was the prototype of the big-city gangster. Others followed Capone to prominence after his demise in the 1930s. A few were convicted, and when evidence of criminal acts was lacking, the federal government deported as undesirable aliens some of those born in Italy.

Italian Americans, though, have not monopolized organized crime. Historians and sociologists remind us that various other ethnic groups have been associated with criminal activity. In the nineteenth century the Irish were notorious as criminals in New York City's Five Points District, and crime has always been a part of ghetto life in this country; as the ethnic occupants of the slums change, so do the names on the police arrest lists. One study of the top underworld figures in Chicago in 1930 estimated that 30 percent were of Italian background, 29 percent of Irish background, and 20 percent of Jewish background. While Capone was famous in the Chicago rackets of the 1920s, Dean O'Banion and men like Arnold Rothstein and Meyer Lansky were prominent in New York City.

It should also be kept in mind the extent to which criminal activities were an avenue of social mobility. Old-stock Americans dominated the powerful positions in American industry, banking, insurance, and commerce. With few exceptions they have always been loath to allow the immigrants or their children opportunities for advancement to the middle and upper levels of management. Crime, like entertainment and sports, was a way out of the ghetto and a means of achieving material success. Reluctantly, some chose it, though for others the choice was not always reluctant.

Another point that must be made is that while certain activities are legally considered crimes, not everyone in the country makes the same assessment. Some ethnic groups did not share the old-stock white Protestant aversion to gambling and drinking. Swedes and some pietistic Protestant immigrants did, perhaps, but others did not think it so terribly wrong to gamble or to supply liquor to thirsty throats during Prohibition. Besides, it was the so-called respectable citizens' patronage of illegal liquor suppliers that made Prohibition a failure. President Warren G. Harding drank during his tenure in the White House, and it was rumored that he and his cronies supported private bootleggers. As Al Capone asked: "What's Al Capone done, then? He supplied a legitimate demand. Some call it bootlegging. Some call it racketeering. I call it a business. They say I violate the prohibition law. Who doesn't?"

If crime has been a path upward for older immigrants, there is evidence that more recent migrants to the city will follow a similar pattern as others move into the more respectable occupations. Recent research has indicated that blacks, Puerto Ricans, and Cubans were already moving to take over organized crime as other minorities had done before them. Or as one Italian American said, "I guess it's their turn now."

Even though only a few Italian Americans have been associated with crime, they have left a lasting impression. The revelations of the Kefauver committee and bestselling books like *The Godfather* have produced a sense of shame and indignation at the stereotype of the Italian criminal. In 1972 Frank Sinatra complained in *The New York Times* that "there is a form of bigotry abroad in this land which allows otherwise decent people . . . to believe the most scurrilous tales if they are connected to an Italian-American name."

The experiences and paths of mobility of the other ethnic groups that were part of the great surge from southern and eastern Europe at the end of the nineteenth and beginning of the twentieth centuries vary from those of the Italians and to a considerable extent from one another. The Greeks were apt to be entrepreneurs—restaurateurs, theater owners, food processors—or else they became professionals, such as doctors, lawyers, and teachers. The career of Alexander Pantages was similar to that of other wealthy ethnic minorities. He came from a middle-class background but made his fortune in the entertainment world. After emigrating to the United States and working at odd jobs, he made money in gold in the Yukon country and then made a fortune in the movie-house business, owning at one time a chain of 80 theaters. The Skouras brothers also owned a large number of movie houses, and Spyros Skouras became president of a major Hollywood organization, 20th Century-Fox. Although the careers of Pantages and the Skourases were exceptional, most Greek Americans were ensconced in the middle class by the 1980s.

The Slavic peoples also began largely as unskilled workers in industrial America, but the second and third generations did not improve their positions as fast as some others of European descent. The working-class districts of American cities were often centers of Polish, Hungarian, and Russian life. These were areas of neat and well-kept houses, not prosperous but substantial. Like the Irish before them, they prized home ownership and invested their savings in their homes and neighborhoods. Disproportionately members of the working class, their offspring were mainly trade unionists and blue-collar workers. A survey of Slavs in Connecticut in the 1960s showed, for example, that 40 percent belonged to unions. Slavic Americans generally had incomes lower than those of the Irish or Jews or white Protestants, and their educational levels were also low. They had often found schools—important for mobility—inhospitable, and many dropped out before completing high school.

Although just reaching the middle-income level in the 1950s and 1960s, many Slavs were nonetheless continuing their educations, moving up the economic ladder, and finding better jobs. One scholar has concluded that throughout the 1920s and 1930s college attendance for Polish-American men increased but lagged considerably behind the national norm. By the 1950s, he argues, Polish-American males were just as likely to attend college as other white males, and a decade later Polish-American women reached the national averages for white women. Among the Slovaks, Slovenes, and Croatians, the pace was just a bit slower but similar to that of the Poles.

These upward trends were confirmed by a study the United States Commission on Civil Rights published in late 1986. Based on census and other data the commission found that those Americans of southern and eastern European descent had achieved educational and earning parity with other whites of European background, meaning the Germans, British, Irish, and Scandinavians. The commission noted that when the millions from southern and eastern Europe arrived after 1880, they generally had about four fewer years of schooling than other white Americans and earned considerably less in their unskilled jobs. The third generation coming of age in post–World War II America had caught up and even surpassed other whites. They had better jobs than their immigrant ancestors, earned more, and were well educated. The study found both men and women of southern and eastern Europe to have equaled their white counterparts from other areas of Europe.

Of course the success of the Jews, whose ancestors hailed from Poland,

Russia, and Rumania and who earned relatively high incomes and were quite well educated, would in part explain a good deal of the results of the study, but even the non-Jewish descendants of immigrants from eastern Europe did well. At the bottom of the income scale, the commission discovered proportionately fewer persons of southern and eastern European descent living below the poverty line. The Commission concluded

> The results reveal that along virtually every dimension, Americans of southern and eastern European ancestry have generally succeeded as well or better than other Americans. This does not imply that many individuals of eastern or southern European heritage have not suffered from prejudice; it only suggests that for the groups as a whole, there is no overt indication of current and widespread discrimination against them in the labor market—that is, the existence of group-specific differences that cannot be explained by standard economic variables such as those accounted for in this report.

One should not conclude from this assessment, however, that the achievements of the children and grandchildren of the southern and eastern European immigrants were uniformly successful. Sometimes the children did not do as well as the parents. Many second-generation Jewish businessmen were dismayed that their professionally trained children earned less money than they did. Moreover, among all groups one found poor people. Finally, one should keep in mind that the top positions in American society had not opened up for many minority group members until the 1970s, and most key posts in leading law firms, businesses, and banks are still staffed by old-stock Americans. The trend toward a more open executive suite was evident, but members of twentieth century groups have only recently been hired solely on the basis of talent and ability.

An indication of how fast a person with outstanding skills can progress was demonstrated in 1980 when Coca-Cola chose Roberto C. Guizueta, a Cuban who arrived in the United States in the 1960s, as its chairman and chief executive officer. To be sure, he attended Yale and cannot be compared with someone growing up in a lower-class neighborhood. Nevertheless it is significant that his ethnic background did not keep his unique attributes from being recognized. Guizueta's appointment immediately established him as perhaps the most prominent person of Hispanic origin in American business history.

Just as the Irish, Germans, and, later, Italians used politics to improve their lives, so did the descendants of Slavs, Greeks, and other eastern Europeans become active in political affairs. In the early 1920s Anton Cermak became the first Czech mayor of Chicago, but most breakthroughs occurred later. Like so many other immigrants, Czechs were slow to become involved in politics; but the second and third generations began to assert themselves more effectively. In 1958 the Polish-American press reported that 13 Americans of Polish background had been elected to Congress, and Poles were important politically in cities like Chicago, Cleveland, Milwaukee, and Buffalo. In 1968 Edmund Muskie of Maine became the first American of Polish extraction to run for vice-president, the same year that Spiro T. Agnew, governor of Maryland and the first politically prominent Greek American, was elected to that office. Six years later voters of Massachusetts chose a Greek American, Michael S. Dukakis, as governor. In 1986 he won his third term by the biggest margin of any Massachusetts governor in the twentieth century. After that victory, Dukakis, who speaks Greek, Spanish, and Korean in addition to his native tongue, English, was mentioned as a possible presidential candidate. Besides Dukakis, the other most prominent Greek-American political leader in the 1980s was U.S. Senator Paul Sarbanes of Maryland.

In 1986 the voters of that same state sent Barbara Mikulski, a Polish-American woman, to the U.S. Senate. President Jimmy Carter also elevated Polish Americans to high posts. He chose Edmund Muskie, who had been a U.S. Senator from Maine in addition to being a vice-presidential candidate in 1968, for secretary of state and Zbigniew Brzezinski for national security adviser.

While the descendants of southern and eastern European immigrants were making their marks both economically and politically, so were the descendants of the one Asian group—Japanese Americans—who arrived during the same time as the Europeans. Yet of the immigrants arriving in large numbers between 1880 and 1920, no group experienced such intense prejudice as did these Asians. Moreover, no group except the Japanese had to endure the shock of being placed in virtual concentration camps during World War II. Those interned on the West Coast lost nearly everything they owned, including their stake in agricultural and small businesses. Beginning from scratch after World War II, they rapidly improved their position. The key to much of their success was education. After 1940 the Japanese had a higher educational level than whites, with a considerable segment going to college. In the 1980s nearly 90 percent of third-generation Japanese Americans were attending some college or university, double the national rate and well above the 58 percent figure for second-generation Japanese Americans. Their attainments, combined with lessening prejudice, led to better jobs and higher incomes. Japanese Americans as a group tend to be concentrated in prestige white-collar positions with higher than average incomes.

Even political life beckoned after the war for Japanese Americans. The Issei (the first generation) were ineligible for citizenship and hence excluded from politics. But members of the native-born second generation (Nisei), who were automatically citizens, grew into a potent political force. Sharp increases in the number of registered voters have been translated into electoral victories. In 1968 both members of the House of Representatives from Hawaii as well as the Democratic senator, Daniel Inouye, were of Japanese ancestry. By 1980 another Japanese American, Spark Matsunaga, had joined Inouye in the Senate. Japanese

Americans were also well represented in the Hawaiian legislature, civil service, and business organizations. California, the state that had fostered so much hostility toward Japanese immigrants and their children, in 1976 elected S. I. Hayakawa, a Japanese American, to the U.S. Senate.

Japanese Americans were not the only Asians who succeeded in the United States. As noted, many Chinese Americans were also beginning to make their marks as were Vietnamese, Asian Indians, Koreans, and Filipinos. In fact, the striking accomplishments of Asians were among the highlights of America's postwar ethnic experience. Newspapers, magazines, and television and radio stations carried features in the 1980s such as "What Sends Asians to the Head of the Class?"; "A Look at Success of Young Asians"; "Asians: The Model Minority"; or "The Triumph of Asian-Americans."

Much evidence existed to support the impression that Asian Americans and new Asian immigrants were doing well. Each year in the 1980s the list of winners of the annual Westinghouse Science Talent Search competition revealed a disproportionate number of Asian names. In 1986, for example, the high scorers included Wei-Jing Zhu of New York and Wendy Kay Chung of Miami. The top five prizes that year went to students born in Asia or of Asian origin. Commenting on her success, Wendy Chung observed, "Throughout the history of man there have been questions about what makes things work, how things tick. It's just a natural curiosity." The next year, 1987, David Kuo of New York City became the third member of his remarkable family to be named a Westinghouse Science Talent Search winner.

The Asian Americans scored well on academic tests, and were well represented in the nation's top schools. More than one professor was known to remark that the way to increase the nation's Scholastic Aptitude Test (SAT) scores in math was to increase Asian immigration. In 1986, while Asian Americans made up about 2 percent of the nation's population, they accounted for 19 percent of the Massachusetts Institute of Technology's undergraduates and 8 percent of Harvard's undergraduates. In the top music schools, they also made their presence felt and were disproportionately represented in those schools' enrollment figures. "We have 24 Kims alone. It's incredible," reported Osegnam Fuschi of the admissions department of the Juilliard School of Music. Yehudi Menuhin, the celebrated violinist, called Asians "the Jews of the future," and predicted their achievements would equal those of individuals of eastern European Jewish heritage, such as Jascha Heifetz, Vladimir Horowitz, and Arthur Rubinstein, among other great musicians.

Academic achievements resulted in improved incomes and better jobs. Asians generally were better educated than other Americans, and were more apt to be professionals; thus they earned more money. The 1980 census reported that the median incomes for Japanese, Chinese, and Indian families were all above that for white families, and Koreans were only slightly below the median; and a smaller proportion of Asians lived below the government's poverty line. Yet whites of the same level of education did better financially than Asians; and as noted, the picture was not universally bright in the nation's Chinatowns. There thousands of Chinese immigrants labored in sweatshops and lived in poverty. What the future holds for many of the recent Indochinese refugees still remains unclear.

Leaving individual ethnic groups, we now turn to an area in which the children and grandchildren of immigrants sometimes participated on an equal footing—the world of athletics. In this realm compared to most others, individual skills rather than ethnic background determined success. And once successful, social and economic doors opened wide. (Athletics, in fact, might be compared to entertainment as one of the great levelers in American society except that until after World War II blacks were restricted from most areas of competition.) Sports have therefore been a way for many members of ethnic groups to escape working-class lives. Famed nineteenth-century boxers like John L. Sullivan and James Corbett were Irish, and Notre Dame's great football team of the 1930s, coached by Knute Rockne, was known as the fighting Irish. Gertrude Ederle, the first woman to swim the English Channel, was of German descent. In baseball other Germans found fame and sometimes fortune. Lou Gehrig, Honus Wagner, Rube Wadell, and the greatest German-American player of all, Babe Ruth, born George Herman Erhardt in Baltimore, were idols in their day. Irish, English, and Germans dominated baseball until the 1920s, then Polish and Italian players began to make their marks. The DiMaggio brothers were the most famous of the Italian baseball players. Stan Musial, Ed Lopat, and Ted Kluszewski were of Polish ancestry. In our own day, blacks and Hispanics are finding the world of professional athletics one arena in which they can compete and be judged strictly on the basis of their talents and accomplishments. The Caribbean has also produced major league baseball players. Juan Marichal, a star pitcher for a number of years, was a Dominican. Another Hispanic, Puerto Rican Orlando Cepeda, won the National League's most valuable player award in 1967. In the 1980s Hispanics have also frequently been quite visible on baseball teams' rosters, comprising about 10 percent of all major league players at the start of the 1985 season. Among the stars were Tony Armas, Pedro Guerrero, Fernando Valenzuela, and Willie Hernandez. Valenzuela spoke practically no English when he first came from Mexico to pitch for the Los Angeles Dodgers. After a sensational debut as a rookie he went on to become an established star. In 1986 he won more games than any other pitcher in the National League.

Because baseball is popular in the Caribbean, Mexico, and South America, it is no surprise that many Hispanics play after coming to the United States. Yet Latin Americans entered other sports as well. Boxing was a big attraction and on occasion some played football. Such was the case of Daniel Villanueva, a field goal kicker for the Dallas Cowboys and Los Angeles Rams. After his retirement, Villanueva became general manager of KMEX, a Spanish-language TV station in Los Angeles.

Obviously, most of the descendants of immigrants could not be outstanding athletes and had to take the more usual paths—white-collar and professional positions—to middle-class security. Better jobs provided higher incomes and a route out of the ghettos. At first the move was to better neighborhoods in the city, but since the end of World War II the trek has been increasingly to the suburbs. In New York City in the late 1920s fewer than 10 percent of the Jews still lived on the famed Lower East Side. The completion of the subways stimulated the exodus to the upper reaches of Manhattan and the Bronx and across the East River into Brooklyn. In Chicago the original Italian districts declined in the 1920s. The subsequent depression and the post–World War II housing shortage curtailed movement, but the affluence of the 1950s rejuvenated it. The growth of suburbia in the 1950s and 1960s can be attributed largely to the movement of the children and grandchildren of the Irish, Italians, Poles, Jews, and Scandinavians who had shared in the nation's growing prosperity. So great was the move that by 1970 the census showed more people, who were overwhelmingly white, living in suburban America than in the central cities.

In many cases the pattern of movement went far beyond the neighboring greenbelts. Sunshine and job opportunities drew people to the South and the West. Florida and California in particular more than doubled their populations in the decades after World War II, and the growth in job opportunities in regional centers such as Washington, D.C., and Houston, Texas, also resulted in mushrooming populations.

Although the suburban growth drew many away from the cities, the old ethnic neighborhoods, the little Italies, Polands, Tokyos, and the like, did not disappear completely. The Slavs and Italians, less affluent and strongly attached to their homes and old family neighborhoods, were the last to leave, and many simply remained where they were. As a result there are still ethnic enclaves of Italians in New York City and Newark, New Jersey, as well as Slavic neighborhoods in Philadelphia, Detroit, Milwaukee, Cleveland, Baltimore, Pittsburgh, and Buffalo. Moreover, refugee arrivals since 1945 strengthened some of the old ethnic neighborhoods. Just as the descendants of the original Chinese were moving out of the Chinatowns in America, renewed immigration in the 1960s and 1970s once again swelled their populations. Similarly, refugee Hasidic Jews reinforced the Jewish population of Brooklyn when they settled in the Williamsburg, Crown Heights, and Borough Park sections.

Yet the general trend was clear. The older and more prosperous immigrants' descendants measured their success by their movement. Many of the recent Asian immigrants did likewise. They too headed for the suburbs to live in more substantial housing and to send their children to better schools. In the process they left behind the less affluent blacks, Mexican Americans, Puerto Ricans, and other Latin Americans. This was particularly noticeable in the major metropolises. New York City, the symbol of the nation's ethnic diversity and the port of entry for so many newcomers, was becoming less Irish, less Jewish, less Italian, and more black, Asian, and Hispanic. The borough of Queens, formerly a step up for the second and third generations, now houses immigrant colonies of Maltese, Greeks, Croatians, West Indians, Armenians, Koreans, Thais, Vietnamese, Cambodians, Laotians, Filipinos, and Japanese. Two major differences between most of these more recent settlers and the immigrants of earlier generations are that the newer arrivals are generally better educated and of a higher social status than turn-of-the-century arrivals, and their presence is not resented as much as had been the case in the past. A New York City population analyst observed in the summer of 1980: "The Asians are generally perceived by their neighbors as a stabilizing influence." They open stores, encourage their children in school, and apparently have the same outward goals and values as middle-class Americans. However, Hispanics are not always viewed so favorably.

Whether the newer Hispanics would be able to move up has already been discussed in Chapter 6. As for the other post–1945 immigrants, evidence is already mounting of a traditional pattern of mobility. One scholar found that the immigrants who arrived in the 1940s and 1950s are making more money than many native-born Americans of similar characteristics. It is too soon to tell about the Asians and others arriving in the post–1965 wave, yet some evidence is available. Many have had to work initially in jobs below their training and found an inadequate knowledge of English to be a barrier. The professionals have encountered difficulties in obtaining licenses to practice their skills. Nevertheless, some are already demonstrating an entrepreneurial spirit. In several American cities Koreans have opened small businesses and work diligently at making them a success. One Korean supermarket owner in Los Angeles told a reporter in 1978, "I work long hours. I don't close my grocery store until 9 P.M. I get home late." Although individuals of a number of ethnic groups are equally diligent and determined, a full accounting of the progress of the more recent immigrants will have to await the test of two or three generations.

chapter *9*

Whither Ethnic America? Assimilation into American Life

The massive flow of immigrants after the 1840s bewildered old-stock Americans. They could not agree on how the newcomers could best be absorbed into the mainstream of American life. The proponents of the melting pot had one theory, the Americanizers had another, and the advocates of pluralism had yet a third point of view. Americans eventually did agree on one thing: Immigration must be restricted both in social composition and in numbers. Although they were willing to increase the numbers arriving after World War II and do away with the national origins systems, general restrictions remained.

But what of the immigrants themselves? Did they and their descendants maintain separate subcultures, or did they blend with old Americans to form a new type, or did they assimilate into the larger society? As we have seen, the people who arrived in the colonial era eventually lost their distinct national heritages and became part of the common American culture. There are exceptions, of course, such as the Amish, who still live apart from the rest of society in their separate religious communities. But the Amish number only about 60,000 today. Little remains now of the original Scotch-Irish, Welsh, German, or Huguenot societies of early America. The old immigrants, those coming in large numbers between 1840 and 1890 from northern and western Europe, have largely assimilated and lost much of their original cultures. The new immigrants, coming after 1880 and now producing a fourth generation, have assimilated, although some Jews, Italians, Poles, and others still retain aspects of their traditional heritages. In fact, in the wake of the civil rights movement of the 1960s, there was a renewal of ethnic self-consciousness, which was subsequently reinforced by waves of Italians, Greeks, Portuguese, Croatians, and Russian Jews from Europe; Hispanics from the Western Hemisphere; and Asians. The most recent newcomers are of course still largely unassimilated. The U.S. Supreme Court's 1974 ruling in *Lau* v. *Nichols,* which requires public schools to teach children in a language that they can understand, may inhibit the pace of future assimilation—or, paradoxically, it may hasten change by educating those who had been turned off by the schools. Bilingualism remains one of the most hotly debated topics about ethnicity in the 1980s, and it is not clear whether it has hindered or helped the process of assimilation.

It is important to recognize that the transition from being foreign to being American is not simply a matter of learning the English language. Nor can the transition always be made easily or without turmoil, as those who have already leaped the hurdle can attest. But because of the federal government's concern and financial aid, the national media impact, and the quality of contemporary education, assimilation for the recent arrivals may, on some levels, be less difficult than it was for their predecessors.

Over the years, for some groups external events have forced a wrenching and radical change. The German Americans, for example, opposed American involvement on the side of the Allied powers against Germany after World War I broke out in Europe in 1914. When the United States finally entered the conflagration on the Allied side in 1917, the German Americans suffered anguish. The issues were not clear-cut in spite of the shrill cries about German militarism, stories of atrocities, and the alleged threats to American interests. Moreover, when the United States entered the war against Germany, German Americans were faced with the reality of fighting against a nation in which many of their relatives and friends lived. Despite the acute agony caused by their situation, German-American soldiers fought as valorously as other Americans.

Yet American entry into the war forced all dissidents into an untenable position. The slightest indication of doubt or disagreement about the righteousness of the cause led to accusations of disloyalty and traitorous behavior. Superpatriots were especially critical of German Americans, the Irish, pacifists, and radicals. A few German Americans and some radicals such as Socialist party leader Eugene Debs continued to oppose the war once it came. Two sons of a prominent German Philadelphia brewing family, Erwin R. and Grover Cleveland Bergdoll, refused to serve because "we do not fight our own kind." One of the two was apprehended and sentenced to a federal prison; the other fled to Germany. Upon his return to the United States he too was imprisoned.

After the war some German Americans were bitter, but most accepted the war's outcome. When Hitler's armies marched in the 1930s, few German Americans supported him. American Nazi organizations in the 1930s, with small memberships, did have a few German immigrant members, but the second and third generations turned their backs on Nazism. Antiwar sentiments were vocal in German areas of the Midwest in the 1930s, but when World War II came, the descendants of German immigrants supported the United States without reservation.

The American Irish were also reluctant belligerents during World War I. Why, Irish-American leaders asked, should the Irish fight on the side of Great Britain when she had refused to free Ireland? It was a valid question, especially for Woodrow Wilson, a president who professed to make the war a crusade for democracy and the self-determination of nations. But the answer was relatively simple: As in the past one fought for his own country no matter what his personal preferences might be. Only a handful of Irish in America resisted the war effort, although others grumbled about the Allied powers. The omission of Irish independence from the peace treaty irked the Irish and caused some to desert the Democratic party; but these were political matters, hardly an issue of citizenship or disloyalty. Ireland achieved independence in 1922, before the coming of World War II. Thus the Irish question was largely dead, although some Irish were not overly sympathetic to Great Britain in the 1930s.

The crisis for Italian Americans, a new immigrant group, came later. Italian Americans had reservations about American foreign policy during the 1930s because of the growing friction between the United States and Italy. During the 1920s and 1930s, many Italian Americans as well as many other Americans admired Mussolini, but some bitterly opposed him and the advent of fascism in Italy. The difficulty for the anti-fascists was that they seemed to be "un-Italian" if they attacked Il Duce. An Italian American said: "Whatever you fellows may think of Mussolini, you've got to admit one thing: He has done more to get respect for the Italian people than anybody else. The Italians get a lot more respect now than when I started going to school. And you can thank Mussolini for that." The Italian attack on Ethiopia in 1935 aggravated the divisions. Some Italian Americans turned away from the Democratic party of Franklin Roosevelt, as some of the Irish had done over the question of Irish independence, because of Roosevelt's condemnation of Italy's actions.

The menace of fascism and the coming of the war in Europe doomed such sentiments, however. Although many Italian Americans were uneasy about going to war against Italy, they supported the United States once war came. Even those segments of the Italian-American press that had praised Mussolini and fascism in Italy proclaimed their loyalty to America and endorsed the American war effort.

The most excruciating test of loyalty faced by an ethnic group was that of Japanese Americans during World War II, discussed in Chapter 4. When the government interned the West Coast Japanese in 1942, no distinction was made between those who were citizens (Nisei) and their parents (Issei) who were born in Japan and ineligible for American citizenship. At first the army refused to draft the Nisei and did not allow them to enlist. The government insisted upon testing their patriotism further by making them answer a series of questions. The camp experience and the questionnaire divided many; a few Japanese were classified as disloyal to the United States and segregated at the Tule Lake, California, center. Several thousand of those classified as disloyal asked to be returned to Japan after the war, and some even renounced their American citizenships. Yet it was the familiar story. Most of the 110,000 interned Japanese Americans professed their allegiance to the United States; and, when given the opportunity, the Nisei joined the army. About 33,000 Japanese Americans served, roughly half from the Hawaiian Islands and half from the mainland.

Japanese Americans fighting during World War II were members of the 100-442d Regimental Combat Team, the most highly decorated army unit of the war. In addition to thousands of medals for heroism, they received 9,486 Purple Hearts for their battle wounds. In the 1980s some of the unit's veterans wanted more recognition for their service. The president of the unit's veteran association told the *Los Angeles Times* in 1986, "Our mission today is to get our story retold. . . . We don't want our children and our grandchildren, or the rest of the world to forget what we fought for." Another veteran summed up the unit's patriotism, "All we've ever wanted is for people to know that we are Americans first and foremost and nothing else."

Since World War II there have been no major wars to divide ethnic attachments in America. Groups like the Irish and Italians do have strong loyalties to Eire or Italy, but most of the immigrants' descendants have become too thoroughly Americanized to be as troubled as their forebears had been during World War I. (The exception of the Jews and Israel is discussed later.)

The longer that groups have lived in the United States, the more they have relinquished their Old World cultures. The immigrants retained their native languages or became bilingual. Their children and grandchildren gradually lost the old languages and spoke only English. Typically, when the government searched among second-generation Japanese Americans in the camps during World War II for possible interpreters, it found that not many Nisei could speak and understand Japanese well, and fewer still could read and write it. In 1974 a middle-aged Czech woman had this to say about a declining Czech community in New Jersey.

> The old Czechs are dying and moving away. Our parents are the ones who were very active. The people of my age still had their parents around. They remember the customs, and that is something you can't forget. But you can't pass memo-

ries on to your children. The younger generation marry people who are not Czech and don't keep up the language with their children. I go to see a friend of mine who's 83, and I talk Czech with her. If I didn't I'd forget the language.

Institutions depending on foreign languages began to disappear as the immigrants' descendants could not use them. The German-language press was thriving on the eve of World War I and was the most important of the foreign-language presses, accounting for about 40 percent of their circulation. The war shattered the German-language press and hurt the standing of the language generally; it was driven off the newsstands and out of the schools. In 1910 there were 70 German dailies in America; in 1960 only 6 remained. Other major foreign-language newspapers also declined, especially the Yiddish, Italian, and Scandinavian ones. Italian dailies decreased in number from 12 earlier in the century to 5 in 1960; French dailies decreased in number from 9 to 1 during the same period. From a high of 142 daily newspapers in 1910 the foreign-language press has less than half the quantity today, and the number and circulation of weeklies have dropped about 75 percent in the same time.

In some particularly isolated rural areas such as Minnesota or the Dakotas the weekly journals still survive. Of course, new immigrants from Asia, Europe, and Latin America read papers in their native tongues. Indeed, these newcomers have begun to publish new foreign-language newspapers to serve their growing populations. Hence Korean newspapers appeared in Los Angeles and the circulation of the Spanish newspapers increased greatly as the Mexican-American population of that city grew. In New York City, no fewer than 10 daily Chinese newspapers were being published in the late 1980s.

No doubt if the present immigration trends continue, new foreign-language papers will appear, and some of the older ones catering to the latest newcomers will expand. But in general, the older foreign-language press is on a steep decline in this country.

The loss of the Old World culture can also be seen in the declining use of foreign languages in one of the most important immigrant institutions, the church. The Danish Lutheran churches are a case in point. As the young learned English, the churches began to abandon Danish. It was abandoned first in the Sunday schools in the 1920s, then in youth work, and finally in the services a decade later. Most of the books and periodicals published by Danish Lutherans in the late nineteenth century were in Danish, and as late as 1940 the annual reports for the United Evangelical Lutheran church were about half in Danish, but the use of the language was discontinued after that.

The decline of foreign languages in churches was indicative of the growing Americanization and loss of ethnicity in American religion in the twentieth century. Lutheranism, which was originally divided mainly along ethnic or nationality lines such as Swedish, Danish, German, and Norwegian, is a good example of this process. In 1967 the United Evangelical Lutheran church, of Danish background, merged with two other synods, one German and the other Norwegian in origin, and became the American Lutheran church. Two years later another Danish Lutheran church, the American Evangelical Lutheran church, joined with German, Swedish, and Finnish synods to become the Lutheran Church in America. These various Lutheran groups were no longer using their old languages or recruiting ministers from the Old World, and since they already were cooperating in religious activities, they reached the inevitable conclusion: Merge into an American Lutheranism. The mergers went a step further in 1987. Then the American Lutheran church and the Lutheran Church in America joined with the Association of Evangelical Lutheran churches, originally of German origin, to become the 5.3 million-member Evangelical Lutheran Church in America.

The same Americanization process happened in other denominations as well. In the late nineteenth century a burning issue in American Catholicism was the nationality parish supported ardently by, among others, German, French-Canadian, and Polish Catholics. The Church disapproved of nationality parishes in principle although it continued to allow them in practice. In the twentieth century, however, the nationality issue gradually became less important and so did the issue of national parishes.

The Germans illustrate this change. In the 1890s German Catholics were most insistent upon having their own priests and organizations and fostered the slogan "Language Saves Faith." The largest of these organizations was the Central Verein, founded in 1855. It reached a peak membership of 125,000 on the eve of World War I and was especially strong in New York, Pennsylvania, and the Midwest. The second-generation German Catholics, however, were already losing interest in an ethnic church when the war began. Twenty-three German Catholic publications were discontinued between 1917 and 1923; and in those that remained, English became prevalent during the 1920s. Membership in the Central Verein declined to 86,000 in 1930 and less than half that a decade later. The journal of the Verein, *Central Blatt and Social Justice,* printed more of its material in English (it discontinued German sections entirely in 1946), changed its name to *Social Justice* in 1940, but continued to lose readers; by the late 1960s, circulation barely exceeded 2,000.

As churches lost their national identities, so too did many of the other immigrant organizations. Social clubs, benefit societies, welfare organizations, and the like lost much of their membership and vitality as the old immigrant neighborhoods decayed. They are strongest today among those of new immigrant background, the Poles, and the Italians. The largest of the nationality organizations was the Deutsch-Amerikanische National Bund or National German-

American Alliance, which was organized in 1901 to promote German culture in America and the interests of German Americans politically. At its peak before World War I it claimed a membership of about 2 million. In addition to promoting the German language and German culture, it was an agent of assimiliation, for it urged German immigrants to become citizens and insisted its primary loyalty was to the United States, not Germany. It opposed American entry on the side of England in World War I, came under attack during the war, and had to disband in 1918. It was not only the war that killed the Alliance, however; third-generation German Americans were not as interested in German culture as their parents and grandparents had been. In common with members of other minority groups they were moving out of the ethnic neighborhoods, especially after World War I, and joining assimilationist organizations.

Parents attempted to maintain the old ways through the use of ethnic or religious schools for their children. This was true of the Scandinavians, the Germans, the East European Jews, the Greeks, and the Chinese. Yet many of these schools have gradually dropped language teaching and have had difficulty in attracting students. During the school crises of the 1960s and early 1970s, many parents did remove their children from public schools to prevent racial integration, and as a result some ethnic schools—Jewish day schools, for example—did show a rise in the number of students; but it is questionable whether the main purpose was always devotion to the ancient heritage. The largest parochial school system in the United States is run by the Catholic church. Only a minority of Catholics attend these institutions despite the growth spurt in the 1950s and early 1960s. Financial troubles have beset the parochial schools, however, and since the late 1960s a number have had to close.

As the descendants of the immigrants improved their incomes, jobs, and education, they moved to new neighborhoods in the cities and to mushrooming suburbs. There they absorbed the values of the mass culture preached by the media and in the schools and came into social contact with a broad range of other people. These contacts led to intermarriage among nationality and religious groups. The importance of this cannot be overstated. The family is the primary social unit in society, and as families mix, so do other institutions. In other words, intermarriage is the ultimate form of ethnic assimilation.

For the first generation, on the contrary, intermarriage outside the ethnic group was rare. Many of the immigrants, who were disproportionately male, even returned to the motherland to find a spouse. Marriage within the group provided security and acceptance, outside of it disgrace and ostracism. When the children of orthodox Jews chose a Gentile mate, for example, their parents mourned for their children as though they had died. Roman Catholics were considered to be living in sin when they chose a Protestant spouse and married outside the Catholic church. Many states barred Orientals from marrying Caucasians. When individuals did venture outside their nationality groups, they usually stayed within the same religious group, so that Irish Catholics married English or German Catholics (but rarely Italian Catholics!) and German Jews married East European Jews.

Data on intermarriage are not plentiful, but studies indicate that with assimilation the rates of intermarriage increase. One important study of trends in New Haven, Connecticut, from 1870 to 1940 revealed that 91 percent married within the nationality group in 1870, 65 percent in 1930, and 63 percent in 1940. Thus the investigator found a decreasing tendency to marry within national groups but still a high tendency to marry within religious lines; in effect, national background faded while religion remained important. Eighty percent of the Protestants, 84 percent of the Catholics, and 94 percent of the Jews married within their respective faiths in 1940. The author drew the conclusion that instead of a single melting pot developing in American society, there was a triple melting pot—Protestant, Catholic, and Jewish groups—and intermarriage occurred within the three religious groups. Other scholars confirmed this as the direction of assimilation in America.

More recent data, though, suggest that the triple-melting-pot thesis is out-dated. In Iowa, the only state that kept religious records in the 1950s, over 40 percent of the Jewish marriages were interfaith. A study of Jewish marriages in Washington, D.C., in the 1960s indicated that only 1 percent of the first, 10 percent of the second, and 18 percent of the third generation married Gentiles. Alarmed by the growing rate of outmarriages among Jews, the Council of Jewish Federations and Welfare Funds conducted a national survey of the period 1966–1972. The findings indicated that 31 percent of all Jews who married during that period chose non-Jewish mates. In the middle of the 1980s rabbis estimated that perhaps 20 to 35 percent of Jews in the East, but well over 50 percent of those in parts of the West, were doing so. They accounted for the sectional discrepancy by pointing out that in more traditional and heavily populated areas Jewish roots ran deep, there were greater opportunities to meet others of a similar background, and perhaps family and community pressures existed, while in the western cities many of the Jews were newcomers with fewer ties to tradition or to coreligionists.

Among Catholics in the 1960s about one in three married someone raised as a non-Catholic. The Irish and Germans were more apt to marry outside the nationality and religious group than the French Canadians, the Poles, or the Italians. Only about 40 percent of the Irish and Germans married other Irish or Germans during the 1960s, while the rate for Italians, Poles, and French Canadians was about 60 percent. Among the newest Catholic Americans from Mexico and Puerto Rico, early studies indicate little intermarriage. Data for the 1960s and 1970s, though, show an uptrend in their rates of intermarriage.

Recognizing the fact of increased intermarriage, the Roman Catholic church modified some of its teachings in the mid-1960s. No longer were those who married outside the faith excommunicated. Non-Catholic clergy were also permitted to be present at a ceremony involving an interfaith marriage and to give a blessing after the exchange of vows. In 1973 an Eastern Rite Catholic professor of religious studies and pastor of a Ukrainian Catholic church gave an opinion more sympathetic to the drift of public opinion: "The danger from increasing interfaith marriages is not that Catholics will join some other churches or religions—which would not be bad at all—but that they will become indifferent and estranged from religion in general." He concluded, "Since the tide cannot be stemmed, it is useless to thunder from the pulpit against interfaith marriages. It would be more proficient if books were written and instruction provided so the partners with their children could practice both religions in meaningful, ecumenical understanding."

Among Protestants, despite variations, the trend has also been for increased incidence and acceptance of intermarriage. Among the Scandinavians, for example, the Swedes, like others, originally opposed marriage outside the group but were more apt to do so than the Norwegians. Most of the outmarriages of the Swedes occurred first with other Scandinavians or else with Germans, but those of the fourth generation have chosen partners from a wide assortment of faiths and nationalities.

Questions asked on the 1980 census made it possible to examine trends in intermarriage among nationality groups. After studying the data, one scholar commented, "The melting pot is increasingly the reality for Americans of European descent and particularly for young Americans." He reported that among people of European background only 27 percent were married to persons with the same ancestry. Moreover, younger Americans appeared to be more apt to marry persons of another background. Among Americans of Italian heritage under age 30, for example, he noted that 72 percent of the men and 64 percent of the women married someone with no Italian background. Eight percent of Italians born before 1920 had mixed ancestry, but 70 percent of those born after 1970 were of children of mixed ancestry.

Recent polls indicate that a growing proportion of the American people accepts interfaith marriage. In 1972, for example, a Gallup poll revealed that two-thirds of those asked approved of marriages between Protestants and Catholics; only 13 percent were opposed. The responses were even more favorable among the young and the well educated. Surveys completed after the 1972 poll confirmed the trend as the proportion accepting interfaith marriage increased; in a 1978 Gallup poll 73 percent did so. A strong minority still resisted intermarriage, however. In 1974 Atlanta rabbis organized Jewish Compu-Date, a computer dating service for the city's widely dispersed Jewish singles. One rabbi explained its purpose: "We started Compu-Date . . . to preserve Judaism and our heritage; it is important that Jews meet and marry one another."

Interracial marriages between those of Asian and European ancestries have also become more acceptable and common. Among Japanese Americans, for example, the intermarriage rate has soared. With intermarriage largely prohibited by law as well as custom in their day, the Issei almost always married others of Japanese descent. Among the Nisei the rates of intermarriage rose, and by the late 1960s Japanese Americans were choosing marital partners having other backgrounds about half the time.

Several factors seem to influence the intermarriage rate. Persons who are well educated, mobile, and have good incomes are likely to intermarry. The culture and location of a group can also be important. The French Canadians, who have had a relatively low intermarriage rate, are strongly nationalistic and are somewhat isolated in New England, near Canada; they travel easily back and forth across the Canadian-American border and thereby maintain their sense of identity more than most other groups do. But the most important variable for intermarriage seems to be time; the longer a group remains in the United States, the faster it assimilates. As both the old and new immigrants are now moving beyond the third generation, one can expect to see increasing rates of intermarriage. Of course, not all interfaith marriages are losses to a particular group. Frequently, one partner converts, and the children are raised in that religion. It is too early to say, though, whether the children of these marriages will preserve the culture in which they are being reared.

Ethnic lines were becoming more blurred as the twentieth century progressed. The fall in immigration and the percentage drop in the number of foreign-born in America meant that the second and subsequent generations would have little contact with an Old World culture. The older immigrant institutions that had served the first generation were simply not as important to its descendants. There was of course a constant trickle of immigrants arriving in America to keep some old traditions alive, but ethnicity was of diminishing significance because some immigrants no longer held on to the deeply rooted aspects of Old World culture.

The twentieth-century development of a public school system was certainly another key factor breaking down ethnicity. The immigrants' descendants were being instructed in Anglo-American values. After World War II most Americans attended, and roughly three-quarters graduated from, the nation's high schools. In the post–World War II era colleges and universities rapidly expanded, and by the 1980s nearly half the college-age population could be found in institutions of higher learning. If elementary and high schools were often homogeneous, institutions of higher education were less so and exposed students to diverse ideologies and ethnic strains. Away from the watchful eyes of parents, the youth seemed more willing to learn about different people. No wonder ethnic leaders were concerned about intermarriage on college campuses!

Along with the expansion of education came the development of the mass media in American culture. The printed word was important before World War I in the form of newspapers and journals, but after 1920 came the radio and movies and then, after World War II, television. Of course, many minorities did operate a press and run radio and TV stations, but they could not compete with the dominant corporations. The major networks possessed huge advertising budgets, and national programs beamed identical messages into most American homes. Regardless of ethnic background, children were exposed to this mass culture of national products, common heroes, and similar values. As one professor put it, television "brings the culture of the North American consumer society right into the home."

By and large, the descendants of immigrants have absorbed this common culture. The values of American society propagated by the Puritans—like beliefs in success and individual achievement—have been accepted. National standards in dress and taste have also been observed. Musicians, movie stars, and athletes are almost universally acknowledged heroes and models. Even certain observance of religious holidays are becoming part of the national culture. A study of a Midwestern Jewish community done in the 1950s revealed that many Jewish families sent Christmas cards, exchanged gifts, and set up Christmas trees. We do not mean, of course, that all ethnic differences over values have disappeared and that Americans have become faceless mass men and women. We are suggesting, however, that the differences among peoples of different backgrounds have lessened and that values are often similar, if not homogenized.

The mobility of ethnic groups has also contributed to a loss of ethnicity. Business and professional people, especially the more highly educated, joined organizations having mixed memberships. Upward mobility has also been accompanied by horizontal mobility, with large numbers of the descendants of immigrants moving out of the old neighborhoods and into the growing suburbs. In suburbia, where social divisions commonly follow class and racial lines, it has been more difficult to maintain ethnicity. Common interests over local governmental questions such as education and zoning bring people together in a variety of activities.

One minority, the French Canadians, long known for retention of their culture, illustrates many of the pressures for assimilation. French-Canadian communities in New England since the nineteenth century have been kept vital by a sustained migration and contact with Canada. In recent years that migration has decreased. But as long as French Canadians lived and worked in textile and shoe factories in isolated New England towns, the values of family, church, and local community could be easily maintained. Since 1960, as they have moved from the mills to better-paying jobs in service industries, their attachment to the old culture has lessened. English was a necessity in these new jobs and French strictly a secondary language. As one scholar noted, among French Canadians old values were being replaced by the "increased value which is attributed to work and economic success." Hence since 1960 the use of French has sharply declined among French Canadians in New England. One student recently discovered that about two-thirds of these people over age 15 speak only English. A scholar who found similar results in Lewiston, Maine, a French-Canadian community, said that in 1960 half the conversations in the central business section were in French, but 13 years later only 5 to 10 percent were. French-Canadian culture with its emphasis on Roman Catholicism, the family, and community is not dead in the 1980s; but it has been eroded within the last two decades.

The religious revival that was said to have followed World War II, especially in the suburbs, was in part an attempt to create a bulwark of security in new surroundings. Church suppers and youth programs provided social entry for families until they could put down new roots. But the religious revival was superficial and was played out by the 1960s. More important was the development of new contacts among religious groups. This led to increased toleration, which in turn opened new paths for social mobility and assimilation. Moreover, modern Judaism, Protestantism, and Catholicism have grown together ritually and theologically, thus further reducing differences and conflicts. The modernization movement, especially in American Catholicism, brought changes in practices and beliefs, and a decline in church attendance after 1970. In 1978, with polls revealing that 80 percent of Roman Catholics approved of intermarriages with Protestants, it was not surprising to find that liberal beliefs about controversial matters such as birth control and abortion were shared by Catholics, Protestants, and Jews of the same social and economic background. At the same time, however, Roman Catholics were still prominent in groups opposed to the Equal Rights Amendment and to a woman's right to choose an abortion.

In the late 1960s, just when the European minorities seemed well on the way toward assimilation, ethnicity became chic in American life and politics. Whereas folk customs and costumes used to be an embarrassment to ethnic children, except on festival days, suddenly there were cries for ethnic studies programs on college campuses, proclamations of ethnic heritage days in cities, formation of new ethnic organizations, and political assertions that the melting pot would not and should not work. All these assertions were evidence of a renewed interest in ethnicity. Michael Novak, author of *The Rise of the Unmeltable Ethnics* (1972), national columnist, and editor of several newsletters devoted to ethnic affairs, was a particularly eloquent spokesman for the descendants of southern and eastern European Catholic immigrants; so too was Roman Catholic priest, novelist, and sociologist Andrew Greeley.

Many communities and colleges responded with special events and programs. Czechs in Nebraska got together, and there is now a two-day Czech festival in Wilbur every August. A Sheridan, Wyoming, radio station started airing a weekly two-hour "Polka Party" to honor the Polish heritage of many of its residents; it reputedly became one of the station's most popular shows. A host of people from Wisconsin's "Little Norway" began putting on an annual production of *Song of Norway,* a former Broadway musical based on the works of Edvard Grieg. In 1975 it was done in Norwegian for members of the State Historical Society meeting in Oshkosh. The performers took pride in the fact that they had memorized all the foreign words for the show. In Kearney, New Jersey, which began to attract many Scottish workers in the late nineteenth century, town residents celebrated the Scottish poet Robert Burns's birthday for one week each year.

College campuses around the nation also developed ethnic programs, among them Puerto Rican studies, Jewish studies, Black studies, Basque studies, and Mexican-American studies. At Louisiana State University the foreign language department introduced a new course in the Cajun language. The Louisiana Cajuns, descendants of several thousand Acadians who came to southern Louisiana from Canada in the 1750s, had traditionally maintained their French derivative language and culture by the spoken word; now they have not only a course but also a textbook, first published in 1977.

Not to be outdone by communities and campuses, the politicians, who have usually been aware of ethnic differences only when counting votes, began to take notice. In 1972 the U.S. Congress, as part of the Elementary and Secondary Education Act, established an Ethnic Heritage Program and a National Advisory Council on Ethnic Heritage Studies. Funds were allocated to study and promote the nation's ethnic heritage.

To some degree, politicians responded in this fashion because of the renewed assertiveness of individual ethnics who found the spirit of the times conducive to new crusades. Meir Kahane's Jewish Defense League (1968), although representing only a small minority of Jews, achieved headlines because of its demonstrations. Kahane lashed out at the goal of assimilation and preached a militant brand of Jewish nationalism. Arrested for his activities in the United States, he went to Israel, where his militancy also brought him into confrontation with the law.

The Italians also showed a renewed concern with ethnicity. Joseph Columbo's Italian American Civil Rights League, founded in 1970, attacked alleged insults to Italian Americans and staged marches in New York City. Italian Americans vehemently protested the alleged prejudicial treatment that the media and law enforcement officials displayed. They resented, for example, television programs in which the underworld figure's name always ended with a vowel. They also railed against alleged discrimination by the Federal Bureau of Investigation (FBI), which they claimed unfairly portrayed Italian Americans as criminals. During the summer of 1971, groups of Italian Americans paraded in front of FBI headquarters in New York City chanting

Hi-di-hi
Hi-di-ho
The FBI
Has got to go!

The new manifestations of ethnicity were sharp reminders that Americanization was taking generations to achieve. Old groups like the Amish and new groups like the Hasidic Jews, who chose to remain in secluded enclaves, were at the far end of the spectrum of ethnicity in America. The Amish live as farmers, apart from other Americans. They do not allow carriers of modern culture, such as television or radios, in their houses. And their children drop out of school as soon as state laws permits them to do so.

Unlike the Amish, the Hasidic Jews of New York City, numbering 70,000 or so, are an urban group; they live close to one another in several neighborhoods. There they can control social activities and their children's education. They own their own stores, employing other Hasidic Jews, and sell computers, cameras, and a variety of electric appliances.

At the other end were the older groups that had been thoroughly blended into the Anglo-American culture; in between stood the descendants of the millions who came after 1880. The descendants of the new immigrants had lost much, probably most, of the Old World culture but still had some common bonds of religion, customs, political interest, and family and group life that held them together.

Social scientists are quick to remind us that ethnic voting behavior was and is important in American politics and often transcends class or regional lines. Politicians are clearly aware of ethnic trends in voting and regularly appear at the appropriate parades or events to eat pizza or bagels or chop suey. Orville Freeman, who served as governor of Minnesota and then as Secretary of Agriculture during the Kennedy and Johnson administrations, attributed his defeat for reelection to the governorship in 1960 to the fact that his grandfather had changed the family name from Johnson, a name that strikes a responsive chord among the Scandinavians in Minnesota.

Ethnic politics is usually most intense at the city level, where political parties strive for ethnically balanced tickets. In New York City the three major elective posts—mayor, president of the city council, and comptroller—have usually gone to people of Irish, Italian, and Jewish backgrounds when these votes were most significant. An Irish name is no longer politically significant, and the city's Italians seem to have moved toward the Republican and Conservative parties. Blacks and Puerto Ricans are now the ethnic groups, besides the Jews, to whom New York City Democrats are making appeals. In Buffalo a Polish name is an asset; in Milwaukee a German name is favored; and in parts of the Southwest a Hispanic name attracts votes. In Baltimore Barbara Mikulski, now a United States senator, first came to prominence as a spokeswoman for the Slavs of her city.

The national political parties are also aware of the relationship between ethnic factors and voting. The Democrats had a temporary nationalities division in 1936 and made it permanent in 1948. As blacks, Poles, Italians, and Jews became more important to Democratic success, the party courted the ethnic vote more aggressively. John F. Kennedy brought Cleveland's Mayor Anthony Celebreze into his cabinet as Secretary of Health, Education, and Welfare in 1962, and political pundits surmised that the president did so with one eye on the Italian vote. A year later the Democratic party made its newly named All American Council a more elaborate organization.

The Republican party responded more slowly to the new immigrant minorities, but in 1968 Richard Nixon made an attempt to capture votes from some of the white ethnic groups with promises and appeals to these people and appointments of their members to office. His final choice for a vice-presidential running mate was reputedly between John Volpe, of Italian background, and Spiro Agnew, of Greek ancestry. He chose Agnew, but placed Volpe in his cabinet as Secretary of Transportation. The Republicans also set up a nationalities division under the direction of Laszlo Pasztor, a Hungarian freedom fighter from the 1956 uprising. In 1971 the division, now called the National Republican Heritage Groups (Nationalities) Council, became a permanent part of the Republican party. Its goals before Watergate were "to attract the more than 40 million Americans of ethnic background to all levels of GOP activity; and to formalize the already substantial support among ethnic Americans for President Nixon's domestic and foreign policies."

The largest celebration of ethnicity occurred in the summer of 1986 when the Statue of Liberty was rededicated. Amidst a huge extravaganza in New York City's harbor, the nation heard numerous speeches about the blessings of immigration. Politicians were quick to identify with the nation's immigrant history and join with organizations giving out medals to representatives of America's many ethnic groups.

To understand ethnicity it is important to remember that each ethnic group brought with it a unique life-style. Roles of family members, expectations of spouses and children, and attitudes toward education and religion often determined how quickly and how well various minorities have been absorbed into American society. Members of groups whose economic and educational aspirations were low and who therefore lacked mobility were least likely to be assimilated. Many Slavs, Italians, and Hispanics would be included in this category. Unfortunately, for most people in the immigrant generation the promises of American life remained unfulfilled. Their offspring, though, did have greater opportunities. By the 1960s militant members of the still depressed minorities demanded that the promises of American life become realities—and quickly.

For this and other reasons there was a resurgence of ethnicity in the 1960s. The black civil rights and black nationalist movements emphasized a quest for identity, and some ethnic groups sought to emulate black pressure-group tactics. Mexican Americans, American Indians, and Italians were among the most prominent of the groups that demonstrated for greater opportunities and respect in American society. They did not feel part of WASP America, and they wanted both recognition and celebration of their own backgrounds. The editor of a Polish-American weekly in New Jersey, for example, announced in 1970 the formation of I'm-Proud-to-Be-Polish clubs. Seven years later a Polish-American woman marketed a Polish coloring book. About culture she said, "You have to start with the young. It can't be done later in life."

The ethnic revival movements seemed to have the greatest appeal to those who believed that the intellectuals, the government, and white elite groups (usually of old stock) were giving favors to blacks at their expense. They did not share in the bounties of upper-middle-class America, but they did have respect for the institutions of society and the traditional values of family solidarity, hard work, and patriotism. The inflation that began in the late 1960s aggravated their frustrations with ethnic as well as youthful protest groups of almost every variety, and they vented their anger against the most downtrodden minorities in society, especially the blacks. They wanted politicians to be tough with criminals, demonstrators, and rioters. They were especially concerned about busing their children into different neighborhoods to promote integrated schools. The movement sponsored by Alabama's Governor George Wallace appealed to this resentment, as did Frank Rizzo's law-and-order campaign for mayor of Philadelphia in 1971. Rizzo concentrated his efforts in white working-class neighborhoods. A police officer by occupation, he said that if elected he would not permit riots, marches, and demonstrations. He was elected, and his tenure in office was characterized by conflicts between Rizzo and Philadelphia's black population over affirmative action programs, charges of police brutality, and other racial issues.

Another confrontation occurred in Newark, New Jersey, where a growing black population was pitted against a declining Italian hegemony led by Anthony Imperiale. Italian control of Newark was finally lost when Kenneth Gibson became the city's first black mayor in 1970; voters reelected him in 1974, 1978, and 1982. In the same city, in 1986, popular representative Peter Rodino found himself challenged, unsuccessfully, in the Democratic primary by several blacks who said it was time the district's black majority was represented in Congress by a black.

In the 1970s and 1980s the confrontations were found not only in politics but in the courts as well. Controversies arose not only over busing but also over quotas and affirmative action programs, pitting white ethnic groups against blacks and Hispanics over jobs and coveted places in law and medical schools. The Bakke case in California in the late 1970s was one example. Alan Bakke sued for admission to the University of California's medical school at the Davis campus on the ground that he had been denied admission even though he was more qualified than some blacks who had been admitted. His case, which he eventually won, was supported by some Jewish groups that had traditionally backed the civil rights movement. In 1980 Puerto Ricans and blacks found themselves opposed by Jewish, Italian, and Irish police—both men and women—in a court fight over hiring procedures in the New York City police department.

Not all white ethnic politics and legal fights were manifestations of white backlash. The Calumet Community Congress of Indiana, formed in 1970, tried to bring white ethnic groups and blacks together to deal with common problems. In Detroit, where many blacks and descendants of Poles lived, leaders of both groups organized the Black-Polish Conference in 1968 to work for their common interests. In 1971 the American Jewish Committee formed the National Project on Ethnic America to bridge the gap between whites and blacks. Its director said

> We have a black problem and we have a white reaction to it. You can't solve the one without solving the other. Civil rights gains have been stalemated in many parts of the North and Midwest because the groups who are resisting have been left out. . . . The task is to push whites off a strictly negative anti-black agenda. We have to make them conscious of their own realities. A new breed of ethnic leaders has to be developed who are as visible as the demagogues trying to exploit ethnic fears.

It was not the black movement alone that heightened ethnicity. The question of values after the 1960s also raised issues. Many descendants of the new immigrants had been ardent proponents of American nationalism as professions of their loyalty. They were especially hostile to the Soviet Union and its policies of oppression in eastern Europe. They were perplexed and confused by the war in Vietnam and the divisiveness that it prompted. Appeals to loyalty touched them and their conception of America. And when they came under attack, they were somewhat bitter about the sons and daughters of the affluent. In the confusion of the 1960s they, like so many other Americans, looked for security and a source of identity, and many found it in ethnicity. Ethnic identity was an answer for much of the alienation of the times.

Although ethnic and racial prejudice declined after the 1940s, it has still not been eradicated. It probably never will be. Despite the fact that fewer Americans are victimized by it, prejudice is still with us. Perhaps the outstanding reminder is its strength in the WASP country clubs and social clubs, which are the bastions of corporate and economic power. Although Jews, Japanese, and other minorities find opportunities practically equal elsewhere, they cannot gain access to the private California clubs where significant business transactions occur. The same is true for these establishments in other major cities. Only in the late 1980s did civil rights laws and court decisions begin to challenge the restrictions of private clubs.

The existence of prejudice serves as a reminder that many peoples are simply not accepted by the dominant culture. It also reflects the frustrations of those who are not comfortable with themselves, hence are unwilling or unable to tolerate differences in others. Moreover, one cannot ignore the possibility that no amount of factual data can change the views of ingrained bigots. In the 1970s, for example, a scurrilous doggerel circulated along the East Coast which denigrated an overwhelming majority of New York City's residents. It read

A Quiet Sunday in New York

All the Jews are visiting their relatives on Long Island
All the Irish are sleeping off their hangovers
All the blacks are in jail
All the Italians are at the cemetery placing flowers
All the Puerto Ricans can't start their cars
All the Polish think it's Tuesday.

That such distorted thinking is not restricted to one section or group of peoples can be verified by recent events. In 1979 letters to "Dear Abby," a syndicated columnist in newspapers from coast to coast, ran 200:1 against admitting into this country the Asian boat people, who were adrift at sea. Three correspondents exhibited the vilest character and the most incredible misunderstanding. A West Virginian asked, "Are we going to let overbreeding Asiatics take over our country? We should help them only if they agreed to be sterilized!" A writer from El Paso said, "Let the Chinese go where they can get raw fish, rice, ride bicycles, live 20 in a room and smoke opium!" An Indiana resident expressed the belief that the Vietnamese "are bringing more diseases with them than we have cures for. I think it's a Communist plot to destroy this country!"

These letter writers were especially vicious but not entirely unrepresentative of public opinion. Surveys indicated that most Americans were opposed to taking in refugees from Indochina. When the Cubans began arriving in the spring of 1980, polls again revealed that substantial majorities of the population were opposed to letting them in. In May 1980 the Gallup organization reported that almost 35 percent of those questioned thought the Cubans should be allowed to resettle in this country but that 56 percent opposed the idea.

In 1980, reflecting a conservative and dangerous trend, both Republicans (in Michigan) and Democrats (in California) nominated avowed members of the Ku Klux Klan for seats in Congress. At the same time a right-wing group known as the Moral Majority claimed 60 million American followers. Its program called for the reintroduction of prayers in the public schools, opposition to the Equal Rights Amendment, and denial of women's individual rights to decide on abortion. The Moral Majority also contends that the United States is a *Christian* country that should be run by and for those who possess fundamentalist Christian values.

Individuals and groups like the aforementioned frighten ethnics and immigrants who want the freedom and opportunities that the rhetoric of this nation promises. It also retards assimilation and encourages minorities to remain within their own enclaves where they can be sure of warmth, understanding, and security.

The bigotry and self-righteousness of some Americans also help to explain why a number of ethnic Americans still show great concern over occurrences overseas. They never know whether events in this country might force them to find havens elsewhere. Thus the civil war in Ireland is followed by Irish Americans. American Greeks keep their eye on this country's policies toward Greece and Turkey, and Arabs seem deeply involved with the troubles in the Middle East.

It is sometimes overlooked that the nation's many Arab Americans are deeply concerned about events in the Middle East. Many of them are refugees who fled the constant fighting and violence there. Lebanese especially have tried to keep ties to that ravished land. Arab Americans also believe that other Americans unfairly blame Arabs for all incidents of terrorism in the Middle East. Faris Bouhafa, a director of the American-Arab Anti-Discrimination Committee, told the press in 1986, "It is a time of anti-Arab hysteria. Every time there is a terrorist attack any place in the world, we feel the repercussions in our neighborhoods."

Like other ethnic groups, Arab Americans are sensitive to how they were portrayed in the media and American culture generally. They objected to, among other things, a record album which included a song, "Killing an Arab." Because they are divided into Christians and Moslems and come from different Middle East countries, Arab Americans are sometimes not united in their views. As a result they have not been effective in marshaling public opinion to support their concerns.

Perhaps no group follows foreign affairs with greater interest and concern than do the Jews. The majority have favored a friendly American policy toward Israel ever since that nation was created in 1948. The succession of conflicts between Arabs and Jews in the Middle East, such as the Suez adventure in 1956, the Six-Day War in 1967, and the Yom Kippur War in 1973, drew lavish financial and moral support for Israelis from Jews throughout the world. The emotional tie of American Jews to all other Jews, which is strengthened by the memory of pogroms and of genocide in World War II, cannot be exaggerated. The Jews share a deep conviction that Israel must survive and that all efforts must be made to ensure that survival. In addition to financial and moral support, therefore, American Jews have communicated their views to their political representatives in Washington. One significant foreign policy accomplishment, in fact, which President Jimmy Carter pointed to with pride in 1980, was the Camp David accords in which the Israeli and Egyptian presidents agreed to terms that all three of them hoped would lead to peace in the Middle East.

Attachment to a foreign people or a foreign culture keeps ethnicity alive and seems to blunt the pressures for complete Americanization and assimilation. But what of the future? Will religion remain important or will the nation become increasingly secular? Will national origins be the key issue? Will the new Asian arrivals significantly affect the direction of our country in the twenty-first century? Will the Hispanics add a distinctive Latin flavor to our culture? Will all newcomers follow the paths of the immigrants before them and blend into what is a uniquely American culture?

The forces undermining ethnicity—mass education, social mobility, and an American culture—are strong determinants that no group in the past has been able to withstand indefinitely. For the moment it seems likely that resistance to assimilation may slow the Americanizing process but cannot prevent it.

The agonies contemporary immigrants have to endure during the Americanization process were poignantly discussed in a 1987 article written by Fakhruddin Ahmed, a Rhodes Scholar from Bangladesh living in New York City. The movement into the mainstream of life in the United States, which took previous immigrant groups perhaps two or three generations, has been accelerated by American occupational, educational, and cultural activities. Ahmed pointed out how career opportunities for himself in this country kept his family in America and how the dreams of returning home faded as the years passed. Unlike his own homeland, where the parents decided the course of family action, in America

> The children will decide the issue. They will not like to hear about returning to an impoverished country. To the consternation of the parents, the children, who will not have experienced a second country, will start growing up like American kids. At school they may be subjected to blatant and subtle forms of racism. This they will try to counter by aiming to be superachievers.
>
> Parents will tell the kids they should not forget their heritage, stressing, for example, that they should speak Bengali at home and that if they are born to a Moslem family they should pray five times a day and refrain from eating pork

or sipping alcoholic drinks. To that the children, who will probably understand Bengali but not speak it, may respond: "Spanish would be more relevant to us!"

The coup de grace will usually be delivered by the adolescent daughter wanting to go out on a date. Parents will explain in great detail why it is not allowed in their culture and will insist that she meet, under strict supervision, only with Bangladeshi boys. Sometimes the girl will relent, on condition that it is a Bangladeshi boy born and brought up in the United States. More often, after her 18th birthday, the daughter will politely but firmly inform her parents that according to U.S. law they cannot interfere in her personal life—and that, to avoid further conflict over the boyfriend, she is going to move in with him.

The parents will be devastated. Doubts and questions flood in. The decision to stay begins to haunt them.

Many other immigrant parents have similar experiences today, or have had them in the past, and have wondered whether the opportunities in America were worth sacrificing traditional cultures. The "pull" of American society seems always to be, or to have been, too great a magnet for most of those people born in this country to resist. Fortunately or unfortunately, the goals of today's most vocal minority groups coincide with the demands of a majority of other Americans. Those who favor the retention of an ethnic way of life must ask what they can offer that would retard their children's absorption into the mainstream of American society when opportunities to do so present themselves. It does not appear likely that any older minority culture, except for a small and dedicated group like the Amish, can sustain its own way of life in the United States indefinitely.

Afterthoughts

Historically, as British colonies and then as the United States, this land has always been a haven for refugees and a beacon for those seeking a new life. Germans tired of the Thirty Years' War and Huguenots forced to flee France in order to retain their Protestant faith were among the first in a long tradition of non-British immigrants who sought a haven in this country. The German '48ers, political opponents of oppressive governments in 1848 who have received much more attention in our history books than their small numbers may seem to warrant, are among the best known of the nineteenth-century refugees who settled in the United States. And during the past four decades Europeans, Latin Americans, and Asians who fled communist countries like Hungary, Cuba, and Vietnam have similarly been welcomed. It is impossible to predict where turmoil may occur in the future, but there is no doubt that our refugee policy will be expanded to aid some of those in distress. For despite outbursts of biogtry and restrictiveness American policy even in the most economically depressed years has always encouraged some foreigners to join with us. In 1985 more than 570,000 legal immigrants and refugees arrived. Whether Congress eventually raises or lowers the annual quota, it is certain that the legislators will not abolish it.

Which groups will be added to the American mix is not always easy to predict. During colonial times only Germans and Africans came in any sizable numbers from outside the British Isles. In the nineteenth century Germans and Irish predominated, while early in this century Italians, East European Jews, and

Slavs topped the statistics. Before and after World War II eastern European victims of nazi and communist tyranny arrived in droves. Thereafter Hungarians, Cubans, Indochinese, and others fleeing communism captured newspaper headlines. On May 5, 1987, in accordance with the 1986 Immigration Control and Reform Act, the INS began processing applications for immigrant status from people who had arrived, and who had remained, in this country without appropriate documents for the past five years. No one yet knows what mix of new ethnic Americans that opportunity will produce although most observers assume that the majority will be Spanish-speaking.

During the twentieth century, and especially since the end of World War II, Hispanic newcomers increased their numbers in this country. In fact, since 1968 over one third the combined total of legal and illegal immigrants to the United States spoke Spanish. Mexicans in the Southwest, South and Central Americans on the East Coast, and American citizens from Puerto Rico have sought greater opportunities in the mainland economy. This growth of Hispanics in the United States is likely to continue, and so will their influence. Mexico's population is increasing too quickly to sustain itself; and neither political nor economic conditions throughout Latin America warrants confidence in the ability of those nations to sustain their citizenry. Mismanagement, inefficiency, and too small a staff in the Immigration and Naturalization Service and the Border Patrol made it possible for millions of undocumented aliens to cross. In passing the Immigration Reform and Control Act of 1986, Congress meant to cut this flow of undocumented immigrants. How well the law is enforced remains to be seen.

Latin America is not the only place in the world that is growing too quickly to absorb increased population. It is likely, therefore, that more Indians and other Asians, Middle Easterners, and Africans will turn toward the United States as a place to improve the quality of their own lives. Advances in international communication have lessened the psychological distance between the Third World and developed western societies. So have television and movies. And modern high-speed transportation has lessened the physical distances. The influence of television alone in bringing news of America to the rest of the world is staggering. Today most immigrant-sending countries, no matter how poor, have populations exposed to television; and much of what they see is produced in the United States. In 1979 an American government report noted that programs originating in the United States accounted for 25 percent of the television presentations in Colombia and the Dominican Republic and 33 percent in Mexico and Latin America as a whole. U.S. presentations amounted to 95 percent of all imported programs in Korea. In 1986 a British broadcaster in Hong Kong told his viewers about how Americans were replacing the English in that British colony. Noting that 60 percent of Hong Kong's English-language television programs were produced in the United States, he remarked, "A good topic for starting conversation at boring parties is the dreadful state of television in Hong Kong, and particularly how Americanized it's getting. . . . It is still a British colony, isn't it?"

The Americanization of world culture reaches Third World peoples in forms other than television. American troops stationed overseas in places like Korea and the Philippines bring people in those lands news about America. In the British colony of Hong Kong in early 1987 American civilians outnumbered those from Great Britain 16,400 to 14,800 and the signs of American commercialization were everywhere. The colony reported 28 McDonald's restaurants, 3 Kentucky Fried Chicken stores, 6 Pizza Huts, and 168 7/Elevens.

Added to the knowledge of American society, the improved transportation, and the pressures for emigration is the perception of the United States as a land friendly to immigrants. True, Americans have often been hostile to newcomers and since the 1920s have pursued a somewhat restrictive policy. But the nation has become more generous in recent years, and it has a long history of welcoming foreigners.

Today the United States still receives more permanent immigrants than any other nation in the world, as well as the largest number of refugees. During the crisis of the Indochinese boat people this country received hundreds of thousands of refugees, but prosperous Japan took only a few hundred. Speaking of the boat people, one Japanese Foreign Ministry spokesman said, "We really cannot do much more. Our territory is just too small and our customs so different from those of the Vietnamese." Similarly, in the 1980 German election campaign, Chancellor Helmut Schmidt urged his fellow Germans to be generous to the temporary foreign workers and immigrants in Germany and to accept more refugees. But in the next breath he said Germany had enough immigrants and told a cheering audience, "We're not a job placement agency for the entire world." He reminded his listeners, "It's not easy for Germans who live in an apartment house and who don't like the smell of garlic to have to put up with it and even to have a lamb slaughtered in the hall."

Schmidt's statement was not an isolated one. Throughout western Europe in the 1980s governments and political groups expressed opposition to foreigners, and the French, Dutch, Belgian, Swiss, and British joined the West Germans in tightening their laws to limit the number of foreign temporary workers, immigrants, and those seeking asylum, especially from the Third World.

Since the end of World War II the United States has seen a growth in racial, religious, and ethnic tolerance. As a result, Congress has changed the restrictive legislation of the 1920s and made it possible for immigration to the United States to increase substantially. About 4 million people arrived during the 1970s and by the end of the 1980s another 5 to 6 million will have entered. Even allowing for the fact that maybe a quarter of these newcomers later will return to their homelands, immigration has grown considerably compared to the restrictionist days of the 1930s and World War II.

While Americans have become more tolerant, increased numbers of immigrants during the 1970s and 1980s have prompted anxiety. This uneasiness often centered on undocumented aliens, and in 1986 Congress finally passed a law to deal with the situation. Quarrels over bilingualism have led to the growth of U.S. English and an attempt to make English the official language in various states and cities. In the fall of 1986 the voters of California approved a proposition to make English the official language of their state. While perhaps innocent on the surface, the movement for an official language surely is a veiled attack on Hispanics, not too different from arguments directed at Germans and others decades ago.

In addition, the 1980s have seen a rise in hostility toward Asians. Indochinese refugees seem to be the main target of this anger, but it also has been aimed at other Asians as well, including those who are prosperous and successful in business. This "bashing," as the *Wall Street Journal* called it, of Asians has been ugly and has led to several fatalities.

The pressures for emigration from other countries to the United States will be strong in the near future, so Americans must decide what kind of immigration laws the nation wants. Few call for totally open borders and few for shutting them down completely. Any policy is selective and involves moral as well as economic and social considerations. Should immigration be geared to economic conditions in this country? Should it be slanted to uniting families? How many refugees is the country willing to accept? And once the number has been decided, which people will get in? The prevailing attitude toward newcomers is clearly politically motivated and unfair to those who are fleeing reactionary governments that the United States supports. Once choices have been made, how are immigrants to be helped at all? Currently, for example, refugees get financial aid from the federal government, while other immigrants do not.

That these problems arise is perhaps inevitable in this nation of immigrants. If it is not easy to resolve the tensions, we would do well to remember that such diversity is surely one of the major strengths of the American people and their history. And if the resolution of differences is problematic, one can also reflect on the past, for the easing of ethnic conflict has always been fraught with complications. We can only hope that the nation will maintain a liberal immigration policy and continue developing a democratic but pluralistic society, thus maintaining one of its richest traditions.

Bibliographic Essay

The first point of departure for those interested in reading further should be Stephan Thernstrom, ed., *Harvard Encyclopedia of American Ethnic Groups* (Cambridge, Mass.: Harvard University Press, 1980). It is at once scholarly and informative, and it covers every ethnic group from Acadians to Zoroastrians. It has maps, charts, statistics, and topical coverage as well. Moreover, many of the state and local historical journals, especially those in the Midwest and West, have had numerous articles on the ethnic heritage of the people within their states. The *Utah Historical Quarterly* is among the best.

There are several texts on ethnics. Thomas Archdeacon's *Becoming American* * (New York: The Free Press, 1983) is the most comprehensive and is particularly sympathetic to the experiences of the Irish Catholics. Maldwyn Allen Jones, *American Immigration* (Chicago: University of Chicago Press, 1960), is good through the nineteenth century. Maxine Seller, *To Seek America* * (Englewood Cliffs, N.J.: Jerome S. Ozer, 1977) is broader in scope and extremely sympathetic in its treatment of minorities. An older and somewhat biased factual account that pays too little attention to Asian and Latin-American immigrants is Carl Wittke, *We Who Built America,* 2d ed. (Cleveland: Press of Western Reserve University, 1964). Especially good for the European background is Philip Taylor, *The Distant Magnet* * (New York: Harper & Row, 1971). Oscar Handlin's

*Asterisks indicate titles available in paperback.

composite saga, *The Uprooted,** 2d ed. (Boston: Little, Brown, 1973), is controversial, interpretive, and beautifully written. Jay Dolan's *The American Catholic Experience* (Garden City, N.Y.: Doubleday and Co., 1985) gives broad insights into the lives of a variety of people, especially the Irish. A recent work on immigrants in urban America is John Bodnar, *The Transplanted: A History of Immigrants in Urban America** (Bloomington, Ind.: University of Indiana Press, 1985).

The literature on various immigrant and ethnic groups is enormous, but of uneven quality. Some peoples have been the object of excellent scholarship; others have been neglected. The beginning reader might start with Bernard Bailyn's *Voyagers to the West* (New York: Knopf, 1986), then use some of the following studies, most of which include bibliographic suggestions for those interested in penetrating the subject still further. James G. Leyburn, *The Scotch-Irish: A Social History* (Chapel Hill: University of North Carolina Press, 1962), and Ned C. Landsman, *Scotland and Its First American Colony, 1683–1765* (Princeton, N.J.: Princeton University Press, 1985), a work about New Jersey, are model monographs. John A. Hawgood, *The Tragedy of German America* (New York: Putnam, 1940); Kathleen Neils Conzen, *Immigrant Milwaukee, 1836–1860: Accommodation and Community in a Frontier City* (Cambridge, Mass.: Harvard University Press, 1976); and Frederick C. Luebke, *Bonds of Loyalty: German Americans and World War I** (De Kalb: Northern Illinois University Press, 1974), are all excellent treatments of the Germans. Arthur Henry Hirsch, *The Huguenots of Colonial South Carolina* (Durham, N.C.: Duke University Press, 1928), is one of the earliest studies on the group; Jon Butler's *The Huguenots in America* (Cambridge, Mass.: Harvard University Press, 1983), is the best.

Since the publication of the second edition of this book, two outstanding works on the Irish in America have appeared. Both must be looked at for insights into the group: Kerby A. Miller, *Emigrants and Exiles: Ireland and the Irish Exodus to North America* (New York: Oxford University Press, 1985), and Hasia Diner, *Erin's Daughters in America** (Baltimore: Johns Hopkins University Press, 1983). Oscar Handlin, *Boston's Immigrants,* revised and enlarged ed. (New York: Atheneum, 1968), is an outstanding chronicle of the Irish in Boston. Theodore Blegen, *Norwegian Migration to America* (Northfield, Minn.: Norwegian American Historical Association, 1940), and Jon Gjerde, *From Peasants to Farmers: The Migration from Balestrand, Norway to the Upper Middle West* (Cambridge, England: Cambridge University Press, 1985), are both first-rate analyses. Gunther Barth, *Bitter Strength: A History of the Chinese in the United States, 1850–1870* (Cambridge, Mass.: Harvard University Press, 1964), and Stanford M. Lyman, *Chinese Americans** (New York: Random House, 1974), treat the experiences of the Chinese in this country. Jack Chen's *The Chinese of America: From the Beginnings to the Present** (New York: Harper & Row, 1981) is quite readable as is Shin-Shan Henry Tsai, *The Chinese Experience in America**

(Bloomington, Ind.: Indiana University Press, 1986). On the Japanese, Roger Daniels, *The Politics of Prejudice** (New York: Atheneum, 1968), and John Modell, *The Economics and Politics of Racial Accommodation: The Japanese of Los Angeles, 1900–1942* (Urbana: University of Illinois Press, 1977), are both worthwhile.

Italians have benefited within the past generation from renewed historical interest. Alexander DeConde, *Half Bitter, Half Sweet* (New York: Scribners, 1971); Richard Gambino, *Blood of my Blood** (New York: Doubleday, 1974); and John W. Briggs, *An Italian Passage: Immigrants to Three American Cities, 1890–1930* (New Haven, Conn.: Yale University Press, 1978), are readable and insightful surveys. Three more specialized monographs include Donna R. Gabaccia, *From Italy to Elizabeth Street* (Albany: State University of New York Press, 1983), Deanna Paoli Gumina, *The Italians of San Francisco, 1850–1930* (New York: Center for Migration Studies, 1978), and Dino Cinel, *From Italy to San Francisco* (Stanford, Calif.: Stanford University Press, 1982). Virginia Yans-McLaughlin, *Family and Community: Italian Immigrants in Buffalo, 1880–1930** (Ithaca, N.Y.: Cornell University Press, 1977), pays particular attention to the experience of women and children. Josef J. Barton, *Peasants and Strangers: Italians, Rumanians, and Slovaks in an American City, 1890–1950* (Cambridge, Mass.: Harvard University Press, 1974), and John Bodnar, *Immigration and Industrialization: Ethnicity in an American Mill Town, 1870–1940* (Pittsburgh: University of Pittsburgh Press, 1977), are both first rate.

There is no satisfactory overall chronicle of the Jews in the United States, but Nathan Glazer, *American Judaism** (Chicago: University of Chicago Press, 1972), is the best. Moses Rischin, *The Promised City: New York's Jews, 1870–1914** (New York: Harper & Row [Torchbooks], 1970), and Arthur S. Goren, *New York Jews and the Quest for Community: The Kehillah Experiment, 1908–1922** (New York: Columbia University Press, 1970), are outstanding monographs. Thomas Kessner, *The Golden Door: Italian and Jewish Immigrant Mobility in New York City, 1880–1915** (New York: Oxford University Press, 1977), uses both quantitative and traditional methods for comparing the mobility of the two groups. Deborah Dash Moore's *At Home in America** (New York: Columbia University Press, 1981) covers the experience of second-generation Jews in New York between the two world wars, while Charles Silberman's *A Certain People** (New York: Summit Books, 1985) points out how much contemporary Jews have accomplished. Leonard Dinnerstein's collection of his own essays, *Uneasy at Home: Antisemitism and the American Jewish Experience* (New York: Columbia University Press, 1987), dwells on some of the more difficult aspects of Jewish life in the United States.

Theodore Saloutos, *The Greeks in the United States* (Cambridge, Mass.: Harvard University Press, 1964), and Charles C. Moskos, Jr., *Greek Americans:*

Struggles and Success* (Englewood Cliffs, N.J.: Prentice-Hall, 1980), are on a par with the best of the books cited, and so, too, is John J. Bukowczyk's *And My Children Did Not Know Me: A History of Polish Americans* (Bloomington: University of Indiana Press, 1987). Jacques Ducharme, *The Shadows of the Trees: The Story of French-Canadians in New England* (New York: Harper & Row, 1943), is the best treatment we have on the French Canadians; new studies are needed. Many aspects of the history of the Swedes, Danes, and Armenians are still awaiting their chroniclers.

The East Central European Slavs have found a brilliant historian to analyze their culture and experiences both in Europe and America—Ewa Morawska. Her study of Johnstown, Pennsylvania's Slavic peoples, *For Bread with Butter* (Cambridge, England: Cambridge University Press, 1985), is much broader in its insights than the subject might suggest and certainly ranks with Oscar Handlin's *Boston's Immigrants* as one of the best works ever written about American ethnic groups.

The easiest introduction to Mexican-American history is through two quite readable surveys: Carey McWilliams, *North From Mexico** (New York: Greenwood Press, 1968), and Matt S. Meier and Feliciano Rivera, *The Chicanos** (New York: Hill and Wang, 1972). Monographs like Mark Reisler, *By the Sweat of their Brow: Mexican Immigrant Labor in the United States, 1900–1940** (Westport, Conn.: Greenwood Press, 1976); Abraham Hoffman, *Unwanted Mexican Americans in the Great Depression: Repatriation Pressures, 1929–1939* (Tucson: University of Arizona Press, 1974); Albert Camarillo, *Chicanos in a Changing Society: From Mexican Pueblos to American Barrios in Santa Barbara and Southern California, 1848–1930** (Cambridge, Mass.: Harvard University Press, 1979); and Juan Ramon Garcia, *Operation Wetback* (Westport, Conn.: Greenwood Press, 1980), are excellent. Thomas Muller and Thomas J. Espenshade, *The Fourth Wave: California's Newest Immigrants** (Washington, D.C.: The Urban Institute, 1985), and Silvia Pedraza-Bailey, *Political and Economic Migrants in America* (Austin: University of Texas Press, 1985), are the most recent discussions of Mexicans and Cubans in the United States. Virginia R. Dominguez, *From Neighbor to Stranger: The Dilemma of Caribbean Peoples in the United States* (New Haven, Conn.: Antilles Research Program, Yale University Press, 1975), also has some good insights on the Cubans.

The most recent treatment of other groups include William A. Douglass and Jon Bilbao, *Amerikanuak: The Basques in the New World* (Reno: University of Nevada Press, 1975); Michael Laguerre, *American Odyssey: Haitians in New York City** (Ithaca, N.Y.: Cornell University Press, 1984); Alixa Naff, *Becoming American: The Early Arab Immigrant Experience* (Carbondale: Southern Illinois University Press, 1985); Illsoo Kim, *New Urban Immigrants: The Korean Community in New York City* (Princeton, N.J.: Princeton University Press, 1981);

Virginia Sanchez Korrol, *From Colonia to Community: The History of Puerto Ricans in New York City, 1917–1948* (Westport, Conn.: Greenwood Press, 1983); and Parmatma Saran, *The Asian Indian Experience in the United States* (Cambridge, Mass.: Schenkman Books Inc. Publishing Co., 1985).

For nativism and immigration restriction, the standard work is John Hingham, *Strangers in the Land: Patterns of American Nativism 1860–1925* * (New York: Atheneum, 1963). For the early anti-immigrant crusade the reader should consult Ray Billington, *The Protestant Crusade, 1800–1860* * (Chicago: Quadrangle Press, 1964). An excellent account dealing with bigotry generally but also immigration restriction is Seymour Martin Lipset and Earl Raab, *The Politics of Unreason: Right-Wing Extremism in American 1790–1970* * (New York: Harper & Row, 1970). Barbara Solomon, *Ancestors and Immigrants* * (New York: Wiley, 1965), is a probing study of the Immigration Restriction League. An older but still useful work about the immigration acts is Roy Garis, *Immigration Restriction* (New York: Macmillan, 1928). More up to date are Marion T. Bennett, *American Immigration Policies: A History* (Washington, D.C.: Public Affairs Press, 1962) and Edward P. Hutchinson, *Legislative History of American Immigration Policy, 1798–1965* (Philadelphia: University of Pennsylvania Press, 1981). Robert Divine, *American Immigration Policy, 1924–1952* (New Haven, Conn.: Yale University Press, 1957), is a good summary, but his analysis of the displaced persons act is contradicted by Leonard Dinnerstein, *America and the Survivors of the Holocaust: The Evolution of a United States Displaced Persons Policy 1945–1950* * (New York: Columbia University Press, 1982). Post–World War II immigration to the United States is dealt with in considerable detail in David M. Reimers, *Still the Golden Door: The Third World Comes to America* * (New York: Columbia University Press, 1985). Post–World War II refugee policy is discussed in Gil Loescher and John A. Scanlan, *Calculated Kindness: Refugees and America's Half-Open Door, 1945–Present* (New York: The Free Press, 1986).

A great deal about ethnic mobility can be found in the works on various groups already noted. In addition, Niles Carpenter, *Immigrants and their Children 1920* (Washington, D.C.: Government Printing Office, 1927), and Edward Hutchinson, *Immigrants and their Children 1850–1950* (New York: Wiley, 1956), both based on census data, are informative.

These collections of essays give a good deal of insight into ethnic families and their values: *Ethnic Families in America,* * edited by Charles H. Mindel and Robert W. Haberstein (New York: Elsevier, 1976), and *Ethnic Chicago,* * edited by Peter d'A. Jones and Melvin C. Holli (Grand Rapids, Mich.: Erdmans, 1981). Two books by Stephan Thernstrom are useful: *The Other Bostonians: Poverty and Progress in the American Metropolis 1880–1970* * (Cambridge, Mass.: Harvard University Press, 1973) and *Poverty and Progress: Social Mobility in a 19th-Century American City* * (Cambridge, Mass.: Harvard University Press, 1964).

Two penetrating analyses by Francis A. J. Ianni are *A Family Business: Kinship and Social Control in Organized Crime* * (New York: Russell Sage Foundation, 1972) and *Black Mafia: Ethnic Succession in Organized Crime* (New York: Simon & Schuster, 1974). Insight into labor and ethnicity may also be garnered from Vernon J. Briggs, Jr., *Immigration Policy and the American Labor Force* (Baltimore: Johns Hopkins University Press, 1984), and Alice Kessler-Harris, *Out of Work: A History of Wage-Earning Women in the United States* * (New York: Oxford University Press, 1982).

On the subject of assimilation, Milton Gordon, *Assimilation in American Life: The Role of Race, Religion, and National Origins* * (New York: Oxford University Press, 1964), is a good beginning. Although Gordon's conclusions are open to criticism, his work is basic. Andrew Greeley, *Why Can't They Be Like Us?* * (New York: Dutton, 1972), is lively and worth reading, as is Nathan Glazer and Daniel Moynihan, *Beyond the Melting Pot: The Negroes, Puerto Ricans, Jews, Italians, and Irish of New York City,* * 2d ed. (Cambridge, Mass.: Harvard University Press, 1970). Judith R. Kramer, *The American Minority Community* (New York: Crowell, 1970), is less stimulating but rewarding. A profitable study on white Protestants is Charles Anderson, *White Protestant Americans: From National Origins to Religious Group* * (Englewood Cliffs, N.J.: Prentice-Hall, 1970). Yonathan Shapiro, *Leadership of the American Zionist Organization, 1897–1930* (Urbana: University of Illinois Press, 1971), is about the Jews; Harold J. Abramson, *Ethnic Diversity in Catholic America* (New York: Wiley, 1973), is about the Catholics. Perry Wood, *The White Ethnic Movement and Ethnics Politics* (New York: Praeger, 1973), is good on the ethnic revival movements of the early 1970s. A provocative but not totally convincing argument against assimilation is presented by Michael Novak in *The Rise of the Unmeltable Ethnics* * (New York: Macmillan, 1972).

Appendix

TABLE A.1 IMMIGRATION TO THE UNITED STATES BY COUNTRY For Decades 1820–1984

Country	1820	1821–1830	1831–1840	1841–1850	1851–1860	1861–1870	1871–1880
All countries	8,385	143,439	599,125	1,713,251	2,598,214	2,314,824	2,812,191
Europe	7,690	98,797	495,681	1,597,442	2,452,577	2,065,141	2,271,925
Austria–Hungary[a,b]	—	—	—	—	—	7,800	72,969
Belgium	1	27	22	5,074	4,738	6,734	7,221
Denmark	20	169	1,063	539	3,749	17,094	31,771
France	371	8,497	45,575	77,262	76,358	35,986	72,206
Germany[a,b]	968	6,761	152,454	434,626	951,667	787,468	718,182
Greece	20	20	49	16	31	72	210
Ireland[c]	3,614	50,724	207,381	780,719	914,119	435,778	436,871
Italy	30	409	2,253	1,870	9,231	11,725	55,759
Netherlands	49	1,078	1,412	8,251	10,789	9,102	16,541
Norway–Sweden[d]	3	91	1,201	13,903	20,931	109,298	211,245
Norway[d]	NA	NA	NA	NA	NA	71,631	95,323
Sweden[d]	NA	NA	NA	NA	NA	37,667	115,922
Poland[b]	5	16	369	105	1,164	2,027	12,970
Portugal	35	145	829	550	1,055	2,658	14,082
Rumania[e]	—	—	—	—	—	—	11
Spain	139	2,477	2,125	2,209	9,298	6,697	5,266
Switzerland	31	3,226	4,821	4,644	25,011	23,286	28,293
U.S.S.R.[b,f]	14	75	277	551	457	2,512	39,284
United Kingdom[c]	2,410	25,079	75,810	267,044	423,974	606,896	548,043
England	1,782	14,055	7,611	32,092	247,125	222,277	437,706
Scotland	268	2,912	2,667	3,712	38,331	38,769	87,564
Wales	—	170	185	1,261	6,319	4,313	6,631
Northern Ireland[c]	NA	NA	NA	NA	NA	NA	NA
Not specified[c]	360	7,942	65,347	229,979	132,199	341,537	16,142
Other Europe[c]	—	3	40	79	5	8	1,001
Asia	6	30	55	141	41,538	64,759	124,180
China	1	2	8	35	41,397	64,301	123,201
India	1	8	39	36	43	69	163

TABLE A.1 (*Continued*)

Country	1820	1821–1830	1831–1840	1841–1850	1851–1860	1861–1870	1871–1880
Japan[g]	—	—	—	—	—	186	149
Turkey	1	20	7	59	83	131	404
Other Asia[f]	3	—	1	11	15	72	243
America	387	11,564	33,424	62,469	74,720	166,607	404,044
Canada & Newfoundland[h]	209	2,277	13,624	41,723	59,309	153,878	383,640
Mexico[i]	1	4,817	6,599	3,271	3,078	2,191	5,162
Caribbean	164	3,834	12,301	13,528	10,660	9,046	13,957
Central America	2	105	44	368	449	95	157
South America	11	531	856	3,579	1,224	1,397	1,128
Africa	1	16	54	55	210	312	358
Australia & New Zealand	—	—	—	—	—	36	9,886
Pacific Islands (U.S. adm.)	—	—	—	—	—	—	1,028
Not specified	301	33,032	69,911	53,144	29,169	17,969	790

TABLE A.1 (*Continued*)

Country	1881–1890	1891–1900	1901–1910	1911–1920	1921–1930	1931–1940	1941–1950
All countries	5,246,613	3,687,564	8,795,386	5,735,811	4,107,209	528,431	1,035,039
Europe	4,735,484	3,555,352	8,056,040	4,321,887	2,463,194	347,552	621,124
Albania[j]	—	—	—	—	—	2,040	85
Austria–Hungary[a,b]	353,719	592,707	2,145,266	896,342	63,548	11,424	28,329
Austria[a,b]	NA	NA	NA	453,649	32,868	3,563	24,860
Hungary[a,b]	NA	NA	NA	442,693	30,680	7,861	3,469
Belgium	20,177	18,167	41,635	33,746	15,846	4,817	12,189
Bulgaria[k]	—	160	39,280	22,533	2,945	938	375
Czechoslovakia[j]	—	—	—	3,426	102,194	14,393	8,347
Denmark	88,132	50,231	65,285	41,983	32,430	2,559	5,393
Estonia[j]	—	—	—	—	—	506	212
Finland[j]	—	—	—	756	16,691	2,146	2,503
France	50,464	30,770	73,379	61,897	49,610	12,623	38,809
Germany[a,b]	1,452,970	505,152	341,498	143,945	412,202	114,058	226,578
Greece	2,308	15,979	167,519	184,201	51,084	9,119	8,973
Ireland[c]	655,482	388,416	339,065	146,181	210,024	10,973	19,789
Italy	307,309	651,893	2,045,877	1,109,524	455,315	68,028	57,661
Latvia[j]	—	—	—	—	—	1,192	361
Lithuania[j]	—	—	—	—	—	2,201	683
Luxembourg[l]	—	—	—	—	—	565	820
Netherlands	53,701	26,758	48,262	43,718	26,948	7,150	14,860
Norway–Sweden[d]	568,362	321,281	440,039	161,469	165,780	8,700	20,765
Norway[d]	176,586	95,015	190,505	66,395	68,531	4,740	10,100
Sweden[d]	391,776	226,266	249,534	95,074	97,249	3,960	10,665
Poland[b]	51,806	96,720	—	4,813	227,734	17,026	7,571
Portugal	16,978	27,508	69,149	89,732	29,994	3,329	7,423
Rumania[e]	6,348	12,750	53,008	13,311	67,646	3,871	1,076
Spain	4,419	8,731	27,935	68,611	28,958	3,258	2,898
Switzerland	81,988	31,179	34,922	23,091	29,676	5,512	10,547
U.S.S.R.[b,f]	213,282	505,290	1,597,306	921,201	61,742	1,356	548
United Kingdom[c]	807,357	271,538	525,950	341,408	340,780	31,572	139,306
England	644,680	216,726	388,017	249,944	157,420	21,756	112,252

TABLE A.1 (*Continued*)

Country	1881–1890	1891–1900	1901–1910	1911–1920	1921–1930	1931–1940	1941–1950
Scotland	149,869	44,188	120,469	78,357	159,781	6,887	16,131
Wales	12,640	10,557	17,464	13,107	13,012	735	3,209
Northern Ireland[c]	NA	NA	NA	NA	10,567	2,194	7,714
Not specified[c]	168	67	NA	—	—	—	—
Yugoslavia[k]	—	—	—	1,888	49,064	5,835	1,576
Other Europe[c]	682	122	665	8,111	22,983	2,361	3,447
Asia	69,942	74,862	323,543	247,236	112,059	16,081	32,360
China	61,711	14,799	20,605	21,278	29,907	4,928	16,709
India	269	68	4,713	2,082	1,886	496	1,761
Japan[g]	2,270	25,942	129,797	83,837	33,462	1,948	1,555
Turkey	3,782	30,425	157,369	134,066	33,824	1,065	798
Other Asia[f]	1,910	3,628	11,059	5,973	12,980	7,644	11,537
America	426,967	38,972	361,888	1,143,671	1,516,716	160,037	354,804
Canada & Newfoundland[h]	393,304	3,311	179,226	742,185	924,515	108,527	171,718
Mexico[i]	1,913	971	49,642	219,004	459,287	22,319	60,589
Caribbean	29,042	33,066	107,548	123,424	74,899	15,502	49,725
Central America	404	549	8,192	17,159	15,769	5,861	21,665
South America	2,304	1,075	17,280	41,899	42,215	7,803	21,831
Other America[m]	—	—	—	—	31	25	29,276
Africa	857	350	7,368	8,443	6,286	1,750	7,367
Australia & New Zealand	7,017	2,740	11,975	12,348	8,299	2,231	13,805
Pacific Islands (U.S. adm.)	5,557	1,225	1,049	1,079	427	780	5,437
Not specified[m]	789	14,063	33,523	1,147	228	—	142

TABLE A.1 (*Continued*)

Country	1951–1960	1961–1970	1971–1980	1981	1982	1983	1984	Total 165 Years 1820–1984
All countries	2,515,479	3,321,677	4,493,314	596,600	594,131	559,763	543,903	51,950,349
Europe	1,325,727	1,123,492	800,368	66,695	69,174	58,867	69,879	36,604,088
Albania[j]	59	98	329	11	23	22	19	2,686
Austria–Hungary[a][b]	103,743	26,022	16,028	948	981	1,065	2,846	4,323,737
Austria[a][b]	67,106	20,621	9,478	367	339	433	2,351	NA
Hungary[a][b]	36,637	5,401	6,550	581	642	632	495	NA
Belgium	18,575	9,192	5,329	467	559	538	787	205,841
Bulgaria[k]	104	619	1,188	124	207	201	121	68,795
Czechoslovakia[j]	918	3,273	6,023	793	960	946	693	141,966
Denmark	10,984	9,201	4,439	506	463	513	512	367,036
Estonia[j]	185	163	91	22	17	16	2	1,214
Finland[j]	4,925	4,192	2,868	317	346	311	214	35,269
France	51,121	45,237	25,069	1,745	1,994	2,061	3,335	764,369
Germany[a][b]	477,765	190,796	74,414	6,552	6,726	7,185	9,375	7,021,342
Greece	47,608	85,969	92,369	4,361	3,472	2,997	3,311	679,668
Ireland[f]	48,362	32,966	11,490	902	949	1,101	1,096	4,696,002
Italy	185,491	214,111	129,368	4,662	3,644	3,225	6,328	5,323,713
Latvia[j]	352	510	207	39	45	31	5	2,742
Lithuania[j]	242	562	248	44	50	41	16	4,087
Luxembourg[l]	684	556	307	18	26	29	20	3,025
Netherlands	52,277	30,606	10,492	999	1,053	1,152	1,313	366,511
Norway–Sweden[c]	44,632	32,600	10,472	1,163	1,216	1,279	1,455	2,135,885
Norway[c]	22,935	15,484	3,941	331	342	409	403	NA
Sweden[c]	21,697	17,116	6,531	832	874	870	1,052	NA
Poland[b]	9,985	53,539	37,234	5,014	5,874	6,427	7,229	547,628
Portugal	19,588	76,065	101,710	7,049	3,510	3,231	3,800	478,420
Rumania[d]	1,039	2,531	12,393	1,974	3,124	2,543	2,956	184,581
Spain	7,894	44,659	39,141	1,711	1,586	1,507	2,168	271,687
Switzerland	17,675	18,453	8,235	601	626	680	795	353,292
U.S.S.R.[b][e]	671	2,465	38,961	9,223	15,462	5,214	3,349	3,419,240

TABLE A.1 (*Continued*)

Country	1951–1960	1961–1970	1971–1980	1981	1982	1983	1984	Total 165 Years 1820–1984
United Kingdom^f	204,468	214,518	137,374	14,997	14,539	14,830	16,516	5,024,409
England^f	156,171	174,452	NA	NA	NA	NA	NA	NA
Scotland	32,854	29,849	NA	NA	NA	NA	NA	NA
Wales	2,589	2,052	NA	NA	NA	NA	NA	NA
Northern Ireland^f	8,970	7,469	NA	NA	NA	NA	NA	NA
Not specified^f	3,884	696	NA	NA	NA	NA	NA	NA
Yugoslavia^k	8,225	20,381	30,540	2,048	1,418	1,382	1,404	123,761
Other Europe^f	8,155	4,208	4,049	405	304	340	214	57,182
Asia	153,249	427,642	1,588,178	264,343	313,291	277,701	247,775	4,378,951
Cambodia^r	11	85	7,648	12,749	13,438	18,120	6,045	58,096
China^p	9,657	34,764	124,326	25,803	36,984	42,475	29,109	702,000
Hong Kong^r	15,544	75,007	113,467	4,055	4,971	5,948	12,290	231,282
India	1,973	27,189	164,134	21,522	21,738	25,451	23,617	297,258
Iran^r	3,388	10,339	45,136	11,105	10,314	11,163	11,131	102,576
Israel^r	25,476	29,602	37,713	3,542	3,356	3,239	4,136	107,064
Japan^g	46,250	39,988	49,775	3,896	3,903	4,092	4,517	431,567
Jordan^r	5,762	11,727	27,535	3,825	2,923	2,718	2,237	56,727
Korea^r	6,231	34,526	267,638	32,663	31,724	33,339	32,537	438,658
Laos^r	14	213	22,092	15,805	36,528	23,662	6,269	104,583
Lebanon^r	4,496	15,196	41,306	3,955	3,529	2,941	2,974	74,397
Pakistan^r	534	2,698	27,534	5,288	4,536	4,807	5,803	51,200
Philippines^r	19,307	98,376	354,987	43,772	45,102	41,546	46,985	650,075
Thailand^r	458	5,256	44,736	4,799	5,568	5,875	16,034	82,726
Turkey	3,519	10,142	13,399	2,766	2,864	2,263	1,652	398,639
Vietnam^r	335	4,340	172,820	55,631	72,553	37,560	25,803	369,042
Other Asia^{e o}	10,294	28,194	73,932	13,167	13,260	12,502	16,636	223,061
America	996,944	1,716,374	1,982,529	246,340	193,505	204,574	208,111	10,304,647
Canada & Newfoundland^h	377,952	413,310	169,939	11,191	10,786	11,390	15,659	4,187,673

TABLE A.1 (*Continued*)

Country	1951–1960	1961–1970	1971–1980	1981	1982	1983	1984	Total 165 Years 1820–1984
Mexico[i]	299,811	453,937	640,294	101,268	56,106	59,079	57,820	2,507,159
Caribbean	123,091	470,213	741,126	73,301	67,379	73,306	68,368	2,113,480
Cuba[r]	78,948	208,536	264,863	10,858	8,209	8,978	5,699	586,091
Dominican Republic[r]	9,897	93,292	148,135	18,220	17,451	22,058	23,207	332,260
Haiti[r]	4,442	34,499	56,335	6,683	8,779	8,424	9,554	128,716
Jamaica[q]	8,869	74,906	137,577	23,569	18,711	19,535	18,997	302,164
Trinidad & Tobago[q]	2,210	24,765	62,551	4,599	3,532	3,156	2,855	103,668
Other Caribbean[q]	18,725	34,215	71,665	9,372	10,697	11,155	8,056	660,581
Central America	44,751	101,330	134,640	24,509	23,626	24,601	27,626	451,902
El Salvador[r]	5,895	14,992	34,436	8,210	7,107	8,596	8,753	87,989
Guatemala[r]	4,663	15,883	25,882	3,928	3,633	4,090	3,955	62,034
Panama[r]	11,680	19,350	23,528	4,613	3,320	2,546	3,243	68,280
Other Central America	22,513	51,105	50,794	7,758	9,566	9,369	11,675	233,599
South America	91,628	257,954	295,741	35,913	35,448	36,087	38,636	934,540
Argentina[r]	19,486	49,721	29,897	2,236	2,065	2,029	2,287	107,721
Brazil[r]	13,783	29,272	17,842	1,616	1,475	1,503	2,184	67,675
Colombia[r]	18,048	72,028	77,348	10,335	8,608	9,658	10,897	206,922
Ecuador[r]	9,841	36,780	50,078	5,129	4,127	4,243	4,244	114,442
Guyana[r]	1,134	6,001	45,855	6,743	10,059	8,980	8,020	86,792
Peru[r]	7,404	19,052	29,171	4,664	4,151	4,384	4,269	73,095
Other South America	21,932	45,100	45,550	5,190	4,963	5,290	6,735	277,893
Other America[m]	59,711	19,630	789	158	160	111	2	109,893
Africa	14,092	28,954	80,779	15,029	14,314	15,084	13,594	215,273
Australia & New Zealand	11,506	19,562	23,788	1,947	2,009	1,879	2,328	131,356
Pacific Islands (U.S. adm.)[o]	1,470	1,769	1,806	108	138	105	163	22,141
Not specified[n]	12,491	3,884	15,866	2,138	1,700	1,553	2,053	293,893

[a] Data for Austria–Hungary were not reported until 1861. Austria and Hungary have been recorded separately since 1905. From 1938–1945, Austria is included in Germany.
[b] Poland recorded as a separate country from 1820–1898 and since 1920. From 1899–1919, Poland is included with Austria–Hungary, Germany, and U.S.S.R.
[c] From 1820–1868, the figures for Norway and Sweden are combined.
[d] No record of immigration from Rumania until 1880.

Table A.1 (*Continued*)

[e] From 1931–1950, the U.S.S.R. is broken down into European U.S.S.R., and Asian U.S.S.R. Since 1951 total U.S.S.R. has been reported in Europe.

[f] From 1925 to present, data for United Kingdom refer to England, Scotland, Wales, and Northern Ireland. Prior to 1925, data for Northern Ireland are included in Ireland. For the years 1901–1951, United Kingdom, not specified, is included in "Other Europe."

[g] No record of immigration from Japan until 1861.

[h] Prior to 1920, Canada and Newfoundland are recorded as British North America. From 1820–1898, the figures include all British North America possessions.

[i] No record of immigration from Mexico from 1886–1893.

[j] Countries added to the list since the beginning of World War I are included with the countries to which they belonged. Figures available since 1920 for Czechoslovakia and Finland and, since 1924, for Albania, Estonia, Latvia, and Lithuania.

[k] Bulgaria, Serbia, and Montenegro were first reported in 1899. Bulgaria has been reported separately since 1920; also in 1920, a separate enumeration was made for the Kingdom of Serbs, Croats, and Slovenes. Since 1922, the Serbs, Croat and Slovene Kingdom has been recorded as Yugoslavia.

[l] Figures for Luxembourg are available since 1925.

[m] Included with countries not specified to 1925.

[n] The figure 33,523 in column headed 1901–1910 includes 32,897 persons returning in 1906 to their homes in the United States.

[o] Beginning with the year 1951, Asia includes the Philippines. From 1934–1950, the Philippines are included in the Pacific Islands. Prior to 1934, the Philippines are recorded in separate tables as insular travel.

[p] Beginning with the year 1957, China includes Taiwan.

[q] Data for Jamaica and Trinidad & Tobago were not collected until 1953. In prior years these countries were consolidated under British West Indies, which is included in Other Caribbean.

[r] Data not listed separately before the year 1951; therefore, the cumulative total for 1820–present may be understated.

Notes: From 1820–1867, figures represent alien passengers arrived; from 1868–1891 and 1895–1897, immigrant aliens arrived; from 1892–1894 and 1898 to the present time, immigrant aliens admitted. Data for years prior to 1906 relate to country whence alien came; data from 1906–1979 and 1984 are for country of last permanent residence; and data for 1980–1983 refer to country of birth. Because of changes in boundaries and changes in lists of countries, data for certain countries are not comparable throughout.

The periods covered are as follows: from 1820–1831 and 1843–1849, the fiscal years ended on September 30 of the respective year—fiscal year 1843 covers 9 months. From 1832–1842 and 1850–1867, fiscal years ended on December 31 of the respective year—fiscal years 1832 and 1850 cover 15 months. For 1868, the period ended on June 30 and covers 6 months. Fiscal years 1868–1976 end on June 30 of the respective year. The transition quarter (TQ) for 1976 covers the 3-month period, July–September 1976. Since October 1, 1977, the data are for fiscal years ending September 30 of the respective year.

Source: U.S. Immigration and Naturalization Service.

Table A.2   JEWISH IMMIGRATION TO THE UNITED STATES, 1881–1984

Fiscal years[a]	Absolute numbers		Percentage of immigrants who are Jewish
	Jews	Total	
1881[b]	5,692	669,431	0.9
1882	13,202	788,992	1.7
1883	8,731	603,322	1.4
1884	11,445	518,592	2.2
1885	15,389	395,346	3.9
1886	19,936	334,203	6.0
1887	32,064	490,109	6.5
1888	27,854	546,889	5.1
1889	24,394	444,427	5.5
1890	27,880	455,302	6.1
1891	50,201	560,319	9.0
1892	73,636	479,663	12.7
1893	32,079	439,730	7.3
1894	27,279	285,631	9.6
1895	23,292	258,536	9.0
1896	30,743	343,267	9.0
1897	19,251	230,832	8.3
1898	23,036	229,299	10.0
1899	37,415	311,715	12.0
1900	60,764	448,572	13.5
1901	58,098	487,918	11.9
1902	57,688	648,743	8.9
1903	76,203	857,046	8.9
1904	106,236	812,870	13.1
1905	129,910	1,026,499	12.7
1906	153,748	1,100,735	14.0
1907	149,182	1,285,349	11.6
1908	103,387	782,870	13.2
1909	57,551	751,786	7.7
1910	84,260	1,041,570	8.1
1911	91,223	878,587	10.4
1912	80,595	838,172	9.6
1913	101,330	1,197,892	8.5
1914	138,051	1,218,480	11.3
1915	26,497	326,700	8.1
1916	15,108	298,826	5.1
1917	17,342	295,403	5.9
1918	3,672	110,618	3.3
1919	3,055	141,132	2.2
1920	14,292	430,001	3.3
1921	119,036	805,228	14.8
1922	53,524	309,556	17.3
1923	49,719	522,919	9.5
1924	49,989	706,896	7.1
1925	10,292	294,314	3.5
1926	10,267	304,488	3.4
1927	11,483	335,175	3.4
1928	11,639	307,255	3.8
1929	12,479	279,678	4.5
1930	11,526	241,700	4.8
1931	5,692	97,139	5.9
1932	2,755	35,576	7.7
1933	2,372	23,068	10.3
1934	4,134	29,470	14.0
1935	4,837	34,956	13.8
1936	6,252	36,329	17.2

Table A.2 (*Continued*)

Fiscal years[a]	Absolute numbers		Percentage of immigrants who are Jewish
	Jews	Total	
1937	11,352	50,244	22.6
1938	19,736	67,895	29.0
1939	43,450	82,998	52.3
1940	36,945	70,756	52.2
1941	23,737	51,776	45.8
1942	10,608	28,781	36.9
1943	4,705	23,725	19.8
1944	2,400	28,551	8.4
1945	4,160	38,119	10.9
1946	12,774	108,721	11.8
1947	29,274	147,292	19.9
1948	17,581	170,570	10.3
1949	41,222	188,317	21.9
1950	13,057	249,187	5.2
1951	18,239	205,717	8.8
1952	7,800	265,520	2.9
1953	5,353	170,434	3.1
1954	3,933	208,177	1.9
1955	3,253	237,790	1.4
1956	6,513	321,625	2.0
1957	10,876	326,867	3.3
1958	7,160	253,265	2.8
1959	8,098	260,686	3.1
1960	6,622	265,398	2.5
1961	7,102	271,344	2.6
1962	9,325	283,763	3.3
1963	10,750	306,260	3.3
1964	9,300	292,248	3.2
1965	7,800	296,697	2.6
1966	7,500	323,040	2.3
1967	6,600	361,972	1.8
1968	7,800	454,448	1.7
1969	9,300	358,579	2.6
1970	7,700	373,326	2.1
1971	5,525	370,478	1.5
1972	5,520	384,685	1.5
1973	6,625	400,063	1.6
1974	9,300	394,861	2.4
1975	11,800	386,194	3.0
1976	13,600	398,631	3.4
1977	9,850[c]	462,351	—
1978	15,543[c]	601,442	2.6
1979	31,887[c]	460,348	6.9
1980	18,978[c]	530,639	3.5
1981	10,522[c]	596,600	1.7
1982	4,683[c]	594,131	1.0
1983	4,117[c]	559,763	1.0
1984	4,625[c]	543,903	1.0

[a]From July 1 of the preceding year to June 30 of the year stated.
[b]The Jewish figures for 1881–1898 apply solely to East European Jews.
[c]Israelis and Soviet Jews only.
Sources: Moses Rischin, *The Promised City* (Harper & Row [Torchbooks], 1970), p. 270; *Jewish People: Past and Present,* vol. I, p. 407, published by Jewish Encyclopedia Handbooks, Inc., 1946; the *American Jewish Yearbook;* the United Hebrew Immigrant Aid Society; and United States Department of Justice, Immigration and Naturalization Service.

Table A.3 ETHNIC BACKGROUND OF THE AMERICAN POPULATION
Reported Single and Multiple Ancestries: November 1979 (in thousands)

Ancestry	Total	Percent of total	Persons reported single ancestry		Persons reported multiple ancestry	Percent of persons by kind of ancestry response		
			Number	Percent		Total	Single ancestry	Multiple ancestry
Reported at least one specific ancestry	179,078[a]	100.0[a]	96,496	100.0	82,582[a]	100.0	53.9	46.1
Afro-American, African	16,193	9.0	15,057	15.6	1,136	100.0	93.0	7.0
American Indian	9,900	5.3	2,053	2.1	7,847	100.0	20.7	79.3
Asian Indian	182	0.1	156	0.2	26	100.0	85.7	14.3
Austrian	1,070	0.6	385	0.4	685	100.0	36.0	64.0
Belgian	448	0.3	113	0.1	335	100.0	25.2	74.8
Canadian	609	0.3	228	0.2	381	100.0	37.4	62.6
Chinese, Taiwanese	705	0.4	540	0.6	165	100.0	76.6	23.4
Czechoslovakian	1,695	0.9	794	0.8	901	100.0	46.8	53.2
Danish	1,672	0.9	438	0.5	1,234	100.0	26.2	73.8
Dutch	8,121	4.5	1,362	1.4	6,759	100.0	16.8	83.2
English	40,004	22.3	11,501	11.9	28,503	100.0	28.7	71.3
Filipino	764	0.4	525	0.5	239	100.0	68.7	31.3
Finnish	616	0.3	255	0.3	361	100.0	41.4	58.6
French	14,047	7.8	3,047	3.2	11,000	100.0	21.7	78.3
French Canadian	1,053	0.6	582	0.6	471	100.0	55.3	44.7
German	51,649	28.8	17,160	17.8	34,489	100.0	33.2	66.8
Greek	990	0.6	567	0.6	423	100.0	57.3	42.7
Hungarian	1,592	0.9	534	0.6	1,058	100.0	33.5	66.5
Iranian	118	0.1	103	0.1	15	100.0	87.3	12.7
Irish	43,752	24.4	9,760	10.1	33,992	100.0	22.3	77.7
Italian, Sicilian	11,751	6.6	6,110	6.3	5,641	100.0	52.0	48.0
Jamaican	184	0.1	158	0.2	26	100.0	85.9	14.1
Japanese	680	0.4	529	0.5	151	100.0	77.8	22.2
Korean	265	0.1	230	0.2	35	100.0	86.8	13.2
Lebanese	322	0.2	179	0.2	143	100.0	55.6	44.4

Table A.3 (*Continued*)

Ancestry	Total	Percent of total	Persons reported single ancestry		Persons reported multiple ancestry	Percent of persons by kind of ancestry response		
			Number	Percent		Total	Single ancestry	Multiple ancestry
Lithuanian	832	0.5	317	0.3	515	100.0	38.1	61.9
Norwegian	4,120	2.3	1,232	1.3	2,888	100.0	29.9	70.1
Polish	8,421	4.7	3,498	3.6	4,923	100.0	41.5	58.5
Portuguese	946	0.5	493	0.5	453	100.0	52.1	47.9
Rumanian	335	0.2	132	0.1	203	100.0	39.4	60.6
Russian	3,466	1.9	1,496	1.6	1,970	100.0	43.2	56.8
Scandinavian	340	0.2	110	0.1	230	100.0	32.4	67.6
Scottish	14,205	7.9	1,615	1.7	12,590	100.0	11.4	88.6
Slavic	722	0.4	300	0.3	422	100.0	41.6	58.4
Spanish	12,493	7.0	9,762	10.1	2,731	100.0	78.1	21.9
Colombian	117	0.1	101	0.1	16	100.0	86.3	13.7
Cuban	675	0.4	558	0.6	117	100.0	82.7	17.3
Dominican	119	0.1	107	0.1	12	100.0	89.9	10.1
Mexican	6,682	3.7	5,889	6.1	793	100.0	88.1	11.9
Puerto Rican	1,333	0.7	1,107	1.1	226	100.0	83.0	17.0
Other Spanish	3,566	2.0	2,000	2.1	1,566	100.0	56.1	43.9
Swedish	4,886	2.7	1,216	1.3	3,670	100.0	24.9	75.1
Swiss	1,228	0.7	312	0.3	916	100.0	25.4	74.6
Ukrainian	525	0.3	231	0.2	294	100.0	44.0	56.0
Vietnamese	198	0.1	177	0.2	21	100.0	89.4	10.6
Welsh	2,568	1.4	455	0.5	2,113	100.0	17.7	82.3
West Indian	193	0.1	129	0.1	64	100.0	66.8	33.2
Yugoslavian	467	0.3	283	0.3	184	100.0	60.6	39.4
Other specified ancestry groups	4,942	2.8	2,372	2.5	2,571	100.0	48.0	52.0

[a]Number and percent by ancestry groups do not add to total, as persons may be counted in more than one ancestry group.

Note: Numbers refer to the civilian noninstitutional population.

Source: U.S. Bureau of the Census, "Ancestry and Language in the United States: November 1979," Series P-23, No. 116, Table 1.

Table A.4 PROVISIONS OF THE MAJOR UNITED STATES IMMIGRATION LAWS AND PROGRAMS

1819   The federal government requires numeration of immigrants.

1864   Congress passes a law facilitating the importation of contract laborers.

1875   Congress passes the first federal restriction of immigration, prohibiting the importation of prostitutes and alien convicts.

1882   The Chinese Exclusion Act curbs the immigration of the Chinese.

1882   Congress excludes convicts, lunatics, idiots, or persons likely to become a public charge and places a head tax on immigration.

1885   The contract labor laws end.

1891   The federal government assumes the supervision of immigration and the next year opens Ellis Island.

1903   Congress expands the list of excluded immigrants to include polygamists, anarchists, and other radicals.

1907   Congress raises the head tax on immigrants and adds to the excluded list persons with physical or mental defects that might affect their ability to earn a living, those with tuberculosis, and children unaccompanied by their parents.

1907   The United States and Japan agree to the Gentlemen's Agreement restricting immigration from Japan.

1917   Congress codifies previously excluded classes and includes a literacy test banning those over 16 who cannot read some language. Persons escaping from religious persecution are exempt from the literacy test. The law also bans virtually all immigration from Asia.

1921   Congress sets a limit on European immigration of approximately 358,000. National quotas are instituted and based on a formula allowing each nation 3 percent of foreign-born persons of that nationality who lived here in 1910.

1924   Congress enacts the Johnson-Reed Act. This act sets the annual quota of any nationality at 2 percent of the number of foreign-born of each nationality resident in the United States according to the 1890 census. This quota is replaced in 1927 with the national origins provision, basing each nationality quota on its proportion of the population according to the 1920 census. Proportions are based on a figure of 153,714 annually from Europe.

1924   The Oriental Exclusion Act bans immigration from Asia.

1930   President Herbert Hoover directs consuls to enforce strictly the provisions of the immigration acts barring "those likely to become a public charge."

1942   The United States and Mexico agree to the bracero program permitting temporary foreign laborers to work in the United States.

1943   Congress repeals the ban on Chinese immigration.

1946   Congress passes the War Brides Act facilitating the entry of alien wives, husbands, and children of members of the United States armed forces.

1948   Congress enacts the Displaced Persons law allowing the entrance of 205,000 displaced persons in addition to those admitted under the annual quotas.

1950   Congress amends the Displaced Persons Act and adds 134,000 to the numbers that may be admitted under its provisions.

1952   Congress passes the McCarran-Walter Immigration and Naturalization Act. It
    —eliminates race as a bar to immigration and naturalization.
    —reaffirms the national origins system but gives every nation a quota.
    —provides for a more thorough screening of immigrants.
    —establishes preferences for those with relatives in America or those with skills.

1953   Congress enacts the Refugee Relief Act authorizing the admission of special nonquota refugees.

1957   Congress passes the Refugee-Escape Act liberalizing the McCarran-Walter Act and allowing more nonquota immigrants to enter.

1960   Congress passes the World Refugee Year Law permitting the entrance of additional refugees.

1962   Congress enacts the Migration and Refugee Assistance Act facilitating the admission of refugees.

1964   The United States and Mexico terminate the bracero program.

1965   Congress passes the Immigration Act of 1965. The act
    —abolishes the national origins system.

Table A.4 (*Continued*)

	—establishes a limit of 170,000 outside the Western Hemisphere but places a limit of 20,000 on any one country. —admits immigrants on a first-come, first-qualified basis. —establishes preferences for close relatives as well as refugees and those with occupational skills needed in the United States. —places a ceiling of 120,000 on immigration from the Western Hemisphere.
1976	Congress extends the 20,000 limit per country to the Western Hemisphere and establishes a modified preference system for the hemisphere.
1978	Congress establishes a single worldwide ceiling of 290,000 for the admission of immigrants and a uniform preference system.
1978	Congress creates a Select Commission on Immigration and Refugee Policy to study and evaluate existing immigration policy.
1980	Congress passes the Refugee Act of 1980. The act —increases the total annual immigration to 320,000. —increases the number of refugees from 17,400 to 50,000 annually. —defines refugee to include persons from any part of the world and not just the Middle East or communist countries. —creates the office of U.S. Coordinator for Refugee Affairs.
1986	Congress passes Immigration Reform and Control Act. The new law —prohibits employers from knowingly employing undocumented aliens. —grants an amnesty to those residing illegally in the United States since 1982 and makes it possible for them to become resident aliens and U.S. citizens. —provides for the admission of temporary farm workers.

Source: Edward P. Hutchison, *Legislative History of American Immigration Policy, 1798–1965* (Philadelphia: University of Pennsylvania Press, 1981); U.S. Congress, Senate, Committee on the Judiciary, *U.S. Immigration Law and Policy: 1952–1979,* report prepared by the Congressional Research Service, 96th Congress, 1st sess.; and *Congressional Quarterly* (1980, 1986).

Index

U.S. Supreme Court, 83, 86, 132, 174
University of California, 120
University of California (Davis), 189
University of Hawaii, 155
University of Idaho, 62
University of Michigan, 157
University of Nevada, 62
University of Oregon, 62
Upper West Side (New York City), 129
Uprooted peoples, 43
Ursuline Convent, 36
Uruguayans, 123
Utah, 30, 62
Utah Nippo, newspaper, 62

Valenzuela, Fernando, 169
Vambrana, Haydee, 124
Variety, newspaper, 108
Vatican, the, 86
Vermont, 30, 72
Veterans of Foreign Wars, 85
Vienna, Austria, 43
Vietnam, 135, 136, 137, 139, 145, 189, 195
Vietnamese, 91, 92, 94, 135, 136, 137, 138, 168, 171,
    190, 197
Villanueva, Daniel, 170
Virginia, 2, 7, 10, 47, 130
Voice of America, 127
Volpe, John, 187
Voting restrictions, 48
Voting Rights Act of 1965, 86, 132

Wadell, Rube, 169
Wages, 33, 53, 54, 96, 110, 112, 113, 121
Wagner, Honus, 169
Wagner, Robert F., 80, 152
Wagner-Rogers proposal (1939), 80
Wales, 7, 21
Wallace, George, 188
Wall Street, 147, 157
Wall Street Journal, 198
Walter, Bruno, 81
War Brides Act of 1946, 87, 100
Warsaw, Poland, 43
Was Grossmutter Erzählt (1915), 38
Washington, D.C., 47, 115, 122, 130, 131, 138, 142,
    154, 170, 180, 192
Washington, state of, 30, 110, 116
Washington Post, 131
WASPs, 162, 166, 173, 188, 190
Watergate, 187
Weber (pianos), 152
Welfare organizations, 178
Welsh, 12, 21, 30, 173
West Germans, 197
West Indians, 89, 99, 171
Westinghouse, George, 151
Westinghouse Science Talent Search, 168
West Virginia, 52, 150, 190

Wetbacks, 113. *See also* Undocumented
    immigrants
Wheeling, West Virginia, 39
White House, 151, 164
"White slave traffic," 53
Wilbur, Nebraska, 185
Williamsburg (New York City), 170
Wilson, Woodrow, 73, 175
Winooski, Vermont, 30
Wisconsin, 20, 21, 23, 27, 29, 30, 38, 39, 185
Wittke, Carl, 23
Women, 46, 55, 95, 121
    black, 40
    Chinese, 32, 154ff, 155
    Colombian, 130
    French Canadian, 32
    German, 32, 40
    German-Russian, 40
    Irish, 31, 32, 40, 148
    Italian, 181
    Korean, 138
    Mexican-American, 120
    Polish, 165, 167, 188
    Puerto Rican, 125
    Scandinavian, 32, 40
    Vietnamese, 137, 139
Women's rights, 35
Women's wages, 53
Woo, Shien Biau, 155
Woonsocket, Rhode Island, 30
Worcester, Massachusetts, 7
Workingmen's party, 64
World Refugee Year, 89
World War I, 17, 23, 29, 37, 39, 45, 50, 53, 58, 61,
    73, 74, 87, 111, 151, 174, 175, 176, 179, 183
World War II, 17, 56, 77, 79, 81, 84, 85, 86, 87, 88,
    91, 92, 100, 102, 107, 112, 119, 124, 135, 145,
    148, 154, 155, 160, 161, 165, 167, 169, 170, 173,
    175, 176, 182, 183, 184, 192, 196, 197, 198
Wurlitzer (pianos), 152
Wyoming, 30, 46, 110

Xenophobia, 71, 73

Yale University, 166
Yang, Chen Ning, 154
Yang, Stephen, 94
Yankee Stadium, 86
"Yellow peril" scare, 65
Yom Kippur War (1973), 192
Young Lords, 126
Young Men's Serbian Society of Tonopah, Nevada,
    62
Yugoslavians, 61, 89
Yukon, 164

Zavala County, Texas, 122
Zhu, Wei-Jing, 168
Zoot Suit Riots (1943), 118–119